BETWEEN EARTH *and* SKY

BETWEEN EARTH and SKY

100 DAYS
OF DEEP LOOKING *in the* PLACE OF THE DEAD

Foreword by
PAUL DAVID MEYER

JO CONFINO

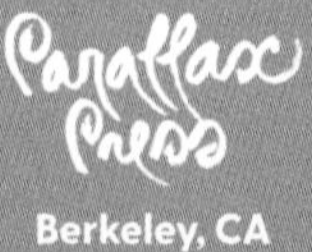

Parallax Press
Berkeley, CA

LAND ACKNOWLEDGEMENT

During my time in San Pablo Villa de Mitla, Mexico, I was an outsider on native Zapotec lands. I acknowledge that the land on which I took these photographs, known as San Pablo Villa de Mitla, is the ancestral and traditional land of the Zapotec peoples. The Zapotec name for this place is Lyobaa, meaning "place of rest" or "place of the dead." I honor and pay respect to the Zapotec elders community, past and present, who have stewarded this land for generations, maintaining a deep and sacred connection to this place. The legacy of Spanish colonialism is embodied in Mitla's cathedral, built with stones stolen from adjacent Zapotec temples. The colonial system destroyed indigenous economic, political, and social relationships. Yet the Zapotec story is also one of resilience. In Oaxaca, roughly 400,000 people still speak a Zapotec language (although many are endangered), and numerous indigenous customs endure in Mitla. Aware of the significant suffering that non-Indigenous peoples have caused to the land and community, I, as a non-native person, take responsibility to advocate for the rights of Indigenous peoples and the preservation of their lands, language, and culture.

TO MY MOTHER AND FATHER,
WHO INSPIRED ME TO SEE LIFE
THROUGH A DIFFERENT LENS

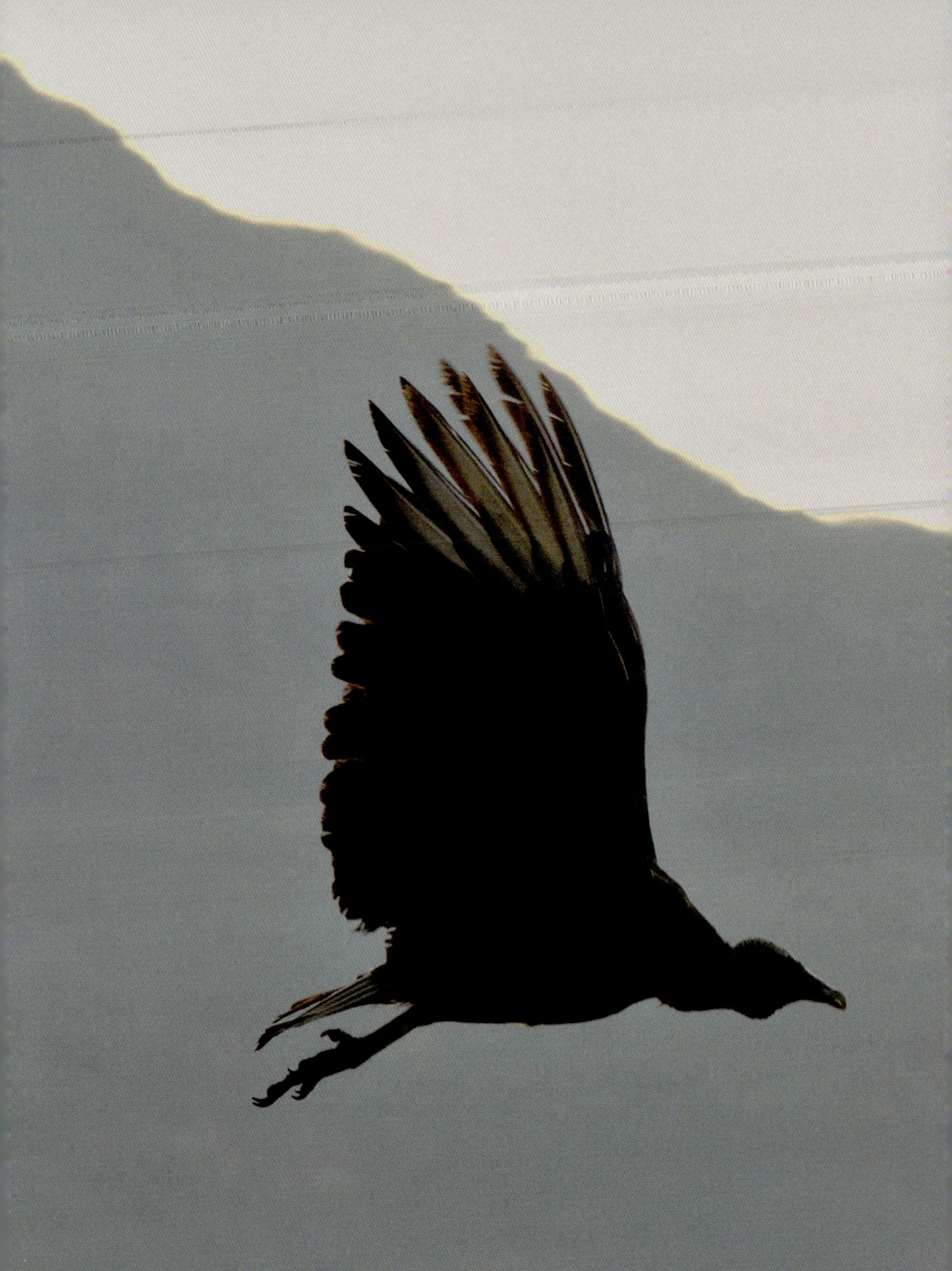

CONTENTS

RECIPROCITY

Jo Confino's images have a quality of veneration, almost sacredness, in their portraits of the natural world—the celebration of a shaft of morning light shattering, prismatic on a spider's web; the consecration of a twig twisted by time; the meditation on a cactus spine. There's a reverence for the land that builds and deepens in these pages as Jo tells his story of personal transformation.

I had a privileged place to witness that transformation. I met Jo in the first days of the pandemic, when he came with his wife, Paz, to stay at our guesthouse in Mitla, Mexico. It's a small town in the state of Oaxaca revered as the "town of the souls" by the local Zapotec families who believe their ancestors return here annually from the underworld. Our home sits at the end of a dirt road that runs into the countryside, set between the ruins of temples to the west and the caves of hunter-gatherers to the east—both portals to the underworld in Zapotec culture. It's here that Jo and I developed a deep friendship during our hundred days of lockdown together. During that time, we lived in-between worlds: the living and the dead, the human and non-human, being and becoming. Lost souls, all of us. Perhaps it's only in such in-between spaces, in a Tibetan Bardo as Jo describes it, that the kind of transformation Jo experienced can take place. Our most powerful personal transformations require being profoundly displaced.

Jo's personal story is indeed a powerful one. And inside of it is another story that's less obvious but no less compelling. It's a story about the local Zapotec community that preserves the land and its cycles. The countryside behind our house where Jo took his daily outings is communally owned, as is much of the land here. And the community has protected that land for millennia. In recent years, I have watched Mitleños band together to defeat a proposal to locate a military base here, prevent a regional landfill that promised groundwater contamination, fight wildfires, and consistently reject lucrative mining activities.

A group of residents patrols the valley and mountains to prevent the poaching of plants and hunting of animals. Hidden springs remain unexploited, even though water security is an ever-present concern in town. A result of that stewardship: Jo's images. Such images are only possible when land is left mostly to be itself—merciless, forgiving, and nourishing in turn, sometimes in the same moment. That's how we get Jo's portrait of a cactus spine impaling a wasp, of black vultures poised expectant on the crowns of mesquite trees, of wings shed by ravenous termites on their annual pilgrimage from inside the earth to feeding grounds. This is the land uncensored.

An astounding fact I recently learned brings all of this into focus. Scientists have extensively studied Mitla's countryside for evidence of Preceramic civilization from roughly 10,000 years ago. Using seeds found in caves, they've identified twenty-one types of edible native plants that were common in the diet then:

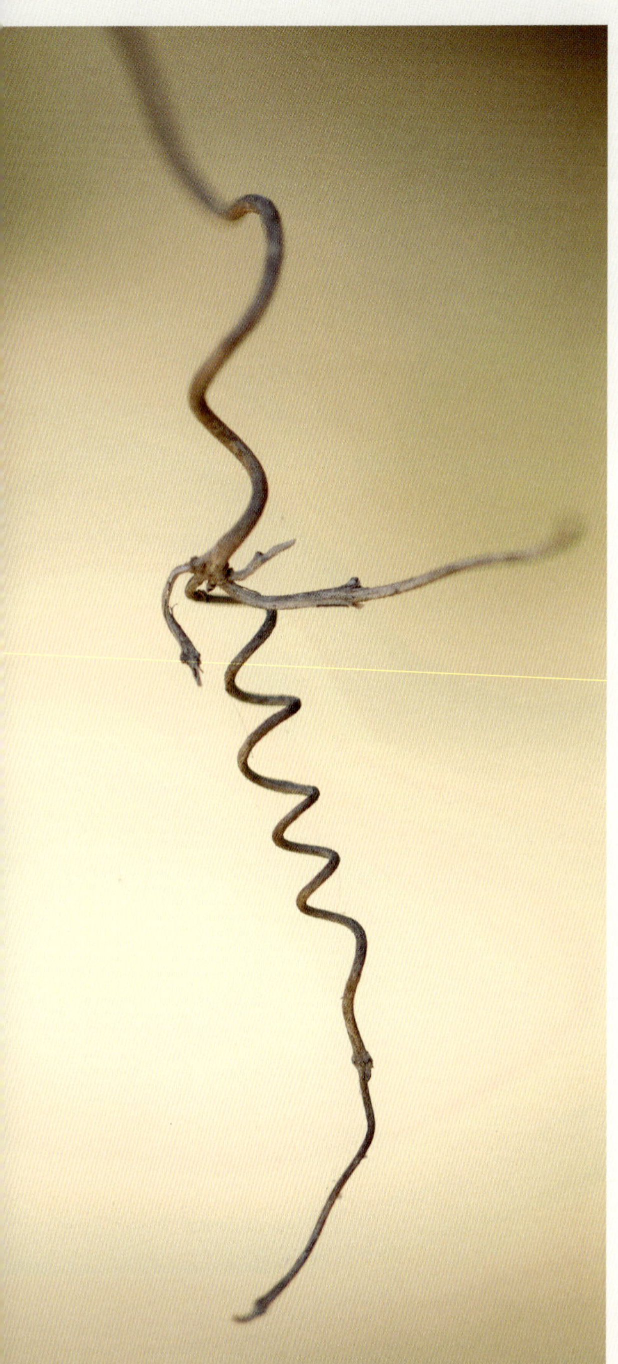

guaje, *Cassia*, *Acacia*, *Mimosa*, copal, agave, *Bromelia*, *Dasylirion*, organ cactus, cholla, nopal, chapuliztle, mala mujer, nanche, wild onions, wild black zapote, mesquite, hackberry, and scattered ocotillo, and piñon pine. Today, all but one remain staples of our countryside, in the same areas. In fact, the local flora is so similar to millennia ago that scientists can use present-day plant patterns as a guide to the past.

To say, then, that the images Jo captures are timeless is not a hyperbole. So, let this book be both a source of personal inspiration and a celebration of the community that made it possible. And, finally, let it be a requiem for the many who died during the pandemic here, from our local doctor who treated one of the first local cases to a weaver who was a repository of local Zapotec history unlike any other. Their legacy, like those of all Mitleños, lives in the land that Jo has so poignantly captured.

PAUL DAVID MEYER
San Pablo Villa de Mitla, Oaxaca, México

If we are able to touch deeply the historical dimension [our everyday life experiences] through a leaf, a flower, a pebble, a beam of light, a mountain, a river, a bird, or our own body, we touch at the same time the ultimate dimension. The ultimate dimension cannot be described as personal or impersonal, material or spiritual, object or subject of cognition—we say only that it is always shining, and shining on itself.

Touching the ultimate dimension, we feel happy and comfortable, like the bird enjoying the blue sky, or the deer enjoying the green fields. We know that we do not have to look for the ultimate outside of ourselves— it is available within us, in this very moment.

THICH NHAT HANH
from an interview with Jo Confino
for *the Guardian*

CROSSING A
THRESHOLD

We came to an emergency stop in the "place of the dead."

After being forced out of my job after five years of frenetic work as a journalist in New York City, I was on my way—with my wife, Paz—to begin a new phase of our life alongside a Zen monastic community in southwestern France.

With my US work visa expiring, we slipped quietly away from Manhattan with hearts heavy on the morning of March 1, 2020. Our original plan had been to spend three weeks exploring Oaxaca City, Mexico, on our way back to Europe, but the explosive arrival of the COVID-19 pandemic threw our time there into disarray.

The speed, breadth, and scale of the outbreak started to become clear during our first few days in Mexico. With so little knowledge of how COVID-19 spread, Paz and I felt anxious and isolated. We were far from our familiar life in New York and we had not yet signed the final contract on our new home, a seventeenth-century French farmhouse next door to the Plum Village monastery of Zen Master Thich Nhat Hanh. When the World Health Organization declared COVID-19 a global pandemic, we hurriedly decided to leave the busy city for what we hoped would be a quieter and safer location. After scouring the internet, I picked a room at random in the tiny town of Mitla—a place we knew nothing about but was within easy reach of Oaxaca City.

It felt like a foreboding sign to discover after booking the room that Mitla means the "place of the dead" in the ancient Nahuatl language of Mexico. Its name in the regional language Zapotec is *Lyobaa*, which means "portal to the underworld." For the Zapotec people, Mitla is a revered sacred site where the newly deceased cross a great river to enter the land of souls.

We arrived as I was crossing my own metaphorical river, facing the painful truth of my redundancy after forty years of secure nonstop work as a journalist. With the media industry rapidly contracting and my advancing age working against me, the likelihood of finding another job was slim at best. I had no plan and no idea of what the future would bring.

With nerves jangling, we arrived in Mitla and drove past the edge of town down a heavily pitted dirt road of half-built houses. My mind raced. *Had I made a terrible mistake? Why had I suggested we go somewhere even more remote rather than simply making a dash onward to Europe?* We reached the very last house before Mitla turned to open countryside and were unsettled to discover the name of the small compound in which we had booked a room: Casa Lyobaa—the house of the portal to the underworld.

We arrived in the depths of the dry season, which lasts at least seven months a year. Scrubland stretched out as far as the eye could see to the foothills of the Sierra Norte mountains, broken only by sporadic candelabra cacti. The countryside, parched and seemingly lifeless, mirrored my own inner landscape.

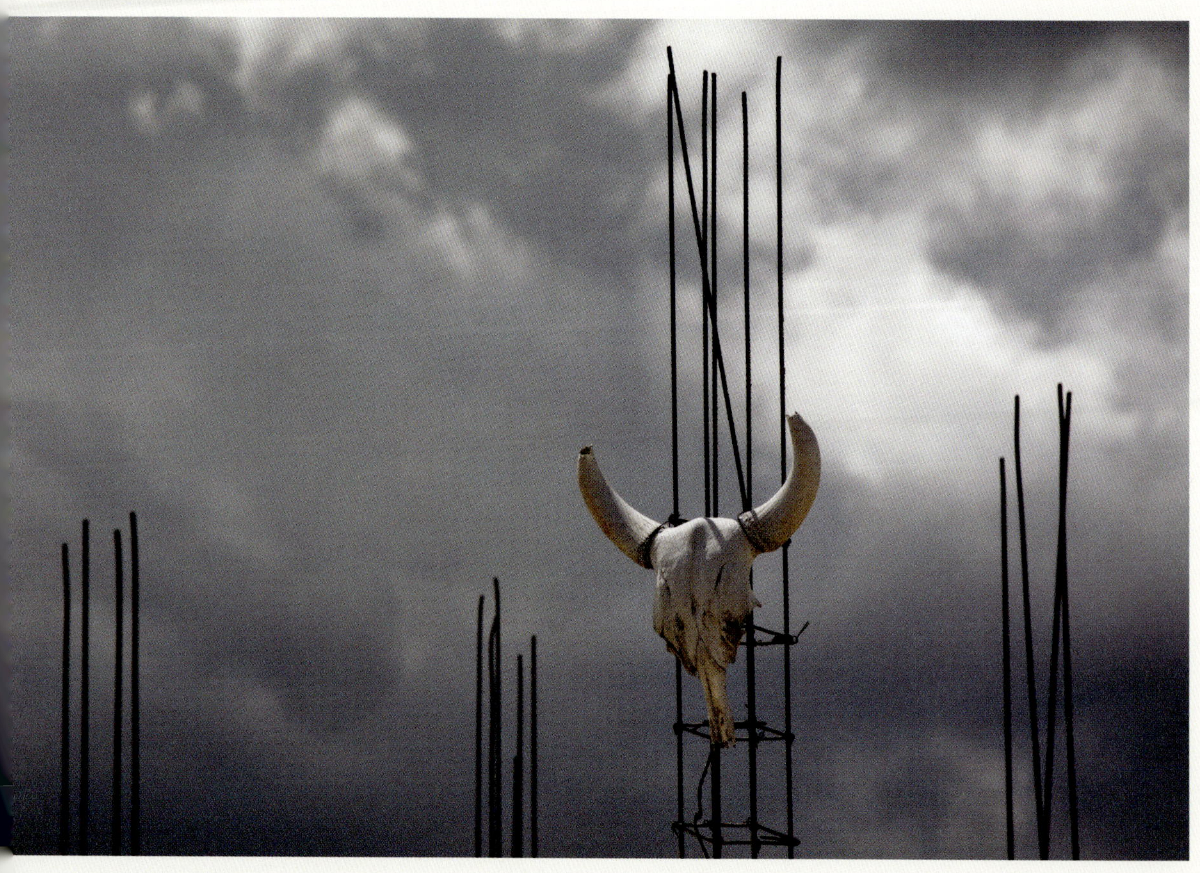

My fear grew as our world shrank. Two days after we arrived, the two other remaining guests, panicked by the rapid spread of the pandemic, hurriedly left for their homes in the United States. Though I presented an air of calm to my wife, my mind and stomach churned. *What if we became stuck in this small town and needed emergency medical care? What if our hosts wanted to isolate themselves and asked us to leave?*

I constantly cycled through backup plans, but a couple of days later, any remaining options evaporated. Flights were canceled en masse, and travel restrictions imposed worldwide. We were stuck. I had booked a room at Casa Lyobaa for three nights, never imagining we would stay for ninety-nine.

My feelings of isolation grew as the owners closed the other rooms within their three-acre garden compound to new guests, but my anxiety eased when we were reassured we could stay as long as we wanted. By the second half of March, it was clear that we—myself, Paz, the owners of Casa Lyobaa, their two young children, and two German Shepherd dogs—would ride out the pandemic together, as family.

We did our best to stay calm, but death surrounded us in the weeks that followed. The suffering in Mitla was immense. There is no reliable count of how many residents died, but nearly every family intimately knew someone who passed.

Three things carried me through and eventually guided me to a grounded resilience and a sense of renewal: the support of my loving partner, the teachings of the Vietnamese Zen master Thich Nhat Hanh (known as Thay, which means "teacher" in Vietnamese, to his students), and my trusty Canon 5D camera.

I have been an avid photographer for over forty years. My frequent use of the macro lens I had brought along allowed me to zoom in on minute details, and focusing my perspective in this way became a refuge for me through these hundred days—a tool in my apprenticeship to the rough ground of this threshold. Looking through my camera's viewfinder, I was surprised to discover islands of calm and flickers of curiosity, potent antidotes to the fear and uncertainty I wrestled daily.

Though the scrublands of this portal to the underworld that I roamed had initially seemed barren, incremental intimacy with the land began to shift my perspective. The more I lingered, the more I noticed life at the margins: a flower's frail bloom amid thorns and dust, the patient carving of an arroyo, the silent resilience of stone. Noticing, in itself, became a kind of participation that tempered my sense of isolation. Day by day, wandering the valley and hills outside of town and composing photographs, I stumbled not into escape but into an unexpected freedom—a recognition that life, death, and renewal braided themselves together in this place, even here, even now. Especially here. Especially now.

Each of us who came through the pandemic physically intact was invisibly transformed, in ways large and small. The following photos, interwoven with their stories, are a visual meditation on seeing the world in a profoundly different way, and being changed beyond measure in the process.

PART 1

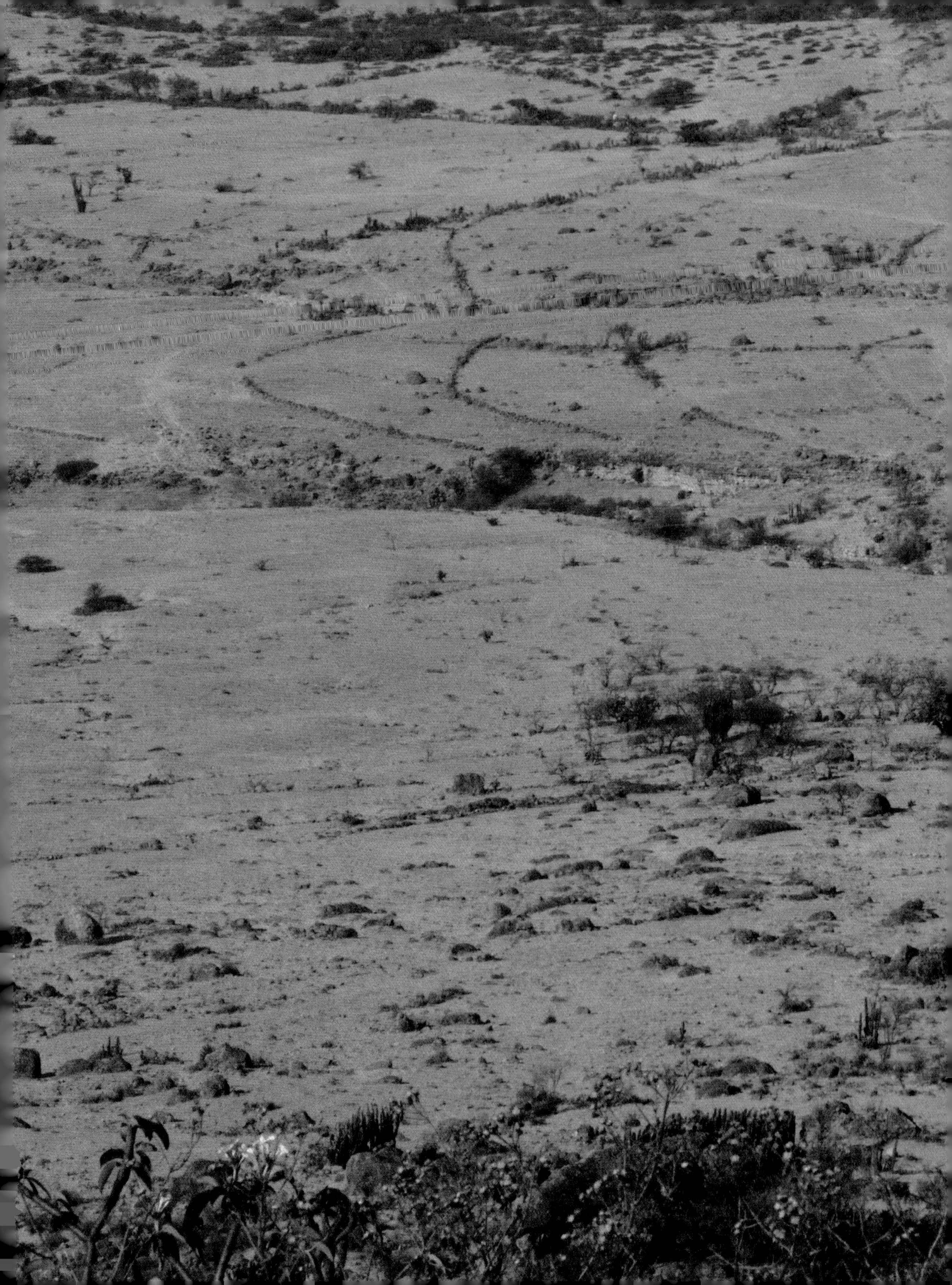

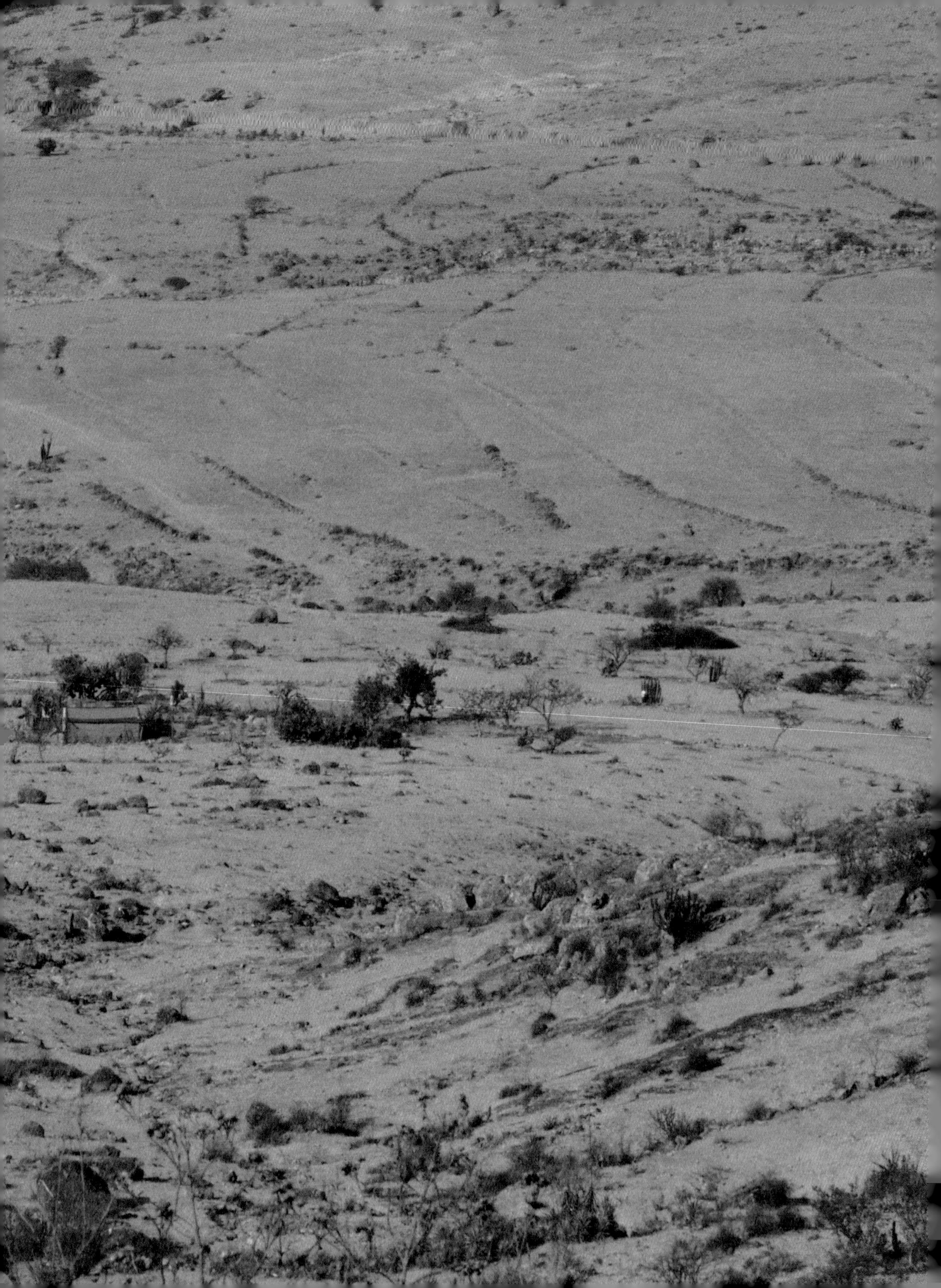

THE ABYSS

Outside, the land is bone-dry, a brown sinew stretched over the crust of the earth. The only distinguishing features are the occasional prickly pear and candelabra cacti.

I wake aimless and empty. My world continues to shrink. Just days after arriving, Mitla is now sealed off, and a travel ban is in place. For the first time in forty-two years, jobless, I am unmoored from schedules and structure. My life has diminished, contracted, to something that feels almost microscopic—a dot. And yet, paradoxically, I feel overwhelmed by an immense and unsettling expanse of time and space. I have no idea how to move through it.

To the Zapotecs who live here, Mitla is the sacred place of the dead. It is where the deceased gather from near and far to enter the underworld—the "land of souls"—inside the earth, accessed through subterranean chambers. Less than half a mile from where we are staying, offerings are still made to the dead and Zapotec burial ruins mark the remains of kings and high priests.

As the pandemic intensifies, fear of the unknown feeds a desperate desire to stay safe. These first few days, I feel like I am clinging to the edge of a vast abyss. Paz and her art practice have helped me to conceptually understand the void not as a dark, bottomless pit to be terrified of getting forever lost in, but as a source of infinite possibility. Yet, no matter how many times I return to this idea, fearful emotions swamp me. I continue to face uncertainty and the fear of death daily in this land where, apart from my wife, I have no family, no friends, and no sense of belonging.

Great kettles of vultures circling ceaselessly overhead, scanning for carcasses, are a constant reminder of impermanence, of the fleeting nature of life.

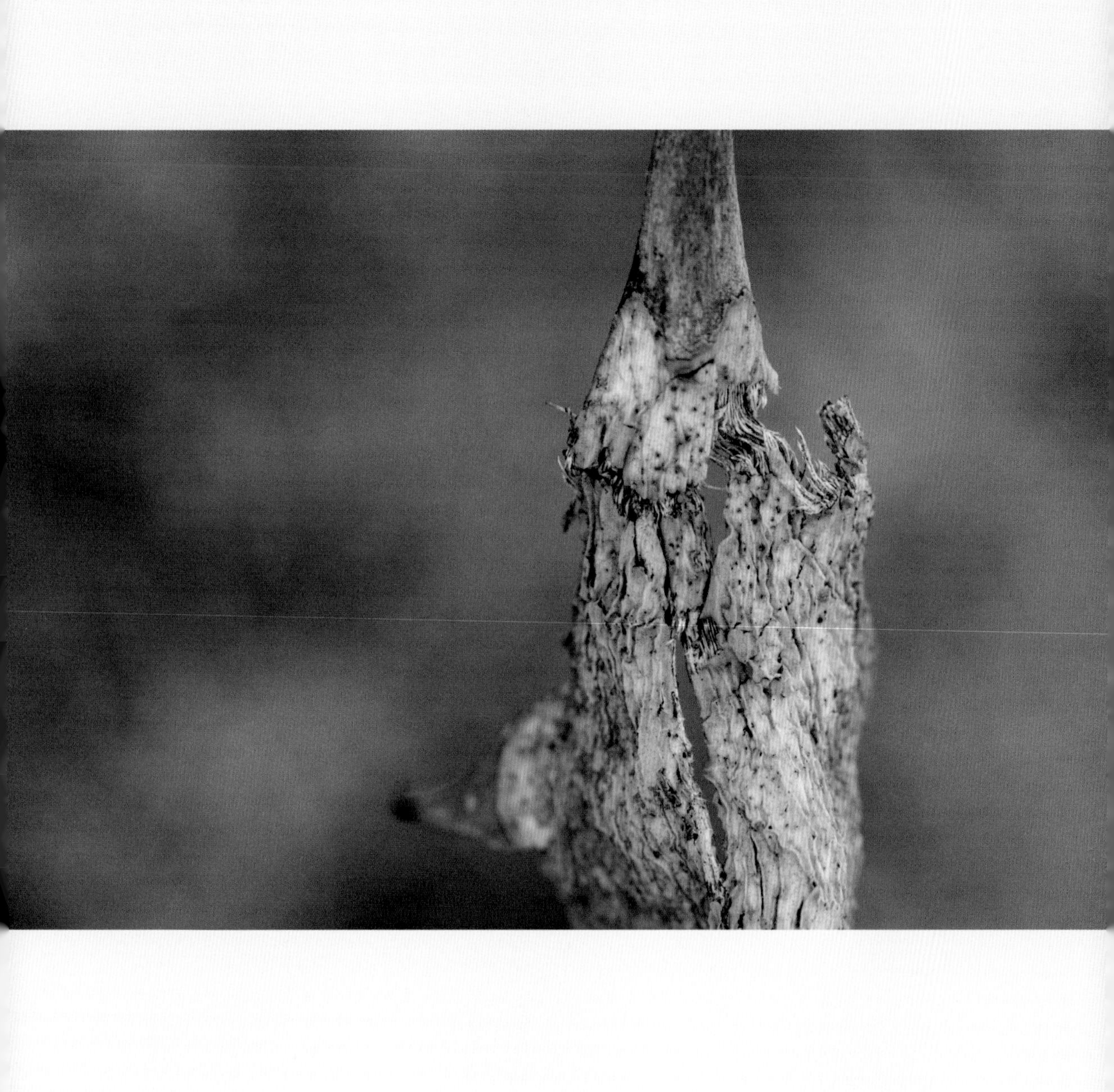

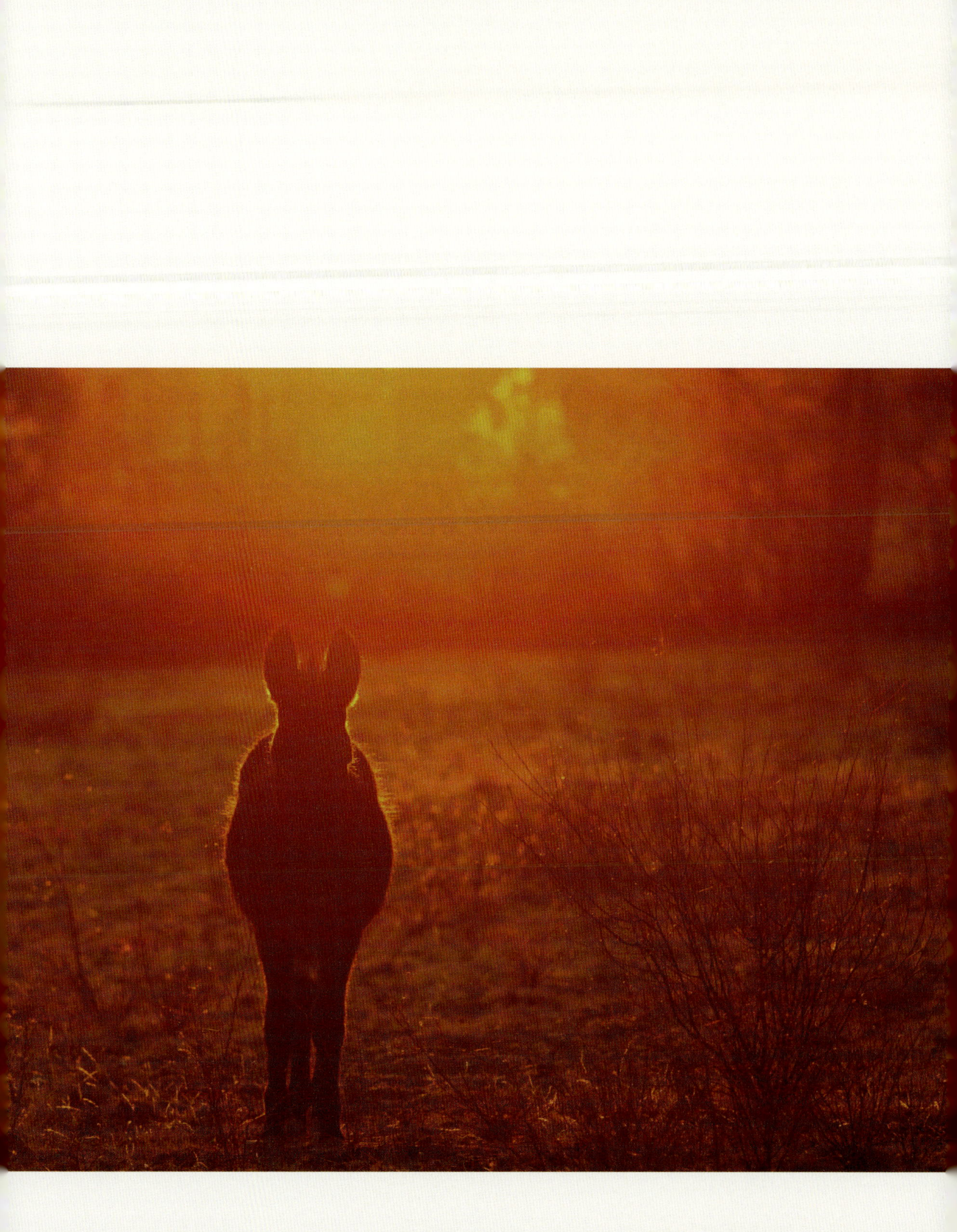

NOWHERE TO GO, NOTHING TO DO

Frustration and boredom stoke my disorientation as the days in Mitla creep by. I miss the buzz of New York City, the constant drumbeat of deadlines, and the camaraderie of being part of a fast-moving team. Living in downtown Manhattan, the city was always in motion and filled with a cacophony of sounds, colors, and textures. I constantly received microdoses of dopamine and adrenaline. Here, the still and quiet is broken only by distant church bells and the occasional braying of donkeys.

The police have barricaded the entrance of town. Physically, we have no way out. Travelers not on official business have no way in.

A memory surfaces. When my older son was thirteen years old, he complained to me that he was restless after I'd forbidden him from playing a computer game. I suggested he reframe boredom as a threshold through which something new could emerge. Of course, the idea was completely lost on him—he walked away annoyed and a little resentful. But now, in Mitla, this recollection arises with an unexpected freshness.

Someone once told me that when you give someone advice, you should be prepared to take it yourself. I decide to sit and be present with the discomfort of not knowing what to do. Thay, Zen master, poet, and peace activist, has been my teacher for fourteen years. He often subverted conventional wisdom. Instead of the usual directive, "Don't just sit there, do something," he suggested, "Don't just do something, sit there!" As I follow his advice, one of his calligraphies rises from the depths of my memory: "The Way Out Is In."

As the days pass and I settle more deeply into myself, the unease within begins to loosen its vise-like grip. I stop looking for tasks and distractions. In the space that opens up, another of Thay's calligraphies, which are like concentrated teachings, comes into focus: "Nowhere to go, nothing to do."

Having been in a hurry to achieve something or other most of my life, this phrase caught me off guard the first time I came across it in Thay's Plum Village monastery. Its gentle invitation intrigued me and touched me somewhere deep inside. Many years later, my old wondering surfaces: *Is it really possible to stop doing and simply be? Is there another path I could walk?*

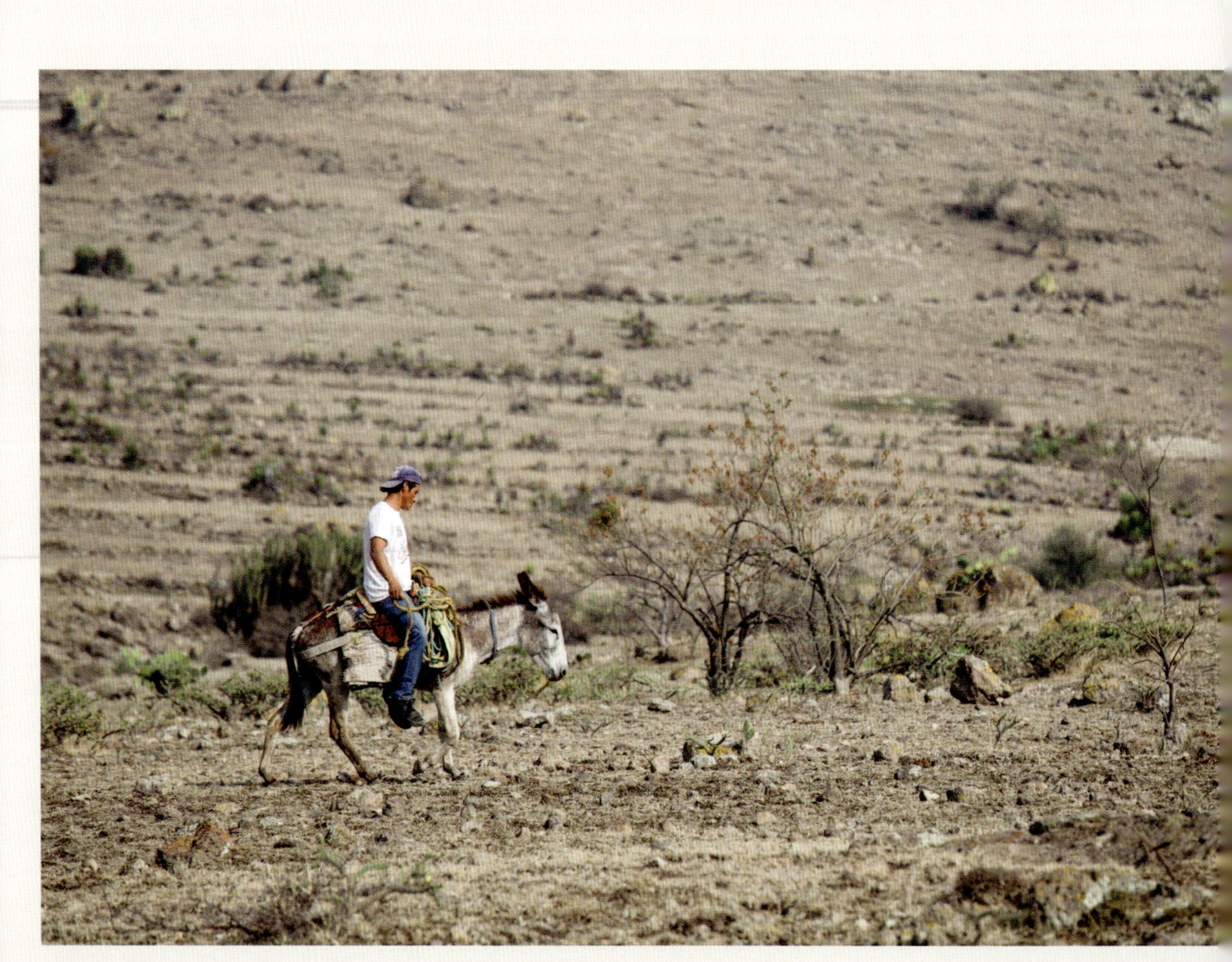

WALKING INTO EMPTINESS

Zen, which my wife introduced me to when we met in 2006, encourages us to go beyond concepts and to viscerally experience whether the meditative and reflective practices offered can help us transform our suffering. In Mitla, I literally have nowhere to go and nothing to do—I can either fight my reality, or flow with it. If I turn toward presence, can my circumstances be an opportunity rather than a constriction? *Nowhere to go, nothing to do* becomes my daily mantra.

Thay unpacks this calligraphy by explaining that it doesn't mean we should sit and do nothing all day, but rather that we should relax into life. It is a reminder: we already have more than enough conditions to be happy; we are already enough. There is no destination to reach, no need to rush, no need to achieve anything, and no need to accumulate more. I give up on recreating my habitual busyness here and instead choose to consciously step into emptiness (a concept, in Zen, that points to the infinite possibilities always ready to be born). I make a commitment to walk aimlessly into Mitla's empty landscape. I will take my camera.

The next day, I rise in the early dawn to hike into the surrounding wilderness while the air is still cool on my skin. I have hiked ever since I was a teenager, and I love to walk long distances. Because of Mitla's closure, I can walk only in one direction: toward the mountains ringing the valley.

As soon as the sun appears over their crest, the temperature rises rapidly. The intensity and oppressiveness of the heat that envelops me by mid-morning limits the area I can explore—if only there were trees to offer shade, streams of water to cool my brow, or at the very least, a little wind to caress my face. I love walking in green and pleasant lands, I realize, places with flower meadows and lakes to joyfully fill my gaze, or along coastal cliff paths, watching the light play on endlessly changing ocean waves.

I am unfamiliar with this monochrome, desert-like scrubland and its accompanying heat. My mind is in a rebellious mood despite my best efforts to calm and soothe it. I would gladly trade this heavy silence for the honking of car horns and the hammering and clanging of construction sites that were my constant companions in New York City. I have gone from sensory feast to sensory famine. How can I conjure joy in a landscape that offers so little variation in color and form? These walks feel more like a test of endurance than a path to spiritual awakening.

After the first couple of hours, I return my camera back to its bag, which stays firmly shut. I feel a quiet disappointment; nothing in the viewfinder stirs me. All I see are slightly varying panoramas of parched land. *Once I have captured one picture, it feels as if I have taken them all.* I imagine myself driving through this terrain without the slightest urge to slow down, let alone stop for a lingering look or photograph. The landscape leaves no imprint in my mind.

I enjoyed two exhibitions of my photography in New York City galleries and love to share my images on Instagram. Trudging toward my temporary home in Casa Lyobaa, I become aware of a hidden part of me that equates taking successful photographs with a hunter proudly returning from a trip with his trophy kill. Inside, I recoil from the disappointment of coming home empty handed.

In the days that follow, I walk each morning but my body protests every time the sun rises in the sky and the light hardens into a harsh glare. My legs involuntarily turn back, even though part of me yearns to press on

toward the distant horizon in the vague hope of discovering something more diverse and interesting. Day after day, I try to find a greater sense of equanimity walking this land. In Zen, emptiness does not mean nothingness. Instead, emptiness captures the insight that everything exists in relation to everything else. Nothing, not even you or me, has a separate, independent self—all things are made of other things. We, for example, are made of the food we eat, the air we breathe, the books we read, the conversations we have, and much more.

"Because of emptiness," Thay would often say, "anything is possible." And yet, despite my intention to step into interconnected potentiality, desert-like scrub is just not for me, and I decide to quit my daily walks. It is too aimless for aimlessness. I feel listless and at a loss. Back at square one.

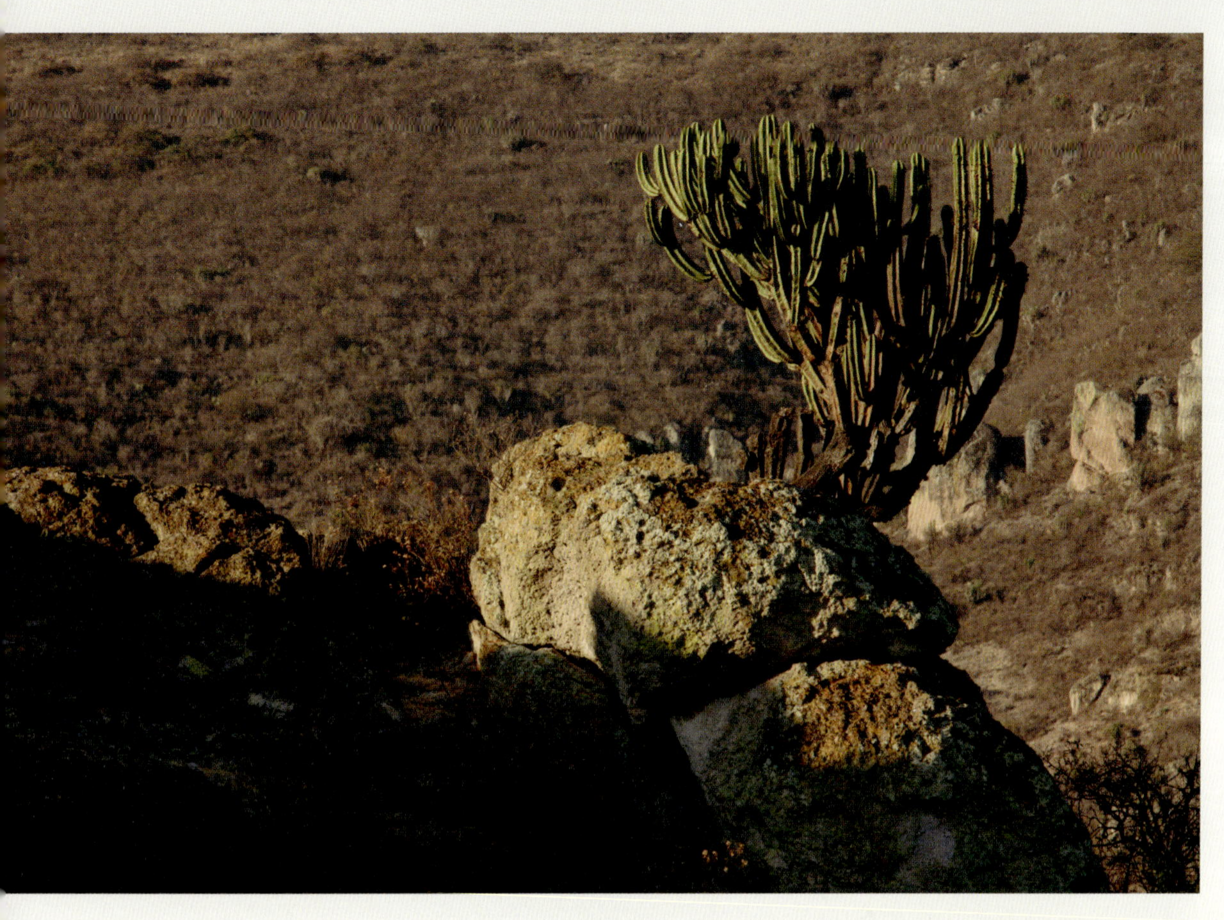

SEEING
IN SILENCE

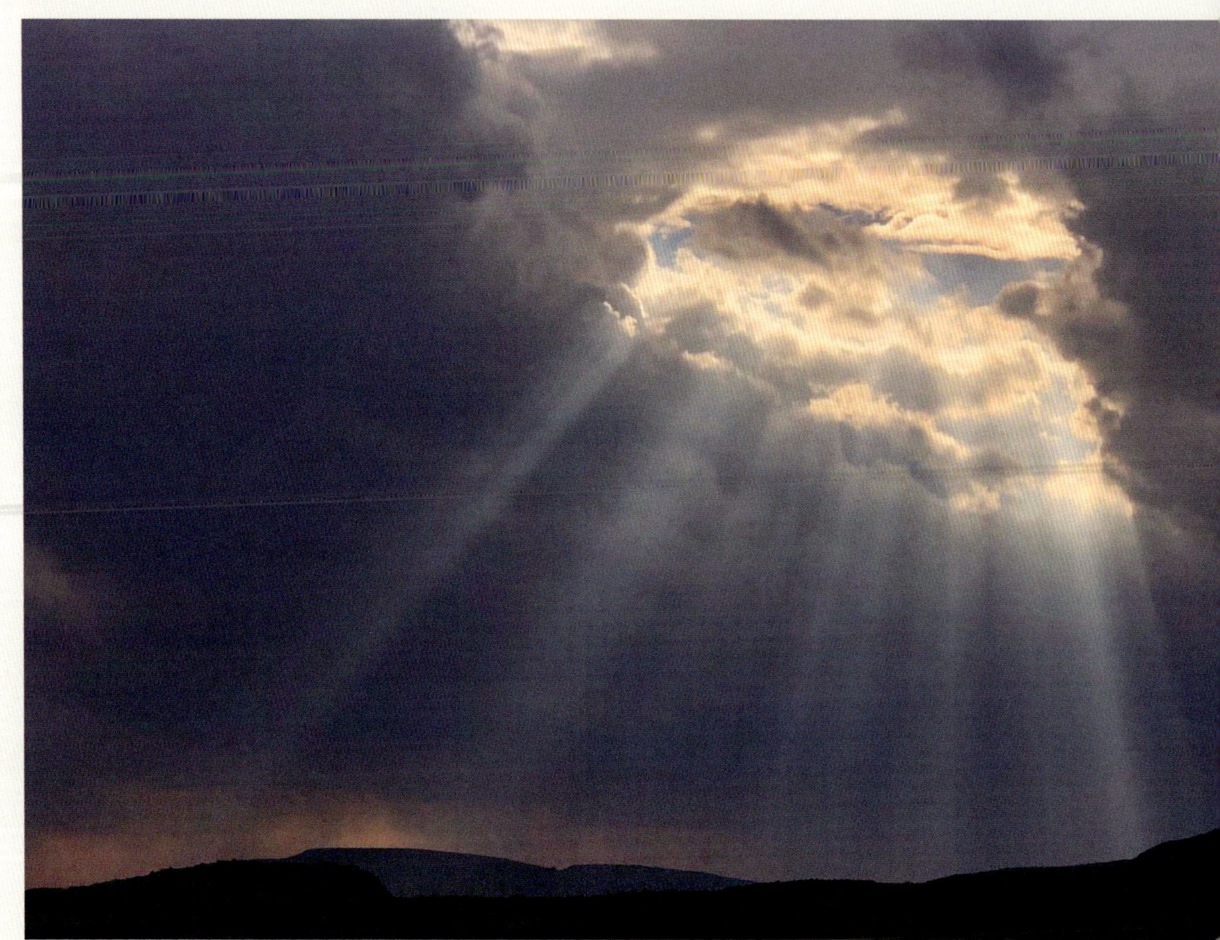

I have learned from my Zen practice that there are no instant fixes. The practice of mindfulness in everyday life needs time to ripen. Patience has been foundational over my fifteen years of practice as I've encountered, again and again; old, embedded habits that keep reappearing. Being gentle, rather than berating myself when I feel I may be taking one step forward and two steps back, has helped me open up to greater self-compassion.

With all this in my mind's eye, I offer room to my feeling of defeat in Mitla. I name it and embrace it. It is not the first time I have experienced a sense of deflation, and almost certainly won't be the last. This acknowledgement, and the tenderness that accompanies it, creates a little spaciousness, and the negative feelings start to ease.

It's hard to pinpoint the exact moment when the very emptiness of this land, its silence, becomes my salvation. Because I have nothing to divert my attention in the quietness of this place, I start to hear the softer and wiser voice within me, the voice that is drowned out most of the time. It suggests, gently, that the problem is not what I see, but the eyes through which I look.

Stephen Mitchell's translation of the Tao Te Ching (the ancient text written by Laozi around 400 BCE), which has accompanied me since I first came across it in my early thirties, surfaces in my mind. It perfectly sums up the gift Mitla is quietly offering me that Manhattan, for all its energy and vitality, never could: "Colors blind the eye. Sounds deafen the ears. Flavors numb the taste. Thoughts weaken the mind. Desires wither the heart. The Master observes the world but trusts his inner vision. He allows things to come and go. His heart is as open as the sky."[1]

Here the sky is all encompassing; can my heart also be that open? More questions come to me: What would happen if I let go of my anthropocentric way of seeing the world, all my demands to be entertained? What if I stopped treating nature as if it were there to meet my needs and instead tried to just be present to what is?

As a journalist, I have written about how our scientific materialist interpretation of the world has contributed to the climate emergency and the destruction of ecosystems—how the belief that we are separate from nature has fueled the pillaging of the earth and severed our connection to the sacred. Trudging through the monotonous scrubland surrounding Mitla, I begin to question whether I have really broken free of this mindset myself. With the sun hot on my back as I head toward the enforced isolation of our home, I realize a question has been quietly ripening in me for many years:

What is my relationship with nature?

1   Stephen Mitchell, *Tao Te Ching* (New York: Harper Perennial, 1988)

This question had first come into focus fifteen years earlier during a week-long course at Schumacher College, the alternative ecology center in Devon, England. Blindfolded and guided through an oak forest, I spent several minutes tentatively feeling my way around, touching the bark of trees, the soft, damp moss underlay of the forest, and experiencing the uneven ground under my feet. Then came an unexpected instruction to shift my perception and see if I could sense nature experiencing me.

Like most people I know, I had been conditioned to believe nature is in service to me, that my relationship with the environment is a one-way street. It came as a shock to suddenly recognize that nature is experiencing me! I felt immediately the truth that we are in relationship, we inter-are—just think of humans and trees breathing in tandem, each inhaling and exhaling what the other gives and needs. My consciousness is in nature, and nature's consciousness is in me.

In that moment, I realized that I was not alone or separate, but part of an intricate web of life. It is a moment etched deeply into my mind. This insight gained greater clarity and depth through conversations I had with Thay at Plum Village. During one interview for the *Guardian*, Thay explained that the mistaken belief that we are separate from nature is a root cause of our alienation and craving. Talking to him was unlike any of the hundreds of interviews I'd conducted before as a journalist—it felt more like a direct transmission, ancient wisdom slicing through my deeply held beliefs like a hot knife through butter.

Looking for inspiration in Mitla, I reread the articles I had written from these conversations many years before. "You carry Mother Earth within you," Thay told me. "She is not outside of you. Mother Earth is not just your environment. Fear, separation, hate, and anger come from the wrong view that you and the earth are two separate entities, that the earth is only the environment. You are in the center, and you want to do something for the earth in order for you to survive. That is a dualistic way of seeing. To breathe in and be aware of your body and look deeply into it, you realize you are the earth and your consciousness is also the consciousness of the earth."

I become inspired to delve into the local culture in Mitla, and I discover the Zapotecs hold a similar view of our relationship to the earth. To them, our planet is sentient. Offerings of food and drink are made to plants, who are spoken to as spiritual interlocutors. Local healers, *curanderas*, offer divine remedies with corn as a spirit plant, and black or blue corn is sacrosanct. Children are assigned spirit animals, *naguales*, at birth. Caves are residences for gods of nature.

These beliefs and customs manifest a connectedness to the earth that has largely been absent from my life, despite the ways I have sought it through my work and my Zen practice.

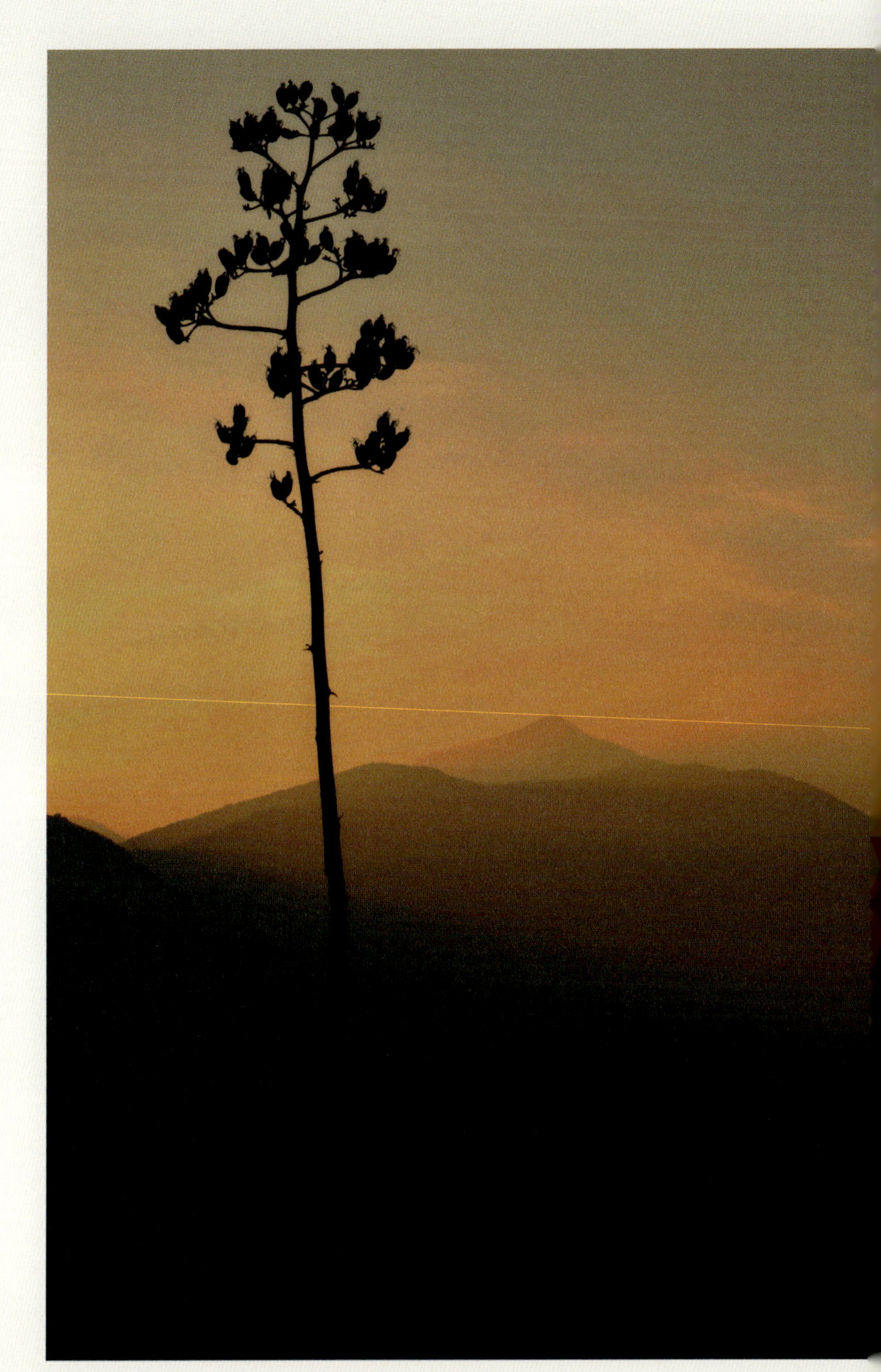

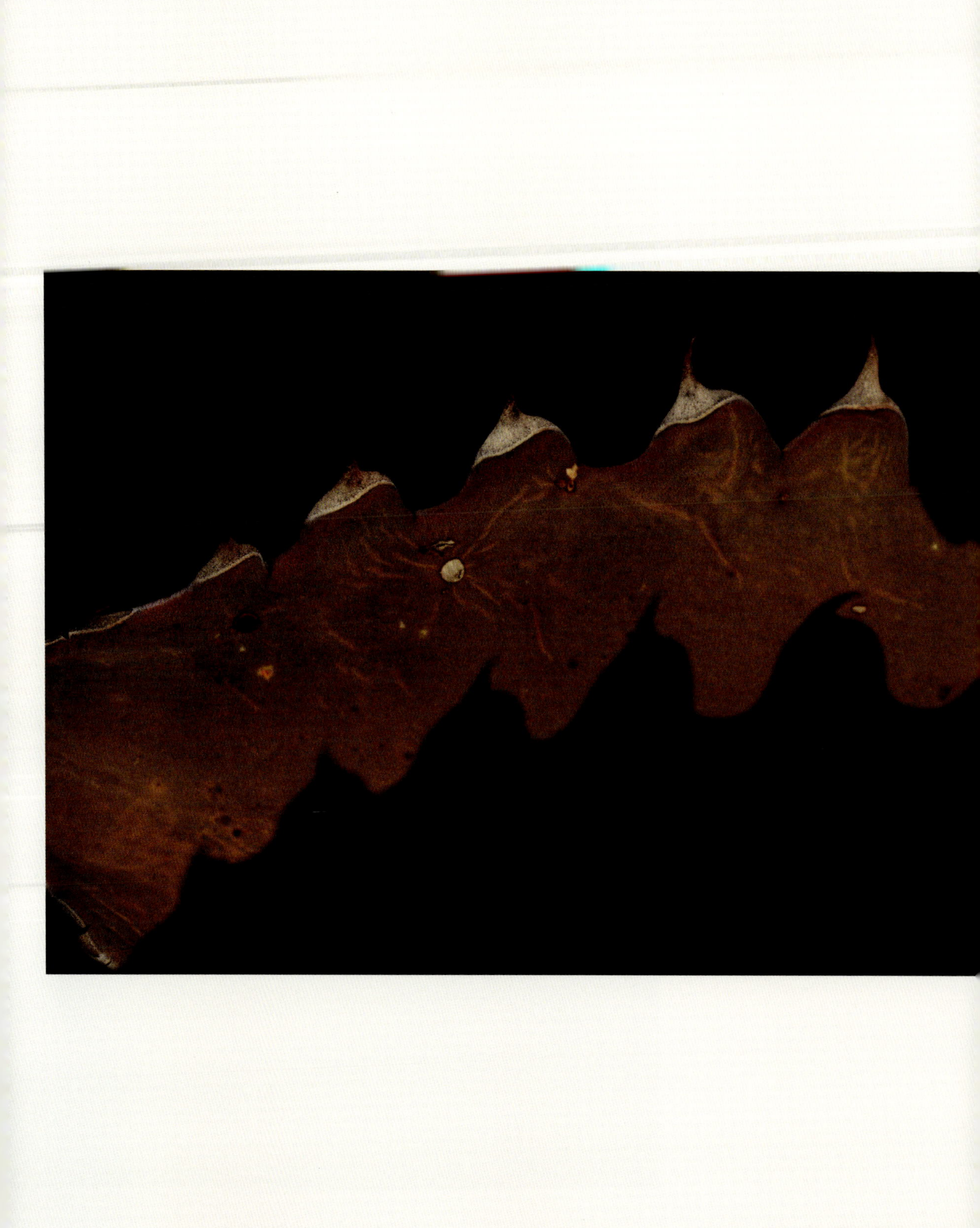

BEING WITH THE EARTH

With my faith rekindled, I recommit to my daily walkabouts. This time I take refuge in the two wings of meditation: stopping and deep looking. Over the coming days, my Western notion of *emptiness* as a feeling of separation and isolation, which persists despite my Zen practice and study, slowly begins to transform.

Slowing down helps. My deeply habituated pattern of rushing is reflected in my hiking. I tend to focus on the distance I travel rather than enjoy the moment. My eyes scan the horizon, rather than look at what is beneath my feet. Outside of Mitla as the days of lockdown continue, I consciously slow my pace. I start to let go. Inspired by the practice of walking meditation, I match my steps with the rhythm of my breaths.

Thay encouraged us to see that "each mindful breath, each mindful step, reminds us we are alive on this beautiful planet. We don't need anything else. It is wonderful enough just to be alive, to breathe in, and to make one step. We have arrived at where real life is available—the present moment."

Every so often I stop, bend down, and look deeply at what is right before my eyes. My relationship to this land, to the sparseness stretching in every direction, begins to change. The separation between myself and what I see begins to blur as a new world unfolds beneath, around, and within me. At least for stretches of time here and there, I no longer need to extract anything, to achieve anything. As the global death count continues to rise, surely it is enough simply to be healthy and alive.

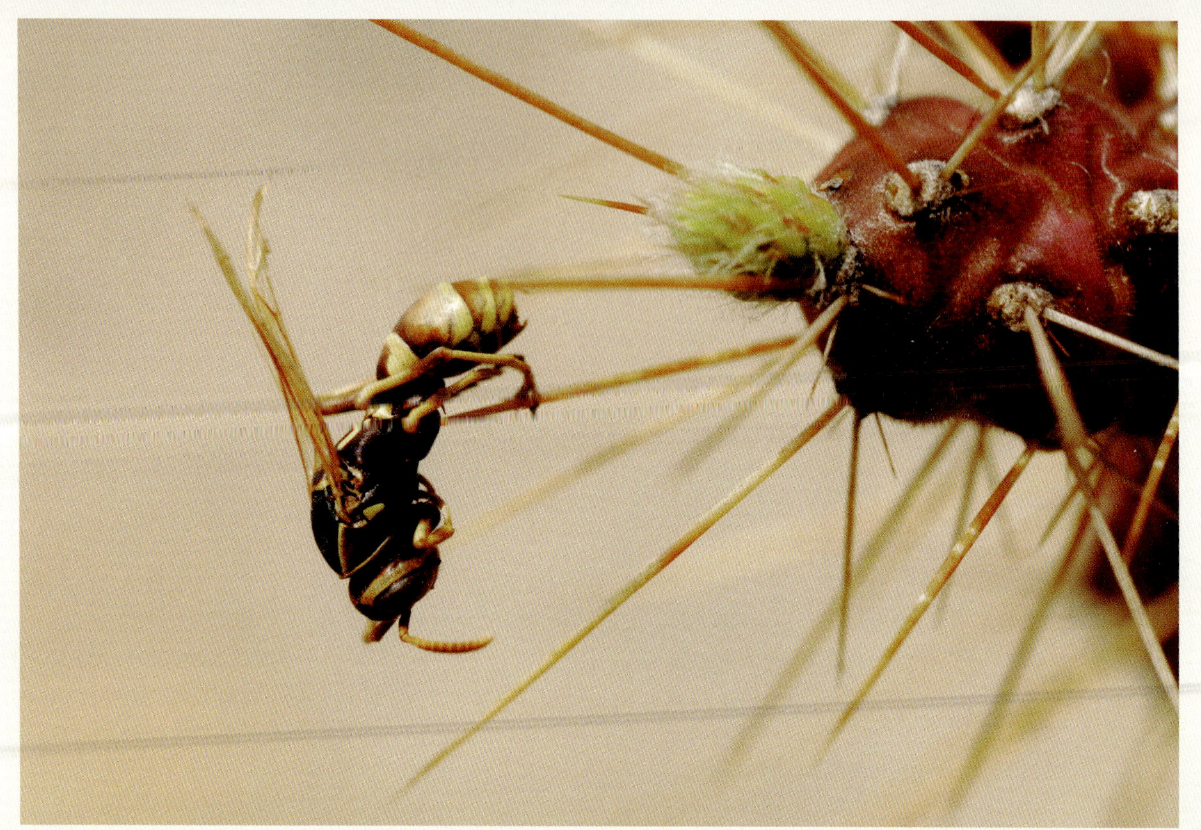

IMPALED

The pandemic sweeps through Mitla with staggering speed, casting a haunting new light on the town's identity as the place of the dead. The most trusted doctor in town is one of the first to die. Black ribbons appear over doors of homes daily, silent markers of loss. The town, which relies on visitors for its livelihood, has shut completely. The streets fall quiet.

My mind, attuned to the pandemic, lingers on dead plants and insects during my daily walking meditations. On my first day of slowing down and looking deeply, I catch sight of a wasp impaled on a cactus spike, perfectly preserved by the dry heat. I wonder if it was blown off course by a gust of wind, or whether a simple, momentary loss of concentration caused its death.

With this wasp, a whole new vista opens up. On closer inspection, I notice back legs still gripping the cactus spine, as if the wasp had struggled to free itself from a slow and painful death. As I focus more intently, the cactus itself begins to resemble some kind of monster. Sitting among the quietness, observing the wasp, I recognize that I have also been impaled by a monster. Living in our extractive capitalist system, I sacrificed my well-being to the relentless demands of work. Only the sudden and forced loss of my job has jolted me free of this unrecognized suffering.

Over the coming weeks, I encounter other insects that have suffered the wasp's fate—the sight of a yellow and black moth, skewered like a fallen dark lord in an epic battle, lingers with me long after I snap the shutter and my understanding deepens of how I have used busyness to reinforce the old belief that I am not enough. Even though I know intellectually that this pattern is left over from my childhood, in practice I have struggled to distance myself from it.

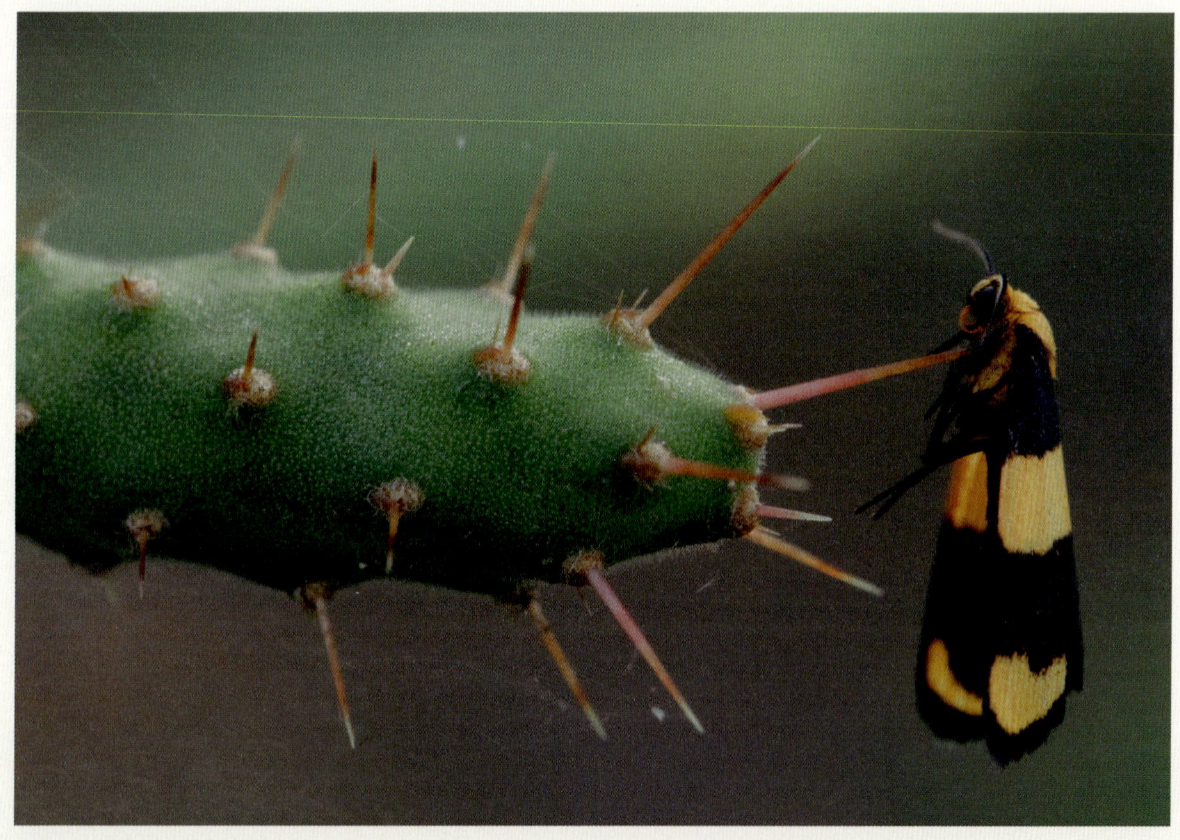

As I continue to wander the hills and ravines surrounding Casa Lyobaa, a new insight surfaces. Throughout most of my journalistic career I sought to drive large-scale impact by educating as many people as possible about the intertwined threats of climate change, biodiversity loss, and social injustice. While this purpose felt noble, it came at a personal cost: the higher I climbed up the career ladder, the more distant I became from feeling personally aligned with the work itself. I sought to help manage change, yet lost my deep personal connection to it.

Layer after layer of understanding and insight opens, leading to new questions that feel as endless as the land stretching beyond the horizon in every direction. I walk, I look, and I see that I have become impaled by my views—stuck. Slowly, I shrank and died inside to new possibilities.

Observing the wasp reveals the difference between having a purpose and having a path. Having a *purpose* brings an objective to strive after, to achieve and live up to—it makes happiness, in part, conditional on meeting

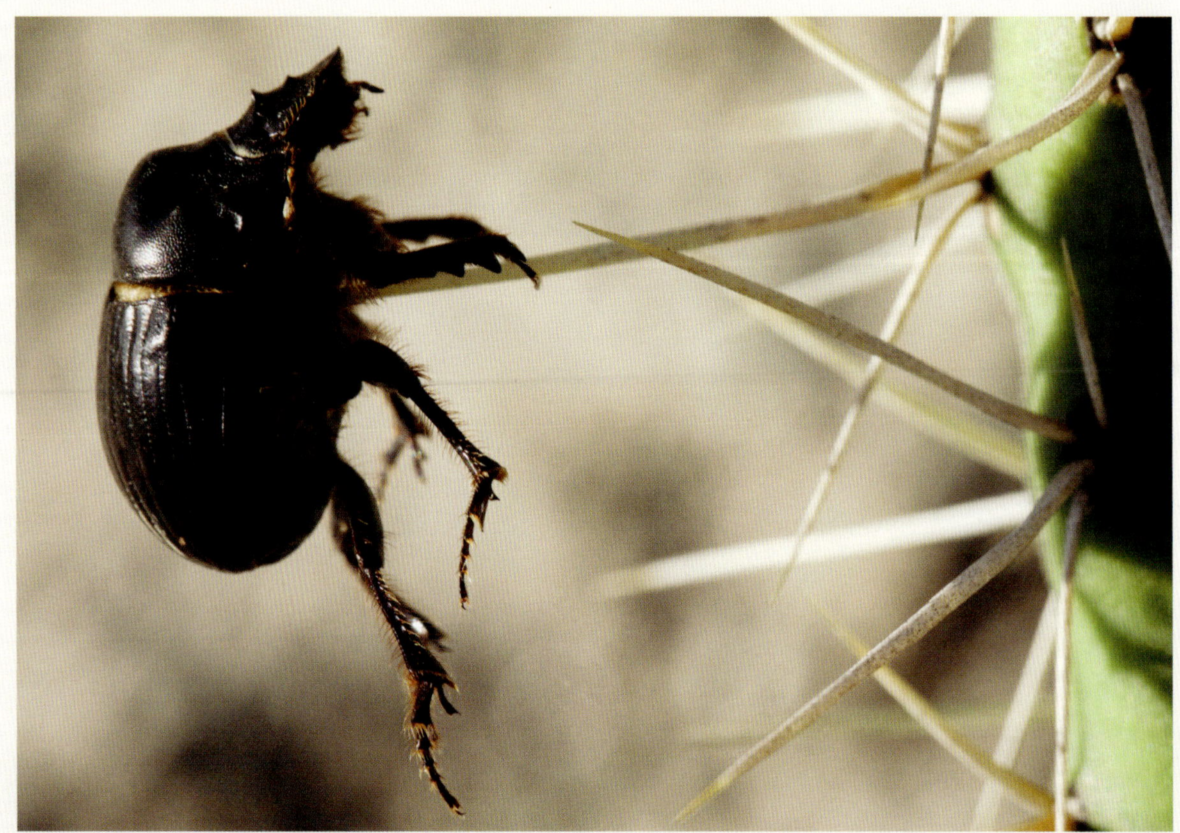

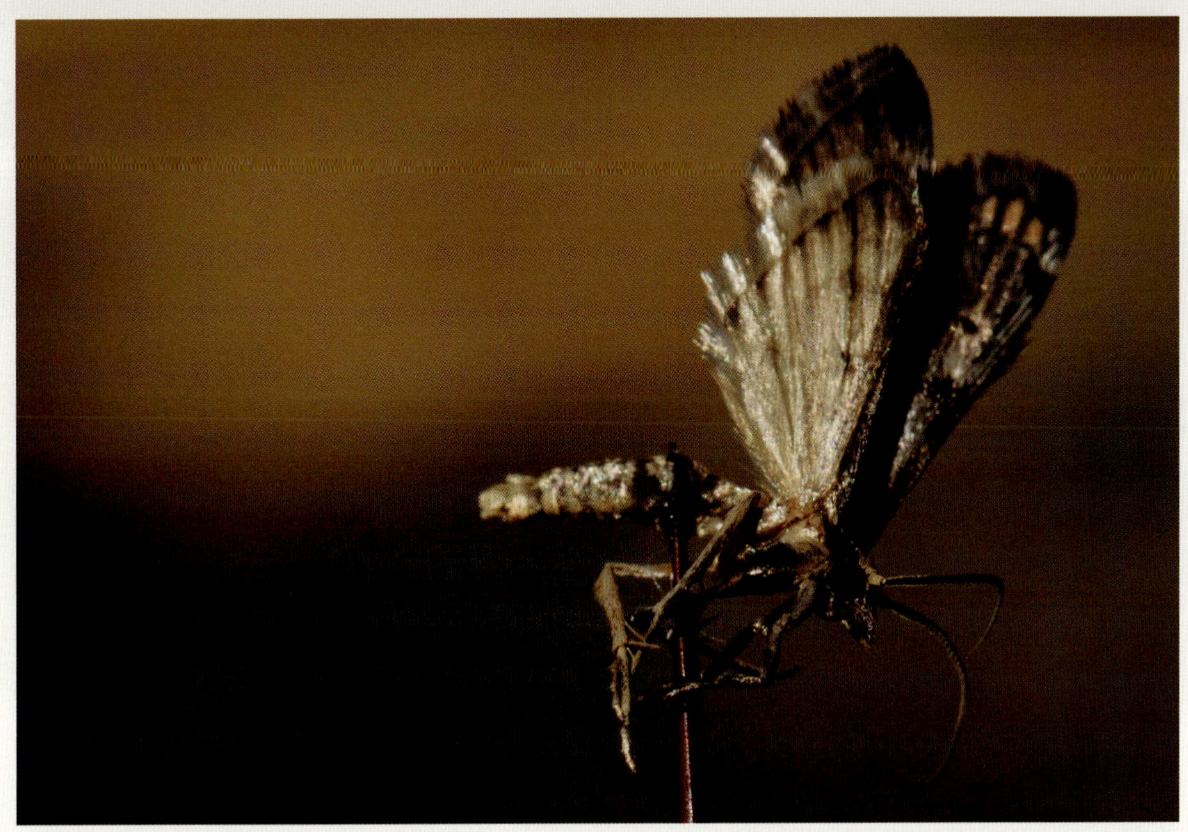

particular goals. A *path* means experiencing reality directly in the present moment. There is no destination, and progress is not measured by success.

The impaled insects stop me in my tracks and teach me: rather than worrying about the past or the future, I have the agency to free myself from the beliefs that keep me stuck. I can walk my path without fear or favor.

To the impaled wasp, I offer my gratitude.

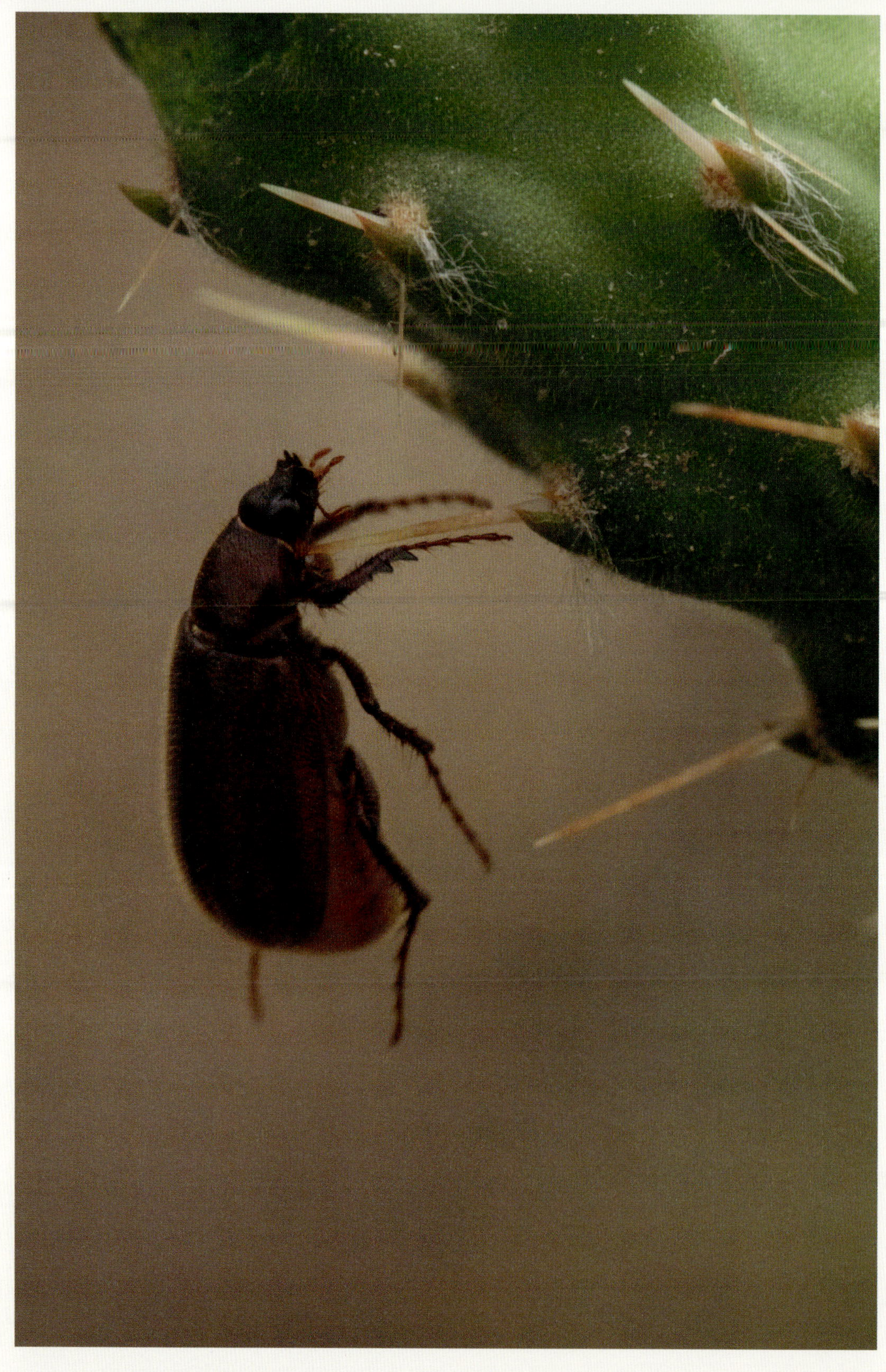

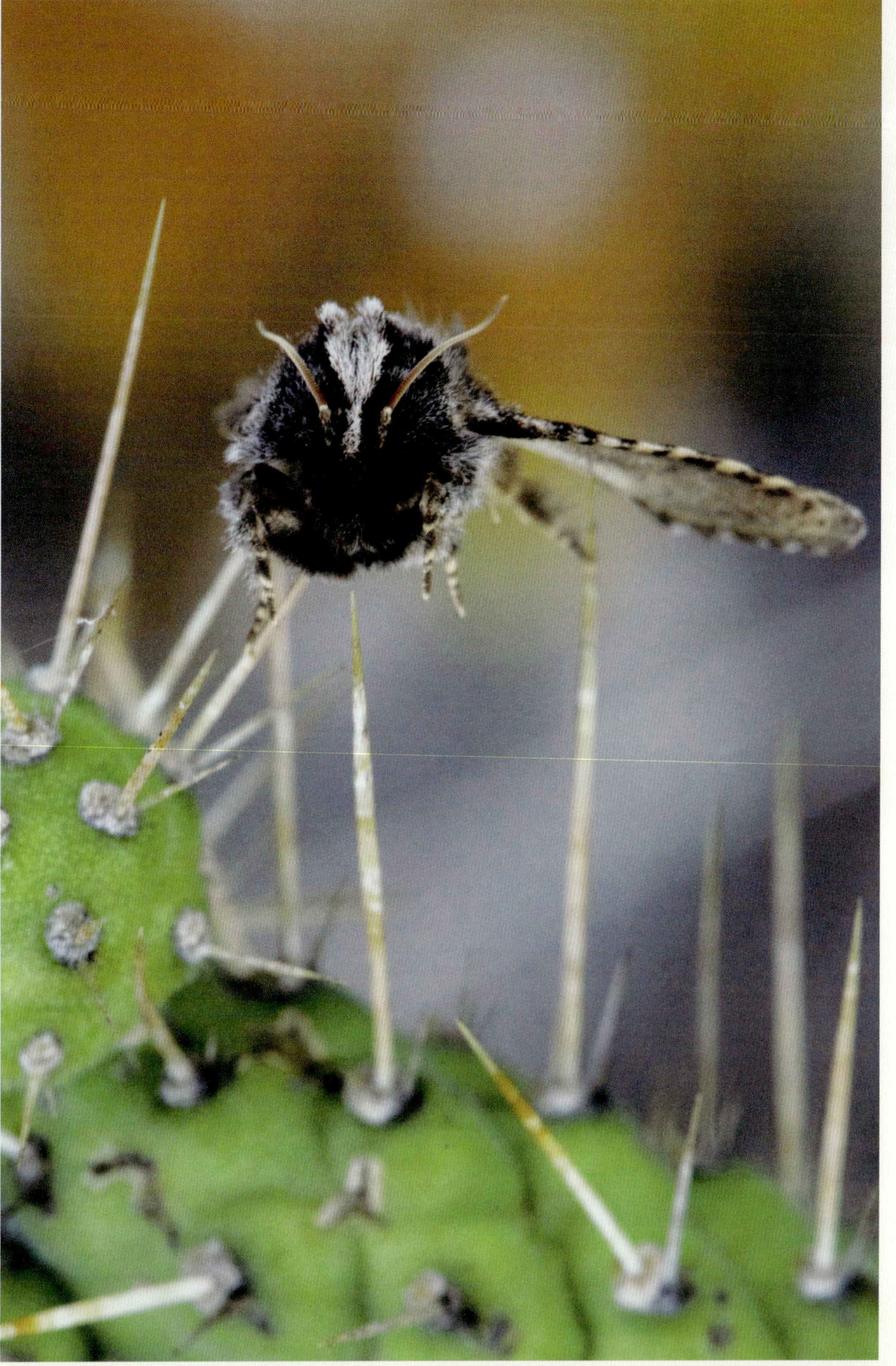

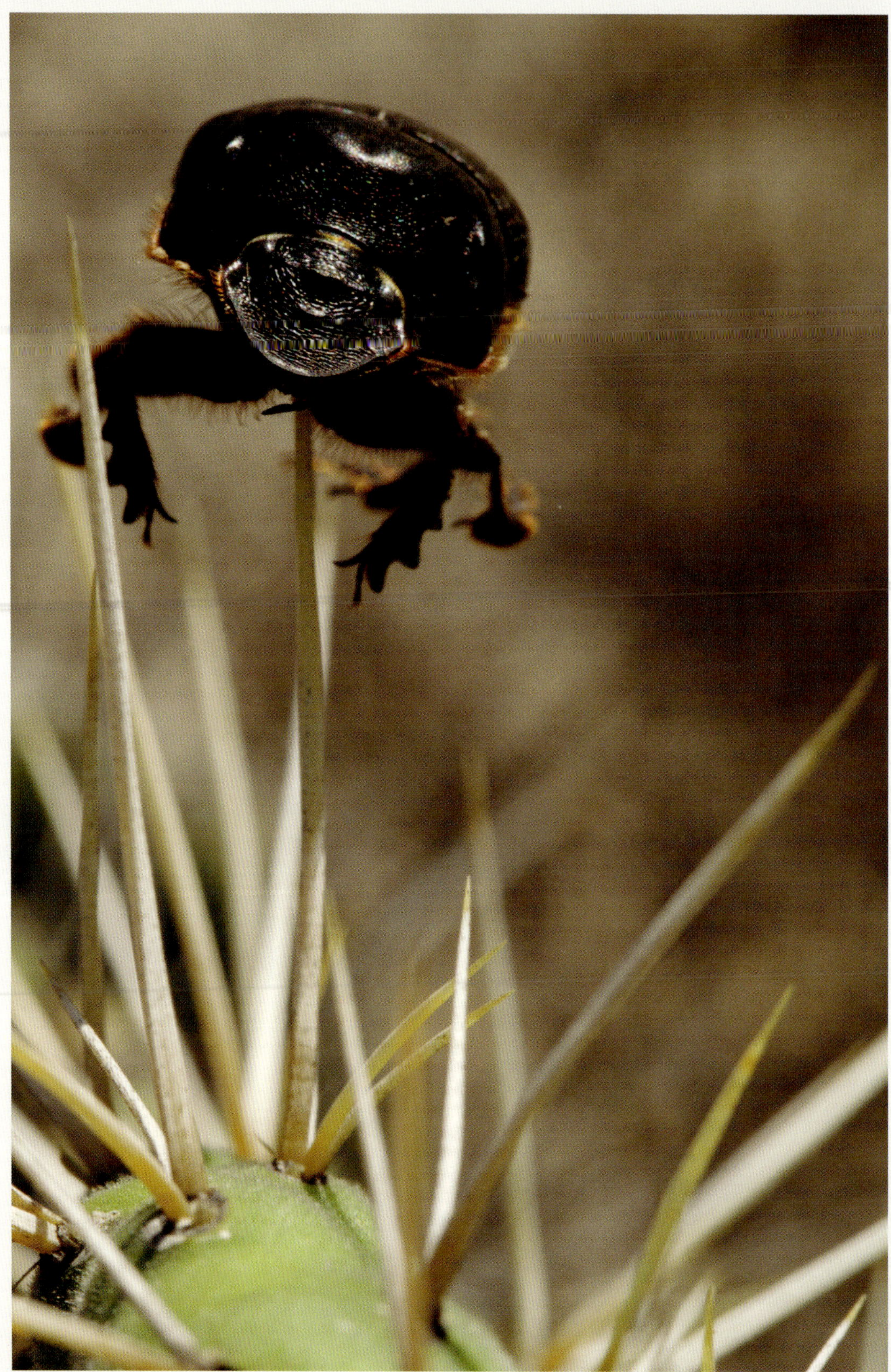

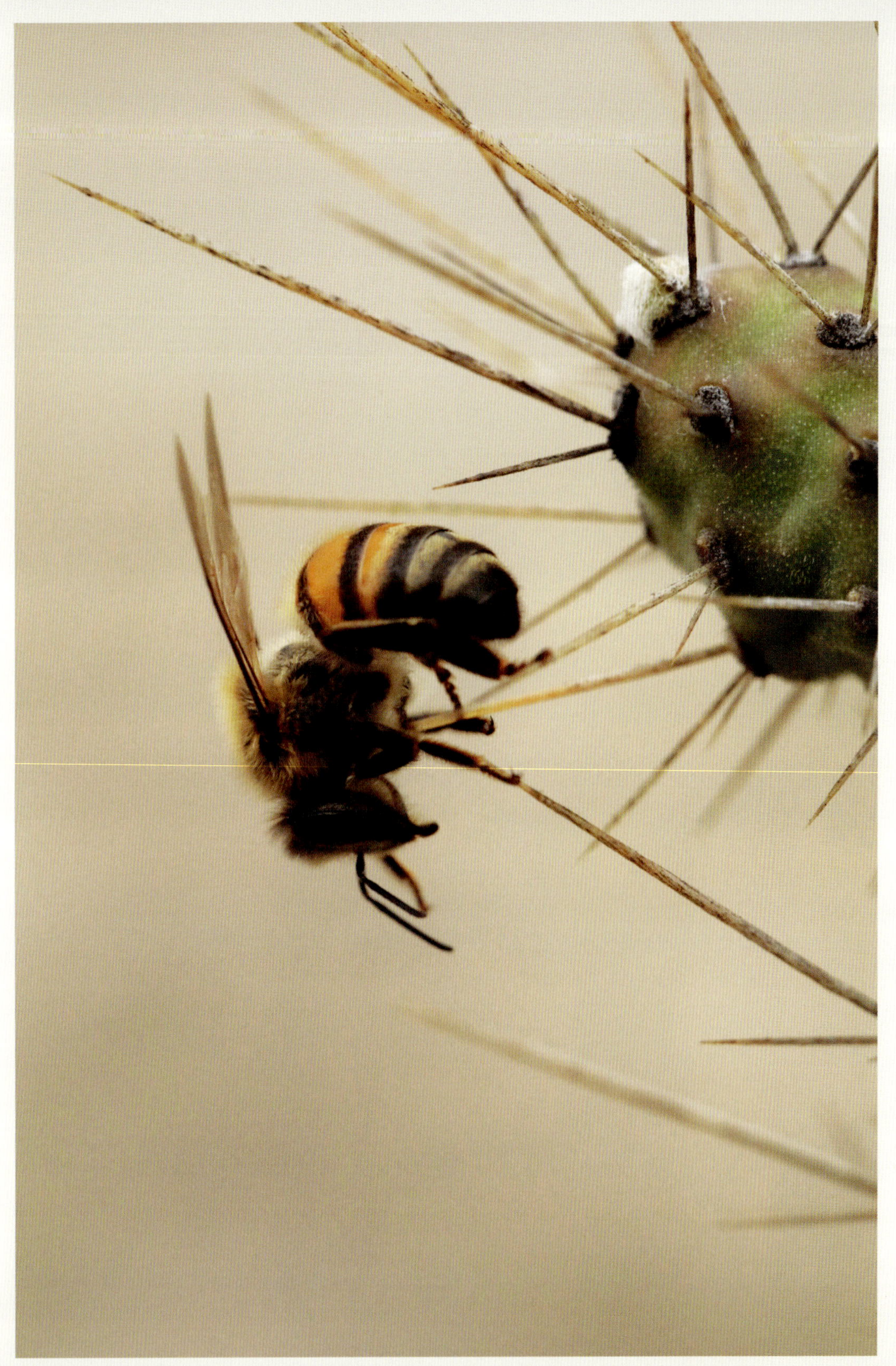

A BELL OF
MINDFULNESS

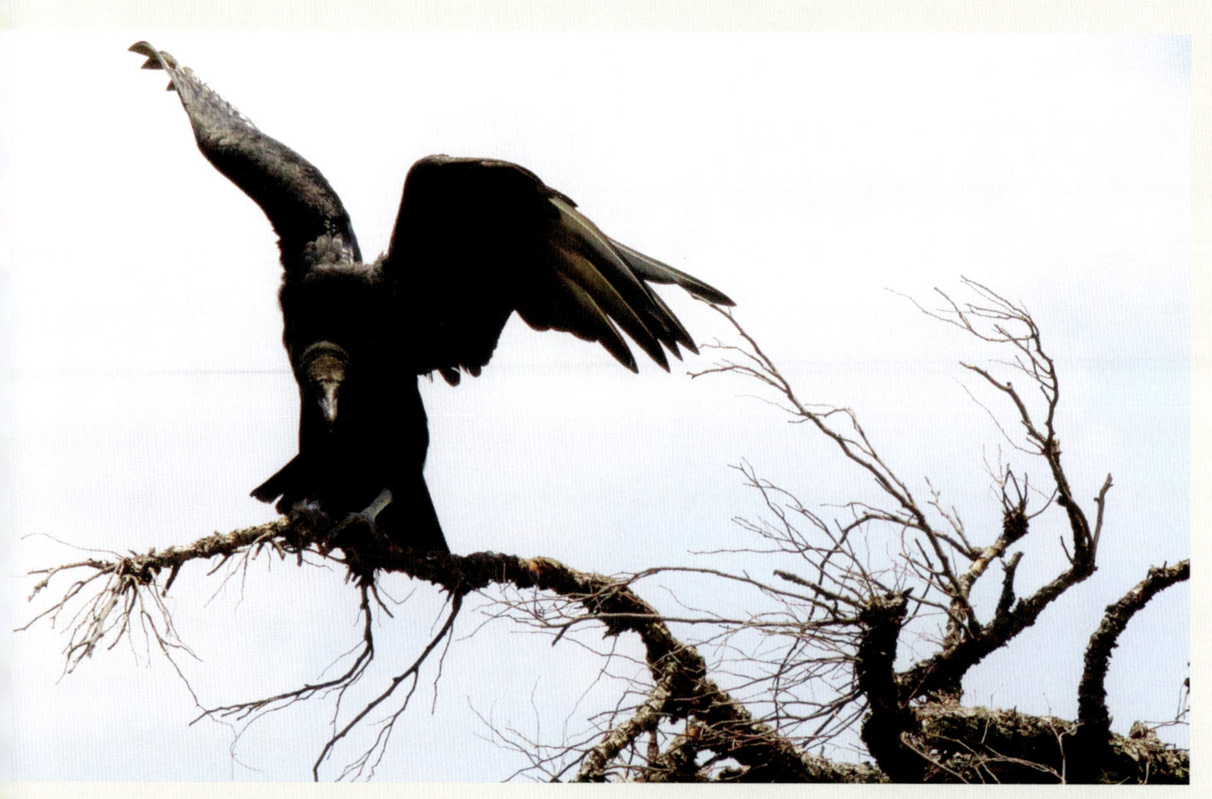

Every morning, as light pours into the valley, I look up at the clear blue sky at the one reliable feature of my time here: multitudes of vultures circling overhead, effortlessly and gracefully riding the thermal currents.

The survival of these birds depends on the decaying remains of the dead. The vultures are the custodians of this place of the dead. They become a daily reminder that life is impermanent—one day I too will die, whether from COVID-19 or if I am fortunate, of old age.

The monks and nuns in Plum Village regularly recite the Five Remembrances, which are an invitation to look this reality directly in the eye:

I am of the nature to grow old. There is no way to escape growing old.

I am of the nature to have ill-health. There is no way to escape having ill-health.

I am of the nature to die. There is no way to escape death.

All that is dear to me and everyone I love are of the nature to change. There is no way to escape being separated from them.

I inherit the results of my actions of body, speech, and mind. My actions are my continuation.

This pandemic is a timely reminder that, while we like to feel in control, we truly do not know what tomorrow will bring. It is an invitation to transform the fear of dying that lies deep within me into the joy and appreciation of being alive.

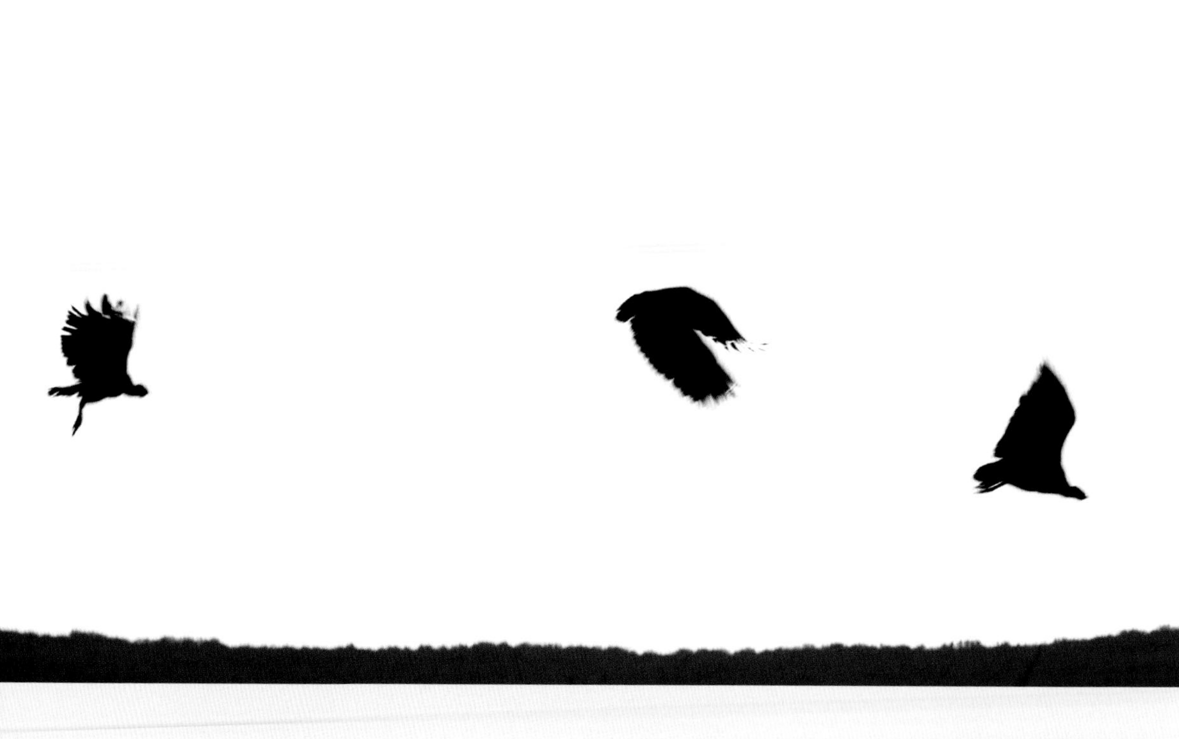

I start to reflect on the contribution I would like to make to life in the time remaining to me. I will soon enter my sixties. After losing my job, I do not yet see a clear path ahead. But, like a carcass that nourishes vultures, I want my actions to sustain the lives of others. A clear wish to help open up blocked minds crystallizes inside of me. I see an opening to integrate my Zen practice with my training as a leadership coach.

I manage to get close to the vultures only once. I stumble across great numbers one morning feasting on a dead goat. After gorging themselves, the huge birds settle on the branches of a nearby tree.

I want to approach during this feeding frenzy, but an irrational fear holds me back, a worry that they may turn on me if I get too close.

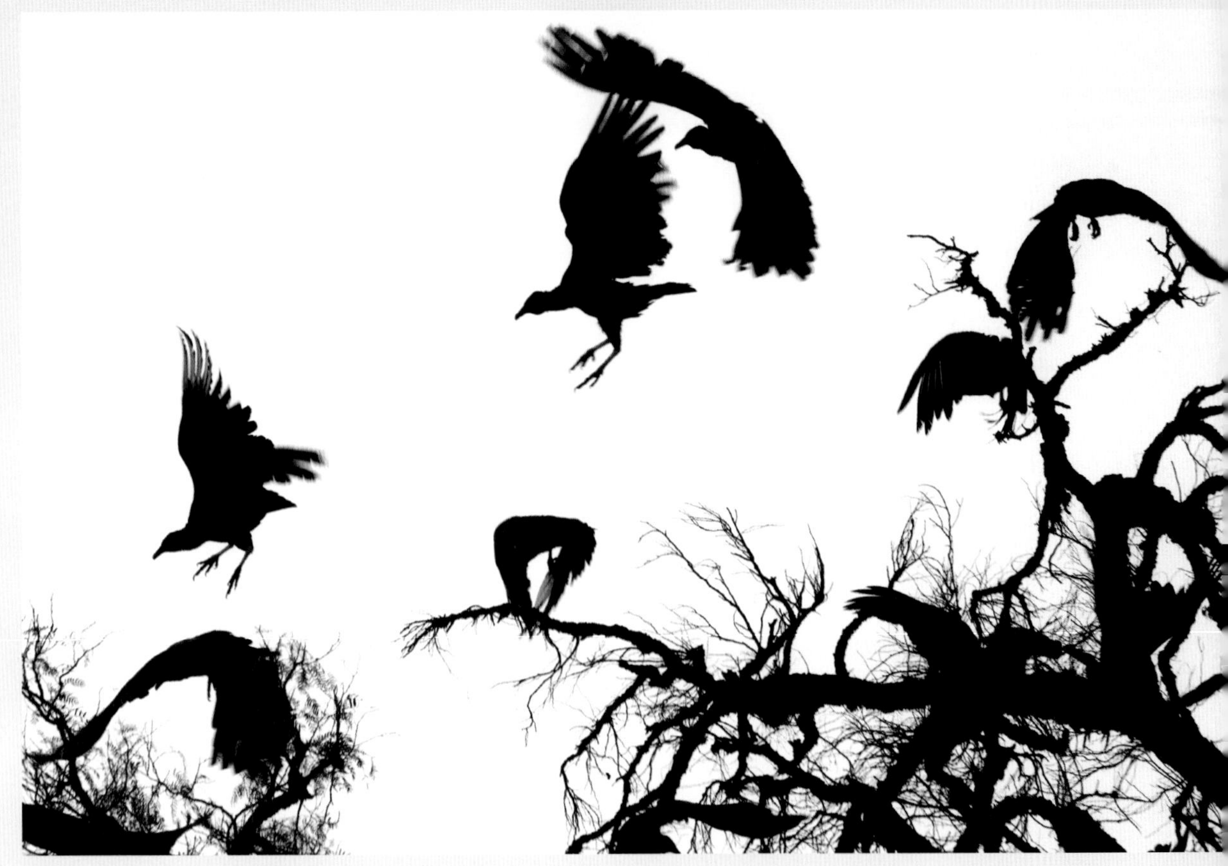

Logically, I know vultures have no interest
in the living, but alone and exposed, I feel
vulnerable. Though I understand the concept
of impermanence and know my life will one
day end, it is hard to embrace here and now. I
am not ready to die just yet.

PATIENCE AND PERSEVERANCE

At first, my untrained eyes fail to see the many spiders scattered across the land. It is only when I slow down and pay close attention that their almost invisible webs come into focus. Unlike vultures, who expend their life energy constantly on the lookout for the dead, I watch spider after spider sit motionless at the center of their delicate, intricate webs—waiting. No chasing, no searching—just stillness and quiet patience.

Their extreme perseverance stands in sharp contrast to my often distracted mind. These spiders remind me of the difficulty I have in balancing action and patience. Deep down, I realize I don't fully trust life. Taught from a young age to be ambitious and strive for what I want, I constantly maneuver to be the one driving change. But now, rather than fighting the reality that I am stuck, I crouch next to spider webs and allow myself to be present for Mitla. When I do, Mitla is able to be present for me.

The spiders teach me life and death are not separate; they are inextricably bound, each giving rise to the other. As I watch the spiders devour their prey, I am reminded that everything is in constant flux. Life transforms into death. What dies gives sustenance to the living. We are all part of this flow of life into death and death into life; there is no beginning and no end.

"Birth and death inter-are in everything— trees, animals, weather, matter, energy," Thay says. "Scientists have already pronounced that there is no birth and no death. There is only transformation. What you call birth and death are only transformation."

This insight resonates in the local Zapotec beliefs, where death is seen as a different kind of transformation. When an individual dies, they pass across a subterranean river, guided by a black dog. They reach the town of souls— located directly under Mitla—where they retain their skeleton, clothes, and persona. Once a year, they return as an incorporeal soul to rejoin their living family for *Dia de Muertos*, a day on which the living prepare the favorite foods and drinks of their dead on an altar inside their home. The belief in this town of souls under Mitla is so strong that families travel hundreds of miles to leave offerings to their dead relatives here.

This flowing connectedness between the living and the dead renders death a fundamentally different (and less terrifying) experience than my Western worldview ever allowed. Nonetheless, my fear of death still runs deep. It's one thing to be at peace with mortality while observing a spider and its prey; it's quite another to accept when it threatens my own life or those I love and cherish. I am thousands of miles away from my two sons, who are under lockdown in London, and I worry daily

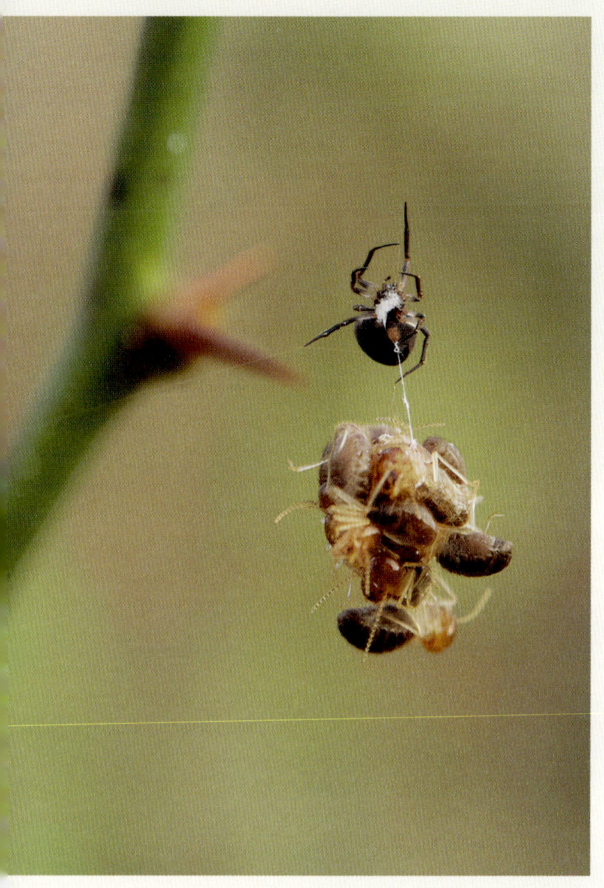

are subject to causes and conditions. Concepts like birth and death are constructs in the mind that we turn to when transformation makes someone or something feel impossible to recognize. Change is not personal, even when we call it *death*.

I once saw Thay demonstrate this by striking a match. He explained that the match catches fire because friction, phosphorus, and oxygen are present; once the phosphorus burns through, the flame vanishes. Life and death are much the same, he finished: they arise, they transform, and they fade according to the conditions that give them form.

Remembering this teaching, I momentarily touch its essence before attachment to the notion of a fixed self crowds in and dominates my mind. While part of me resonates with the truth of no birth and no death, integrating it into my consciousness may well be the work of a lifetime.

for their safety. While it is only human to grieve the loss of those we care about, my fears show me I am still very much caught in seeing death as annihilation rather than part of the natural order of things.

Recognizing my limitations, I wonder whether I can truly grasp the depth of the Buddha's teachings on death. *No birth, no death* is a common Zen phrase, pointing to the reality that birth and death are not personal but they

From all the time I spend observing spiders, one particular scene captures my imagination.

I spot a small spider who has somehow managed to ensnare a cluster of insects many times its size, bundling them into what looks to me like a thief's bag filled with loot. I watch transfixed as the spider slowly but surely hauls its bounty, bound up in a silken net, to the top of a bush for safekeeping: an intimate dance of life and death.

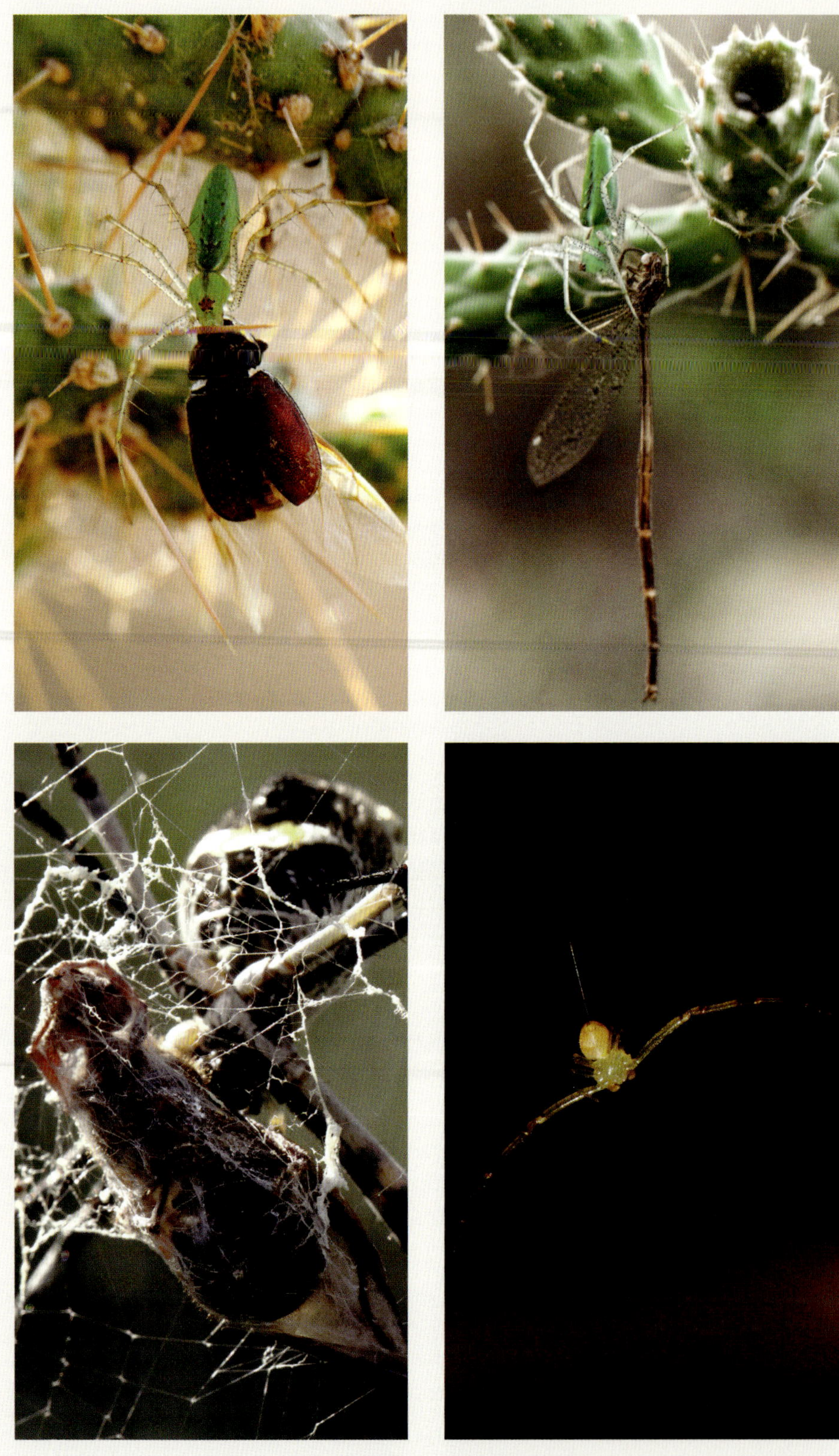

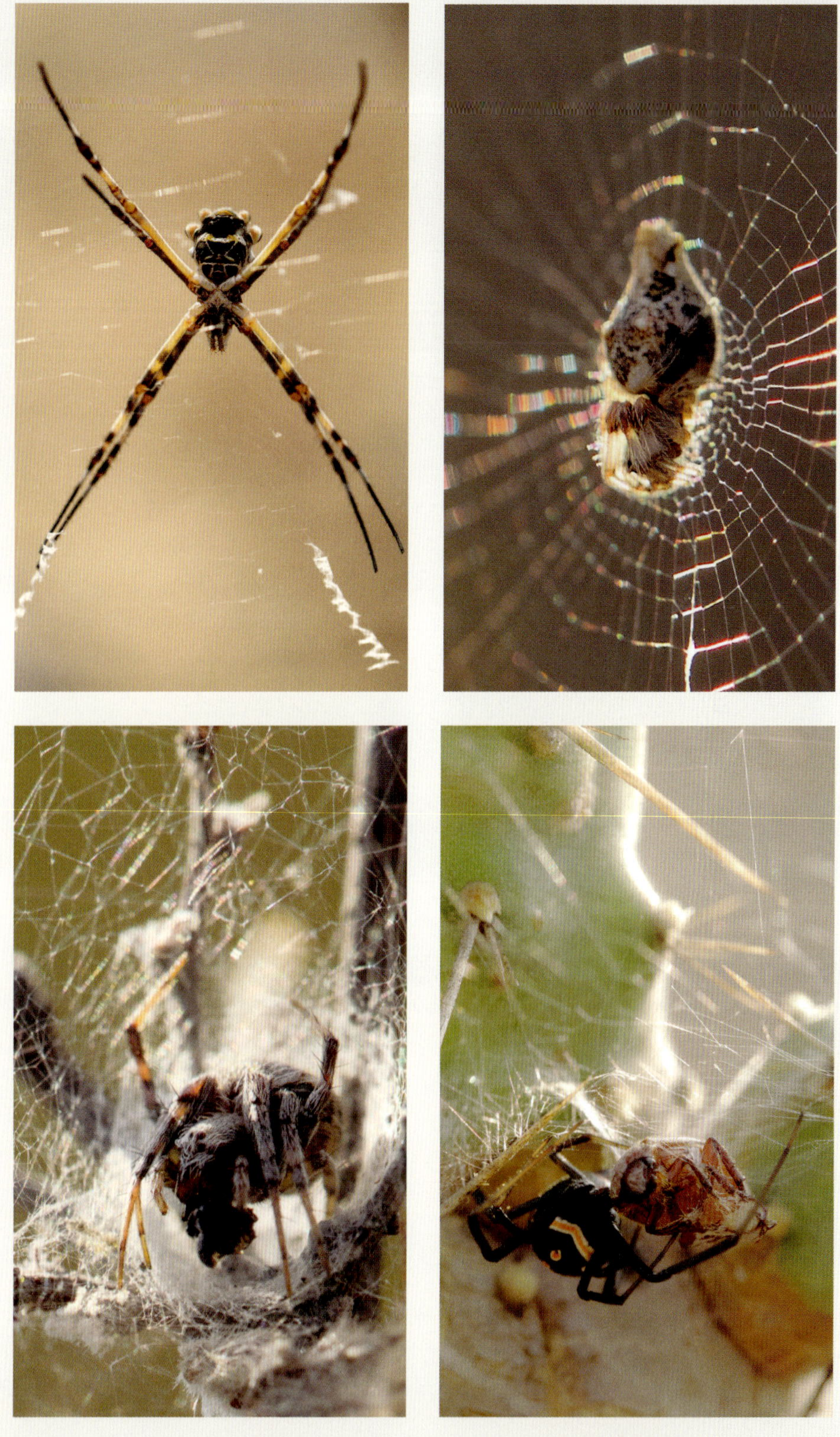

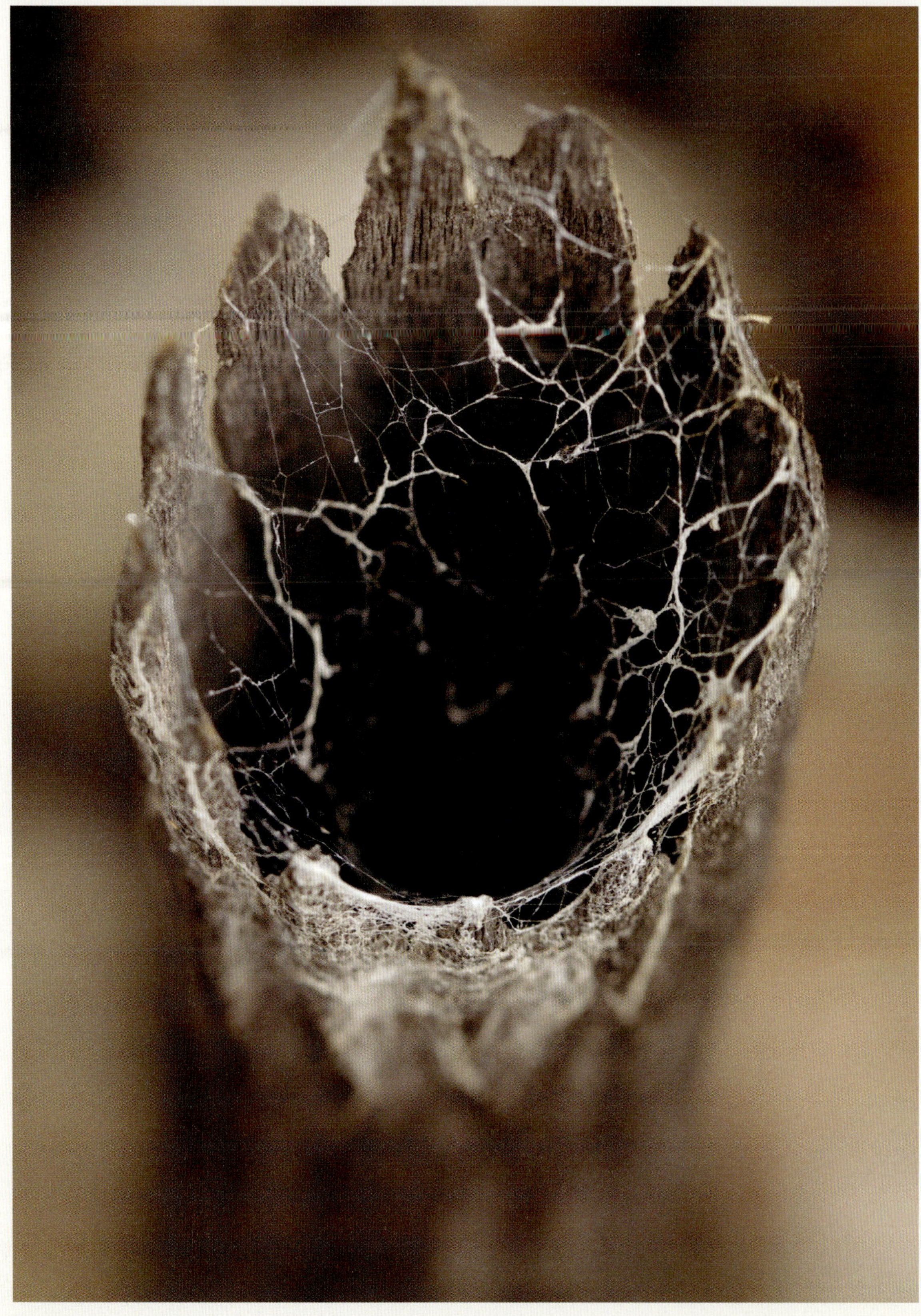

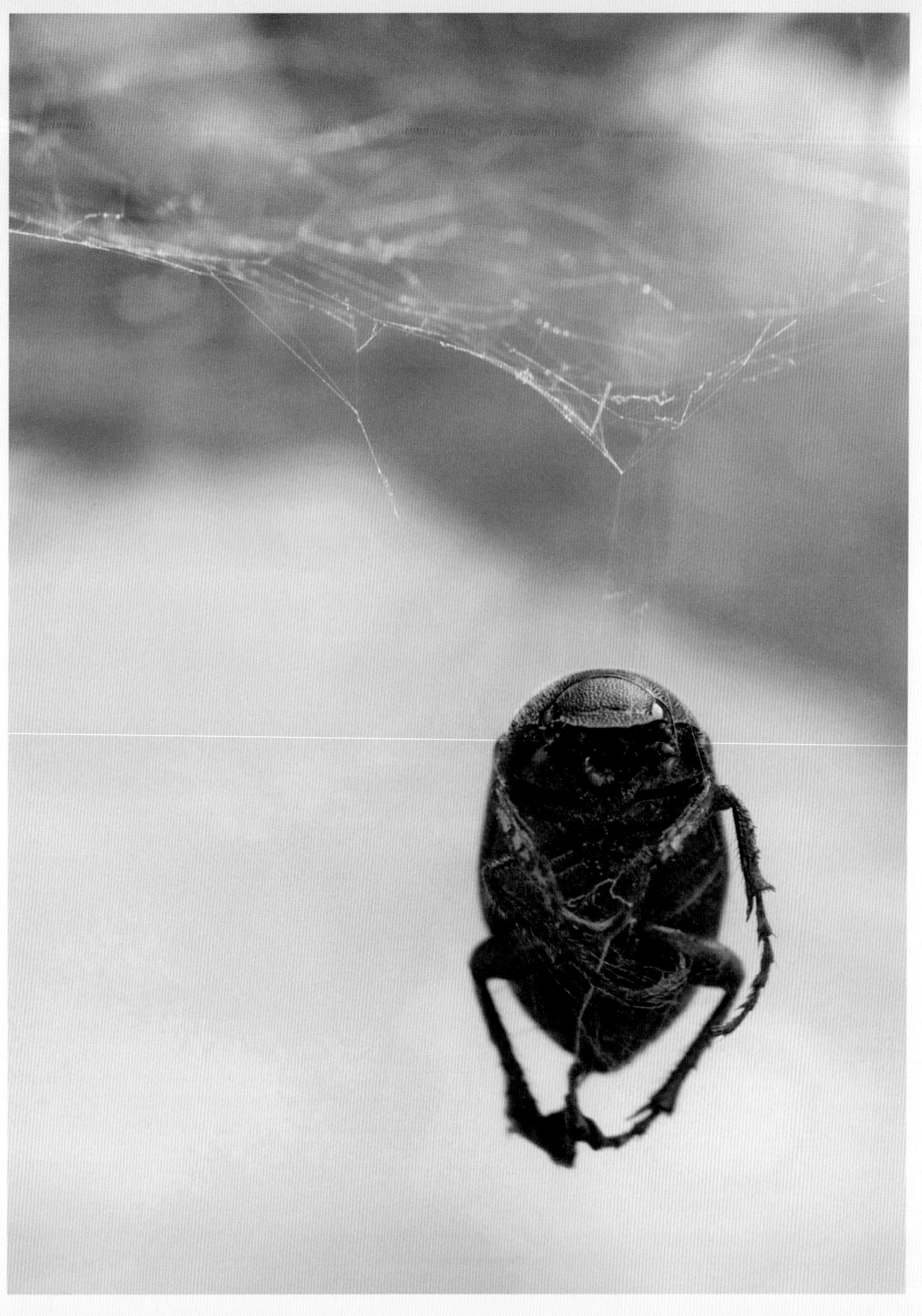

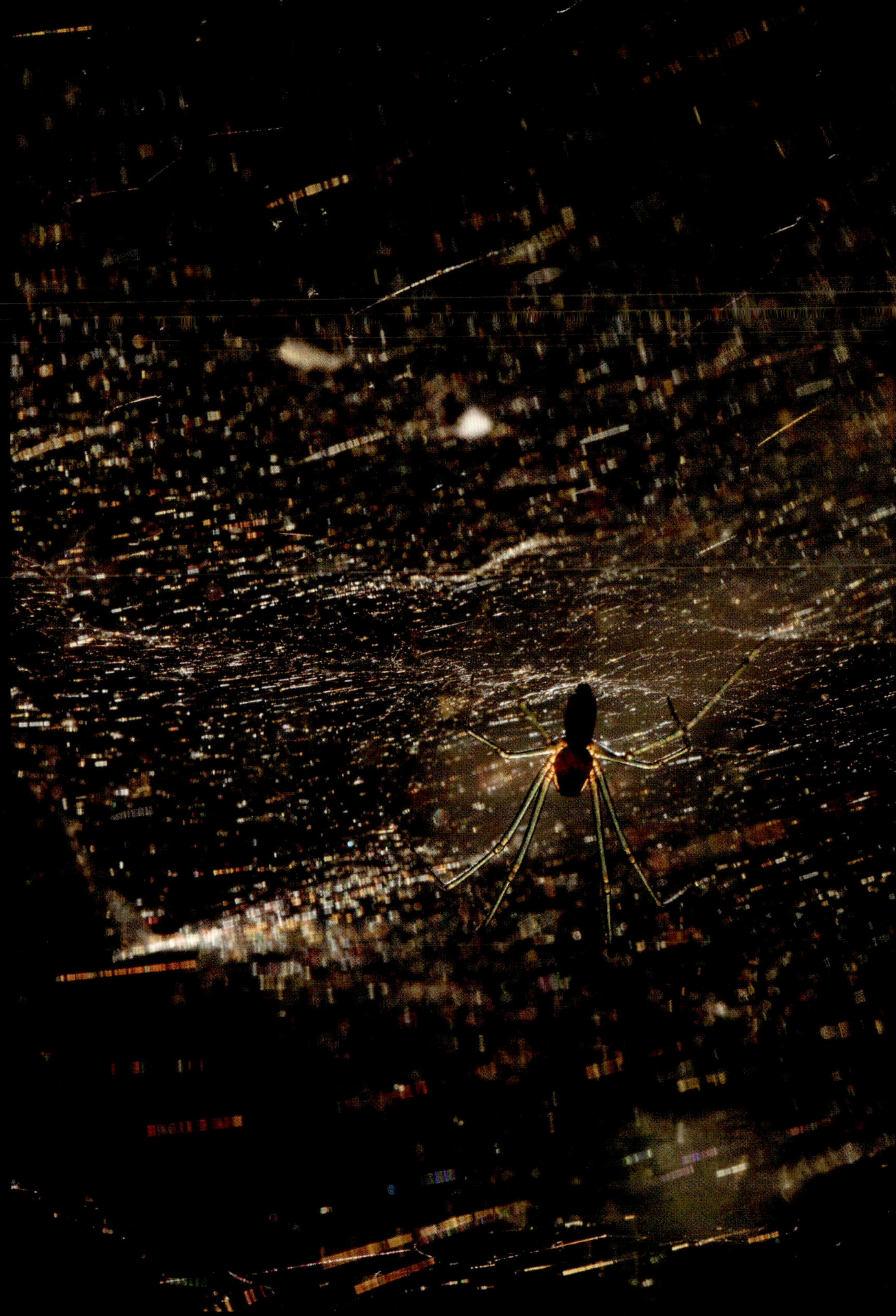

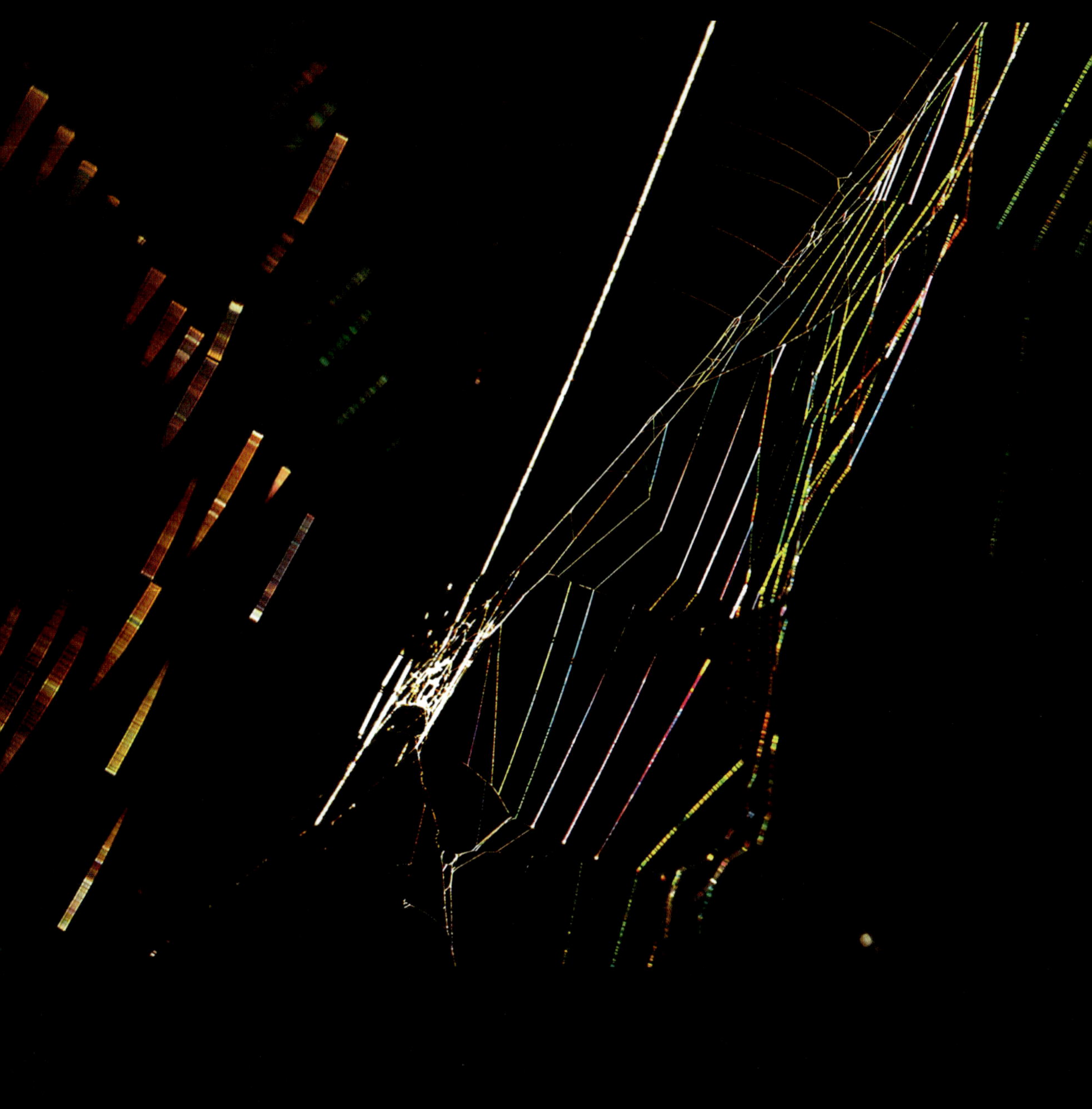

BEAUTY IN DECAY

As my attitude toward mortality begins to shift, I see a greater beauty in the death and decay I encounter on my walks.

The countless objects and creatures around me evoke the Japanese aesthetic of *wabi sabi*, which reveres imperfection, impermanence, and the quiet dignity of decay. This feels a world away from our collective social-media-fueled obsession with superficial beauty and the illusion of perfection.

The spirit of wabi sabi is also evident in the art of my wife, Paz. While I am out walking, she makes her own sense of the pandemic by creating one artwork a day using the basic materials she brought along—ink and paper. She also collects and incorporates objects found in the vicinity of the guest house, each bearing their own marks of decay and transformation—rubber tubing, pieces of old rope, and rusted metal.

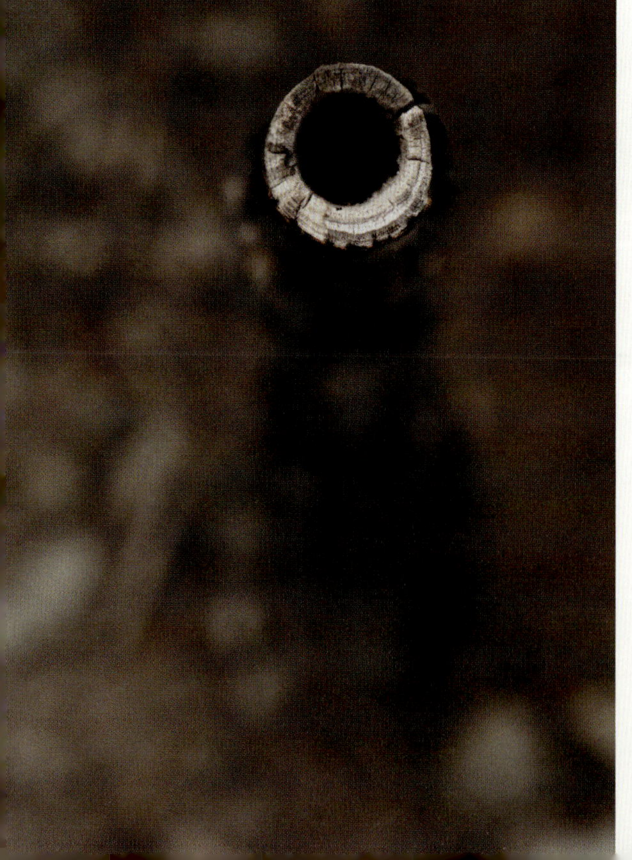

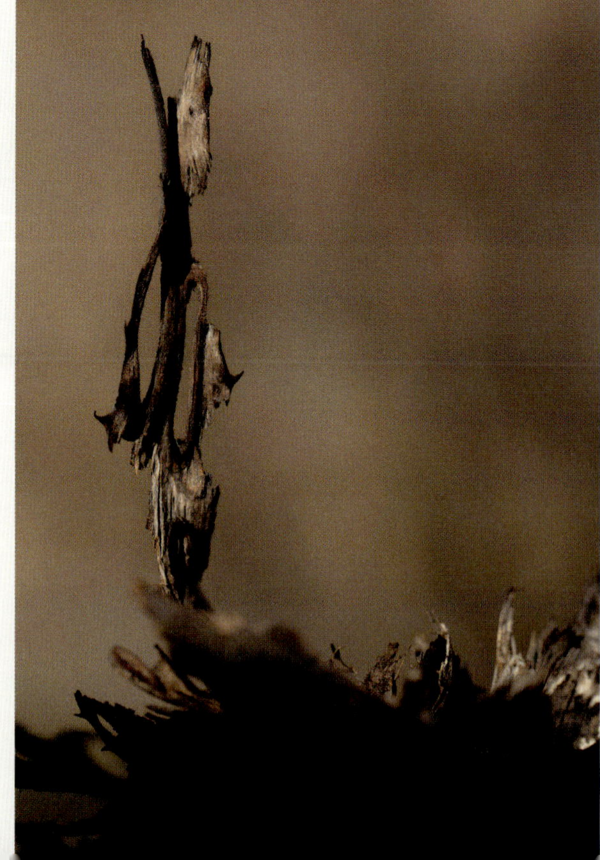

During my wanderings, I start feeling most
drawn to dead cacti—twigs and roots shaped
by time and weather. In this arid landscape,
decay is slow. It can take years for the fiber of a
cactus paddle to return to the soil. That gradual
process lends the decay an extraordinary
sculptural beauty as surfaces become wind-
twisted, sun-bleached, and water-eroded.

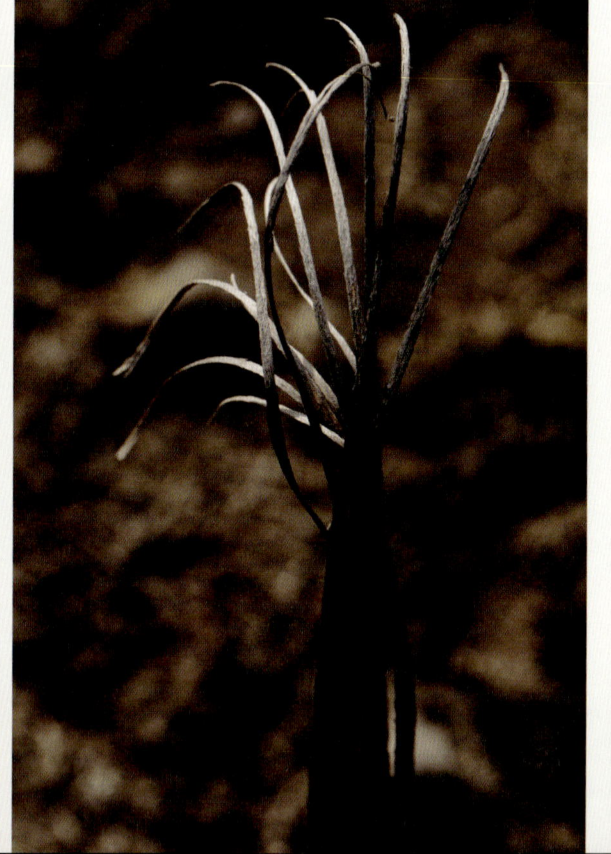

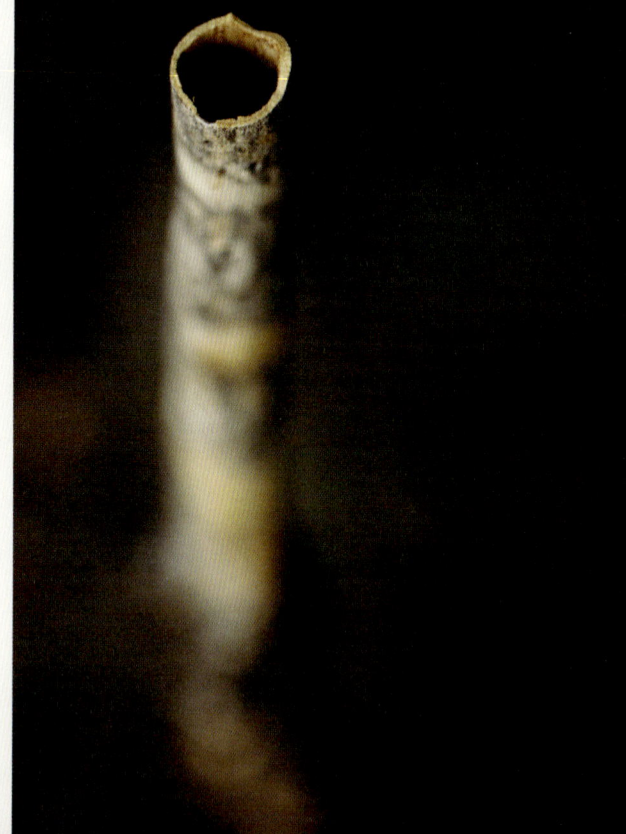

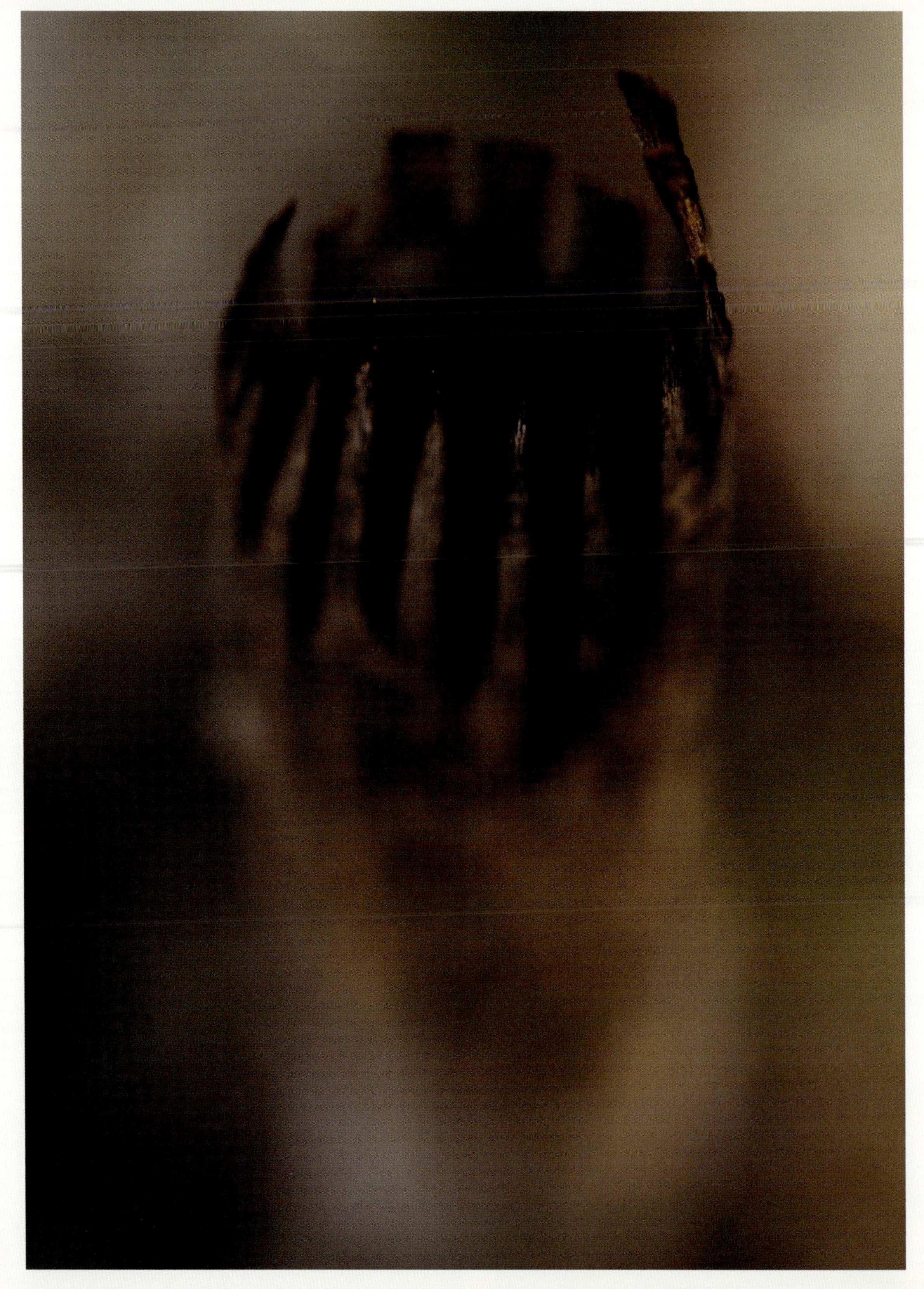

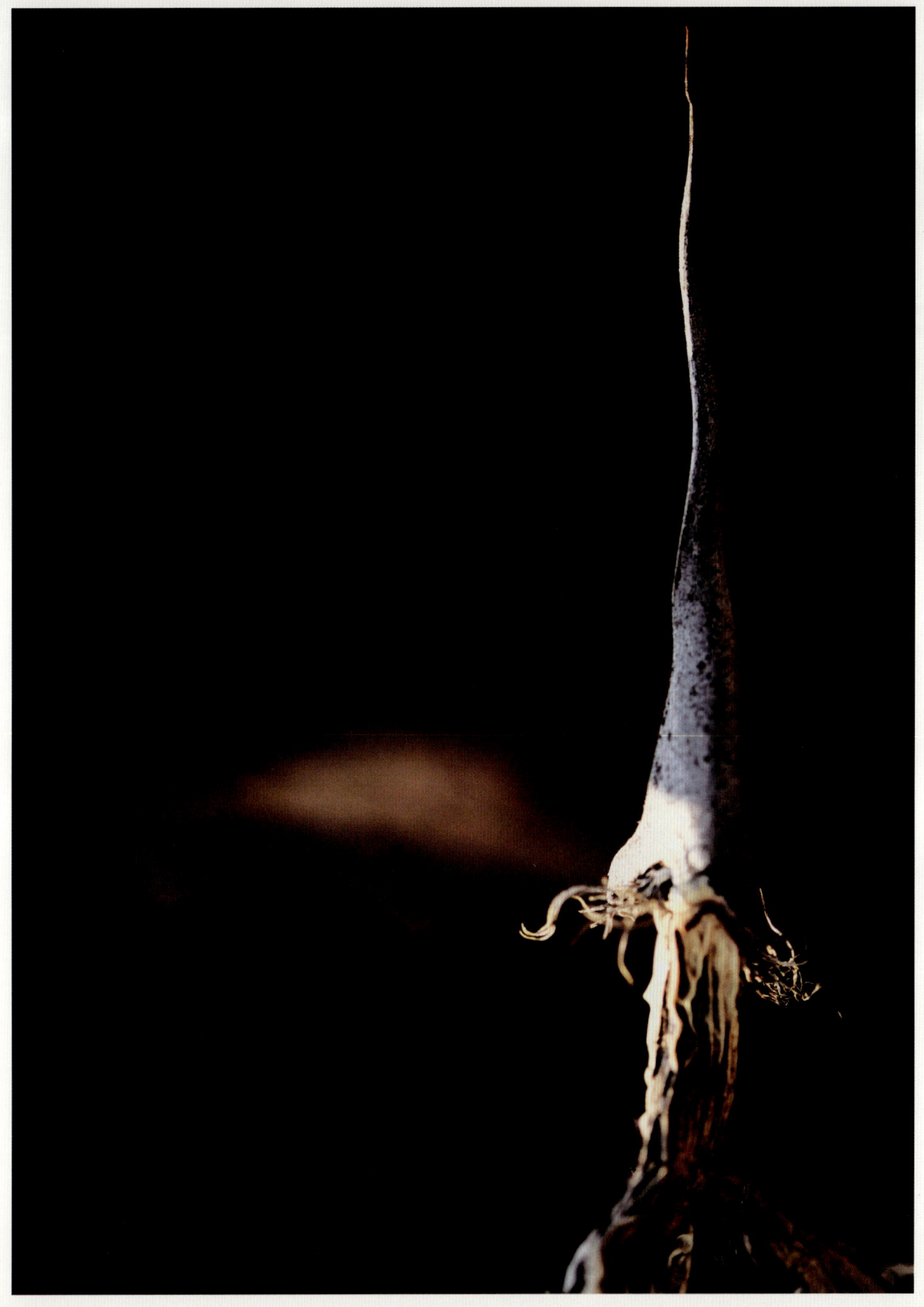

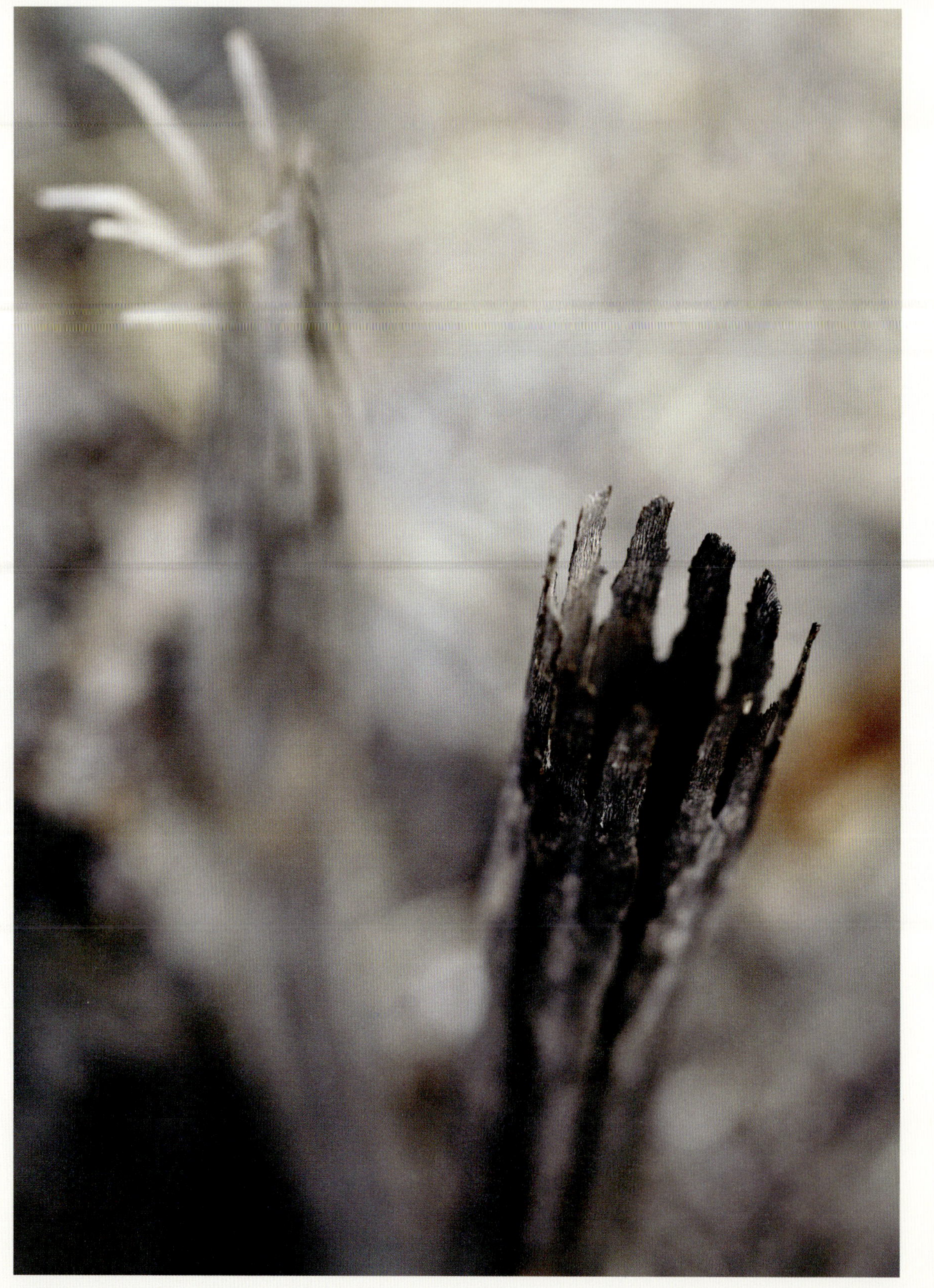

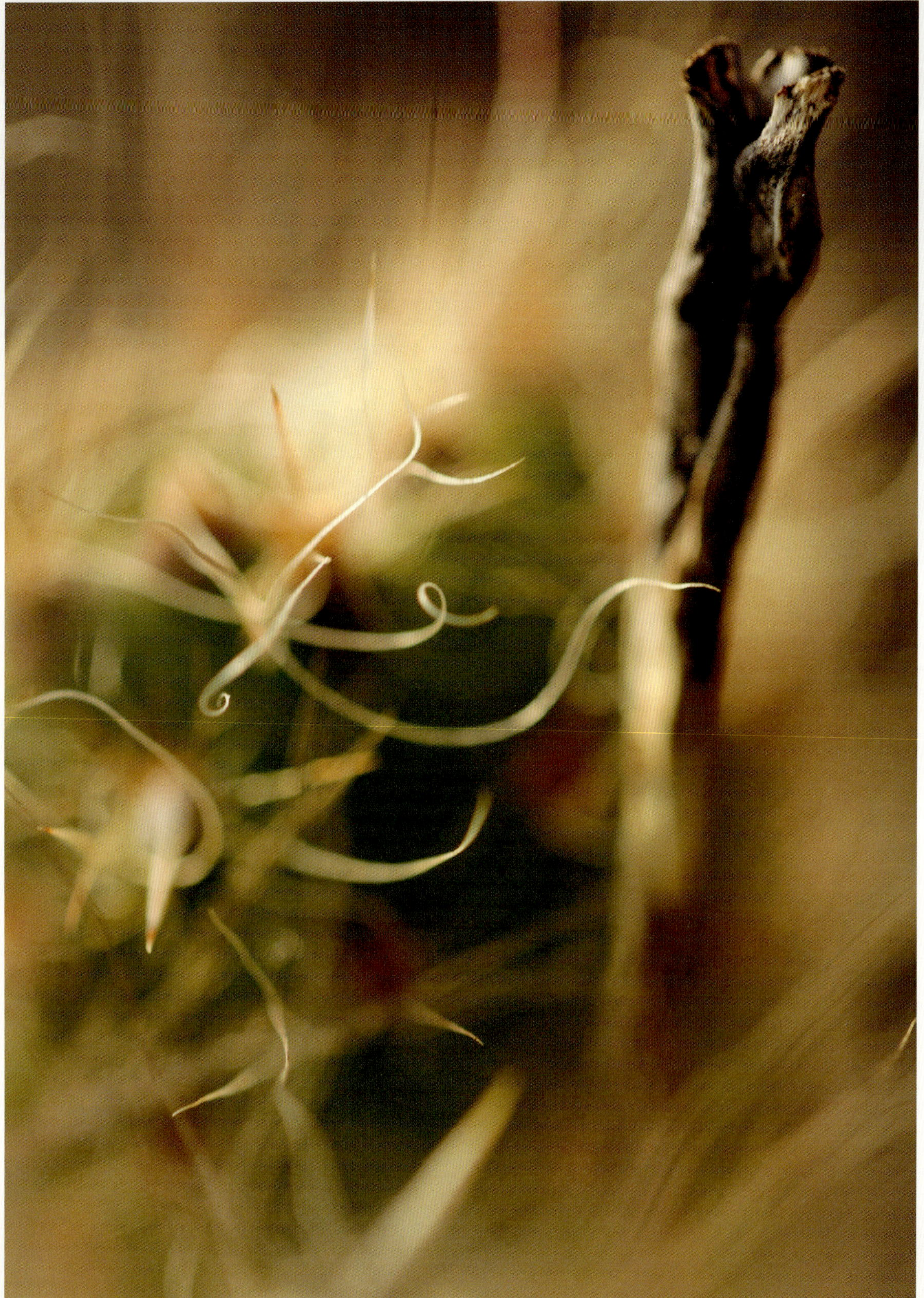

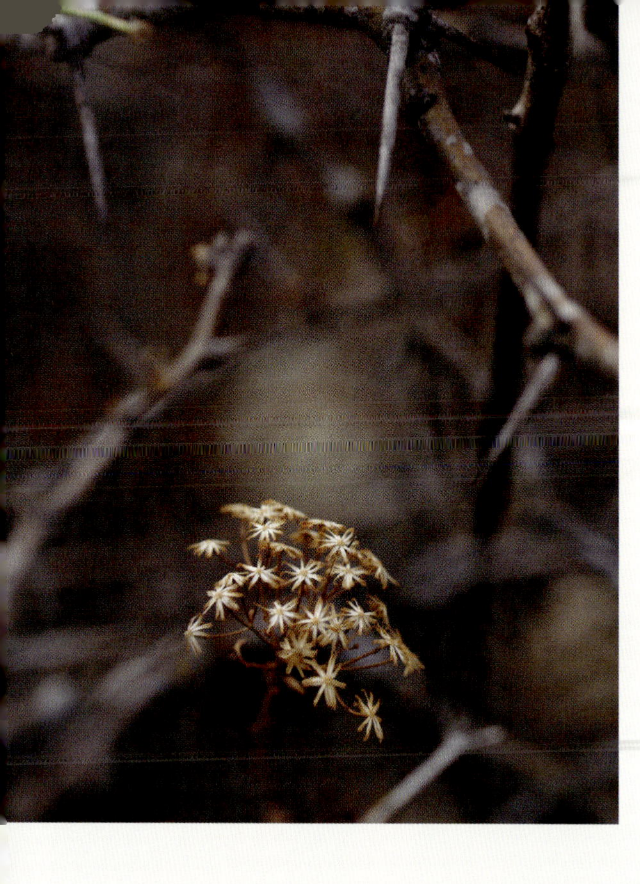

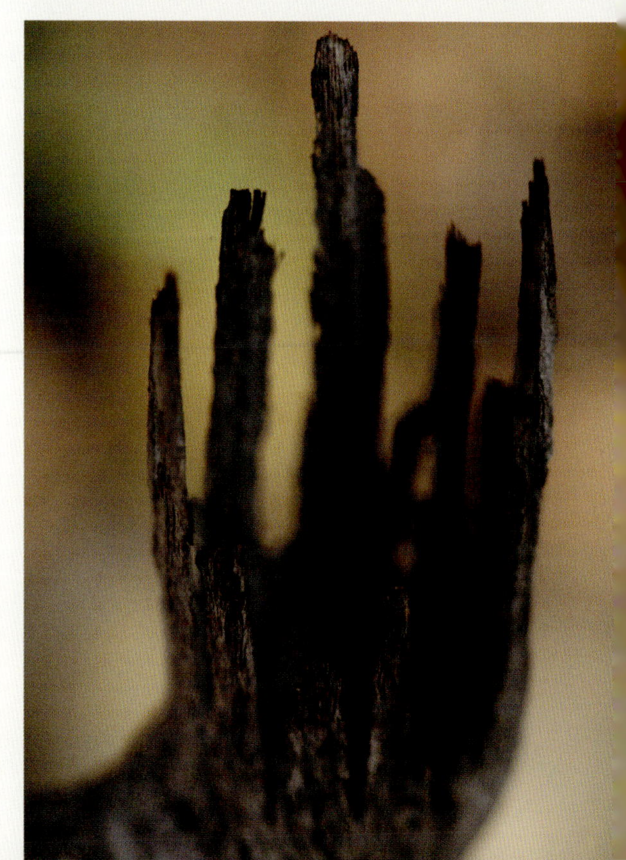

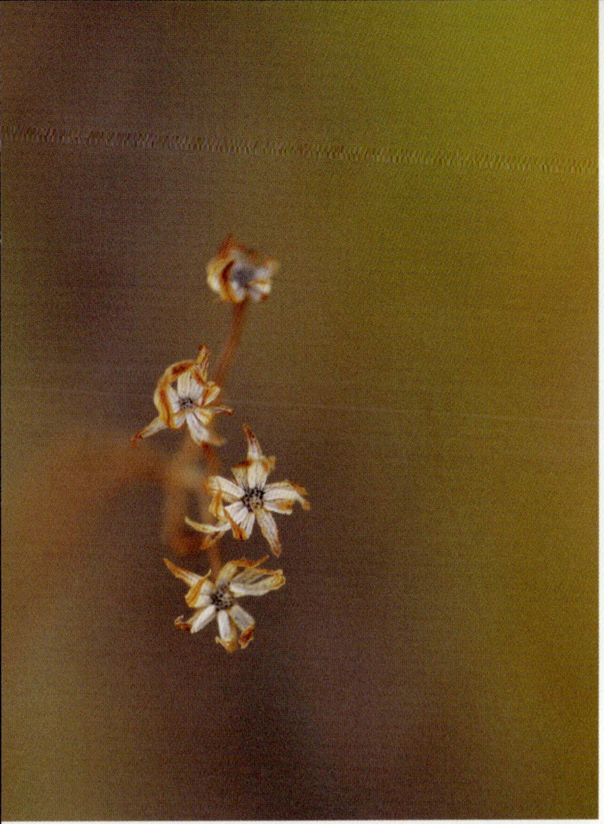

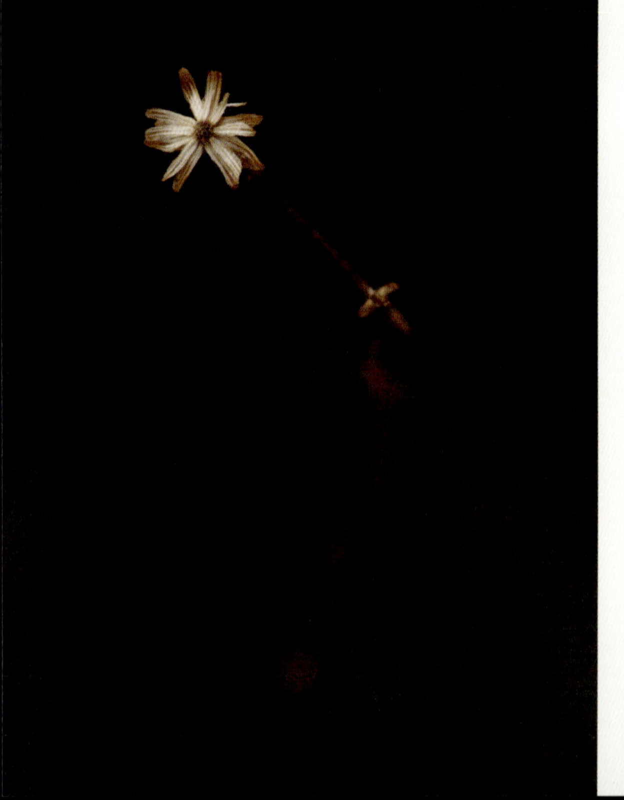
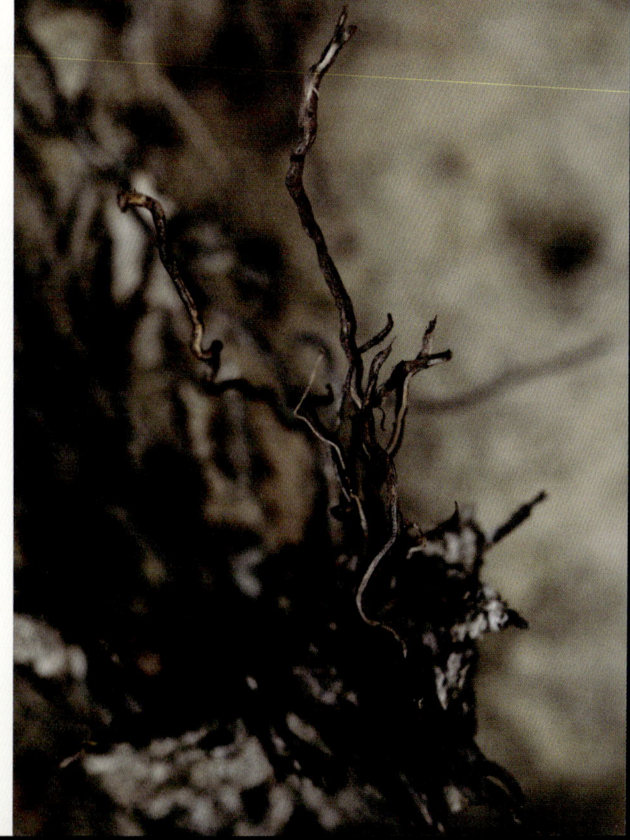

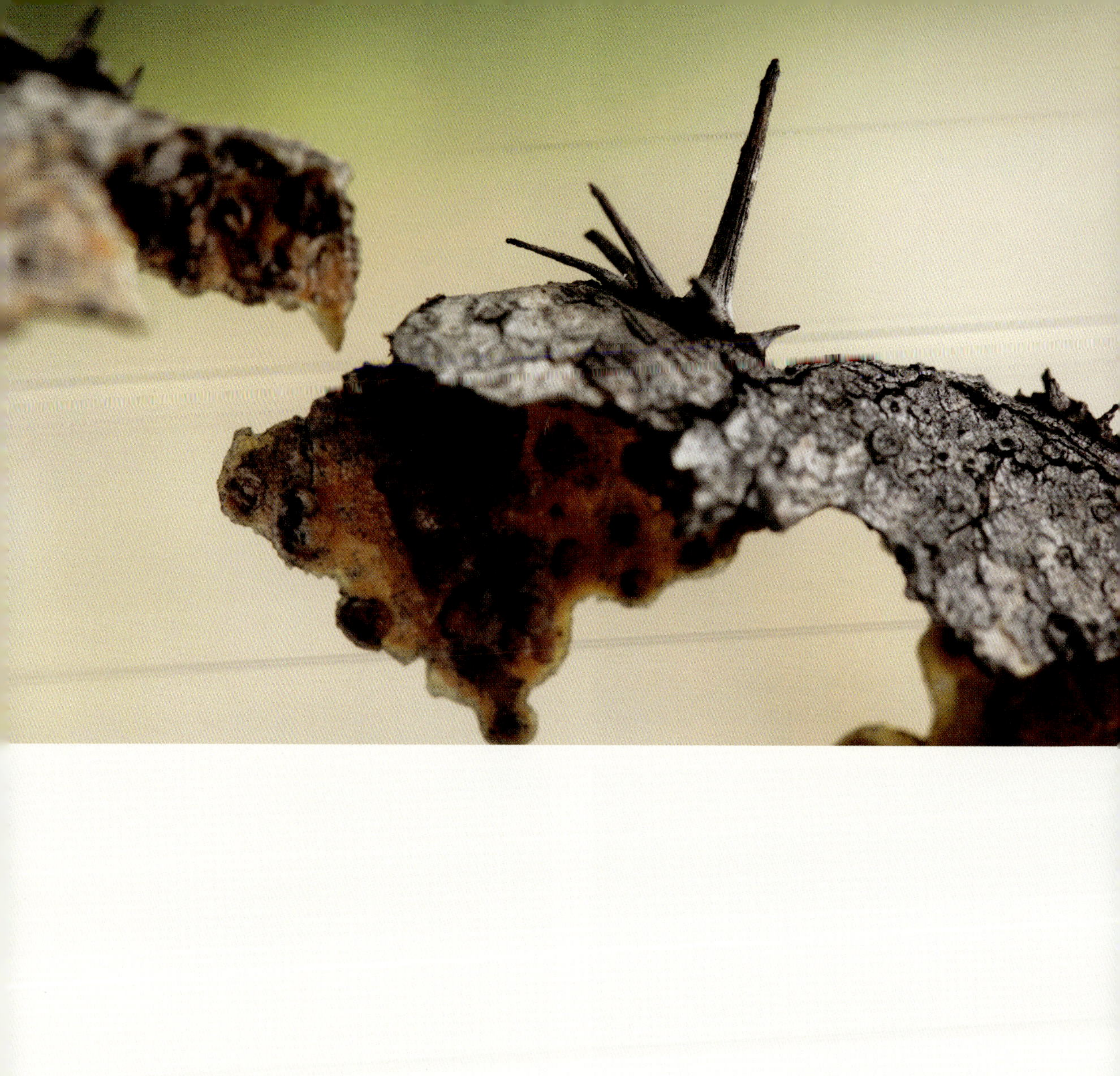

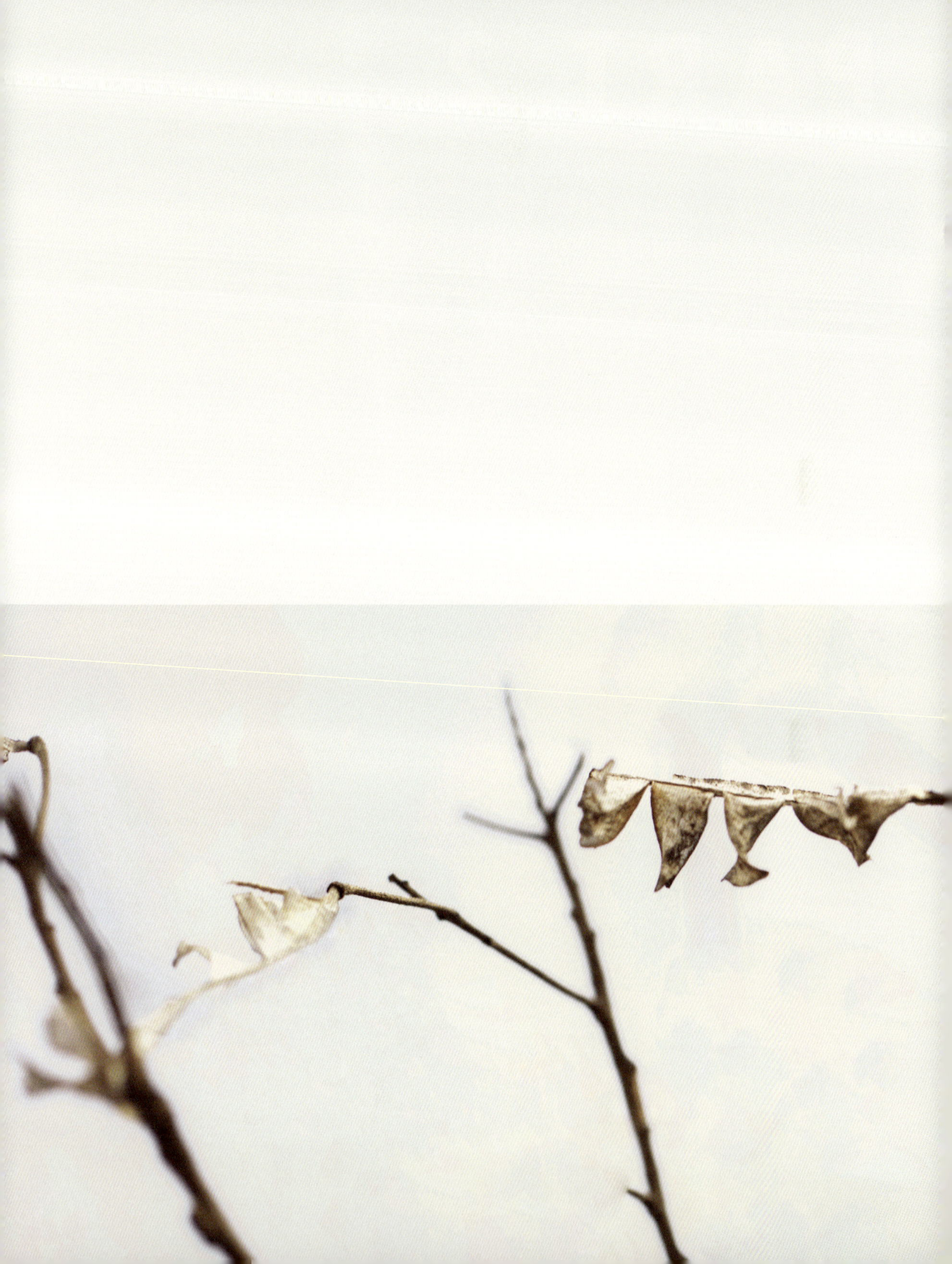

PART 2

LIFE

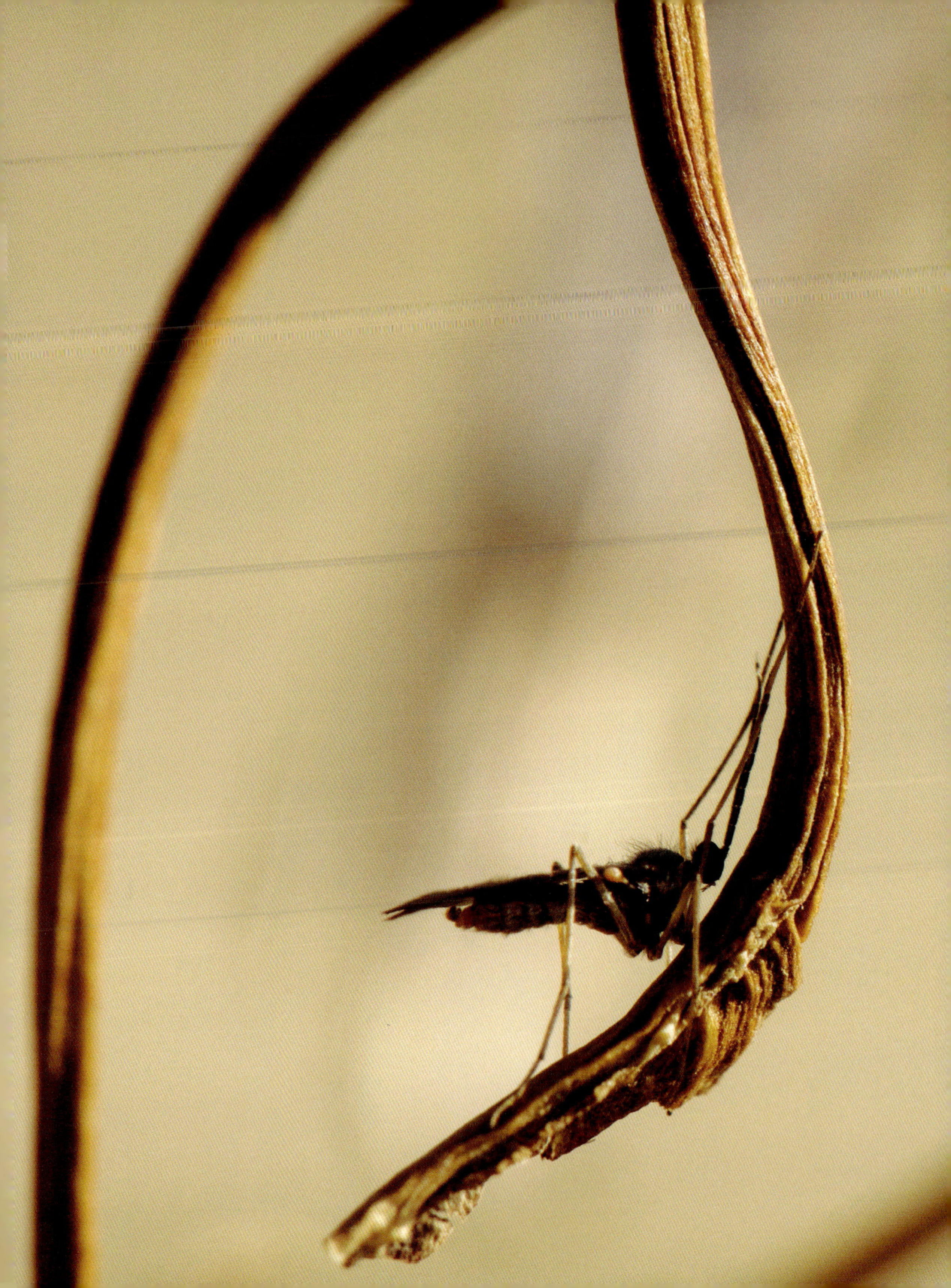

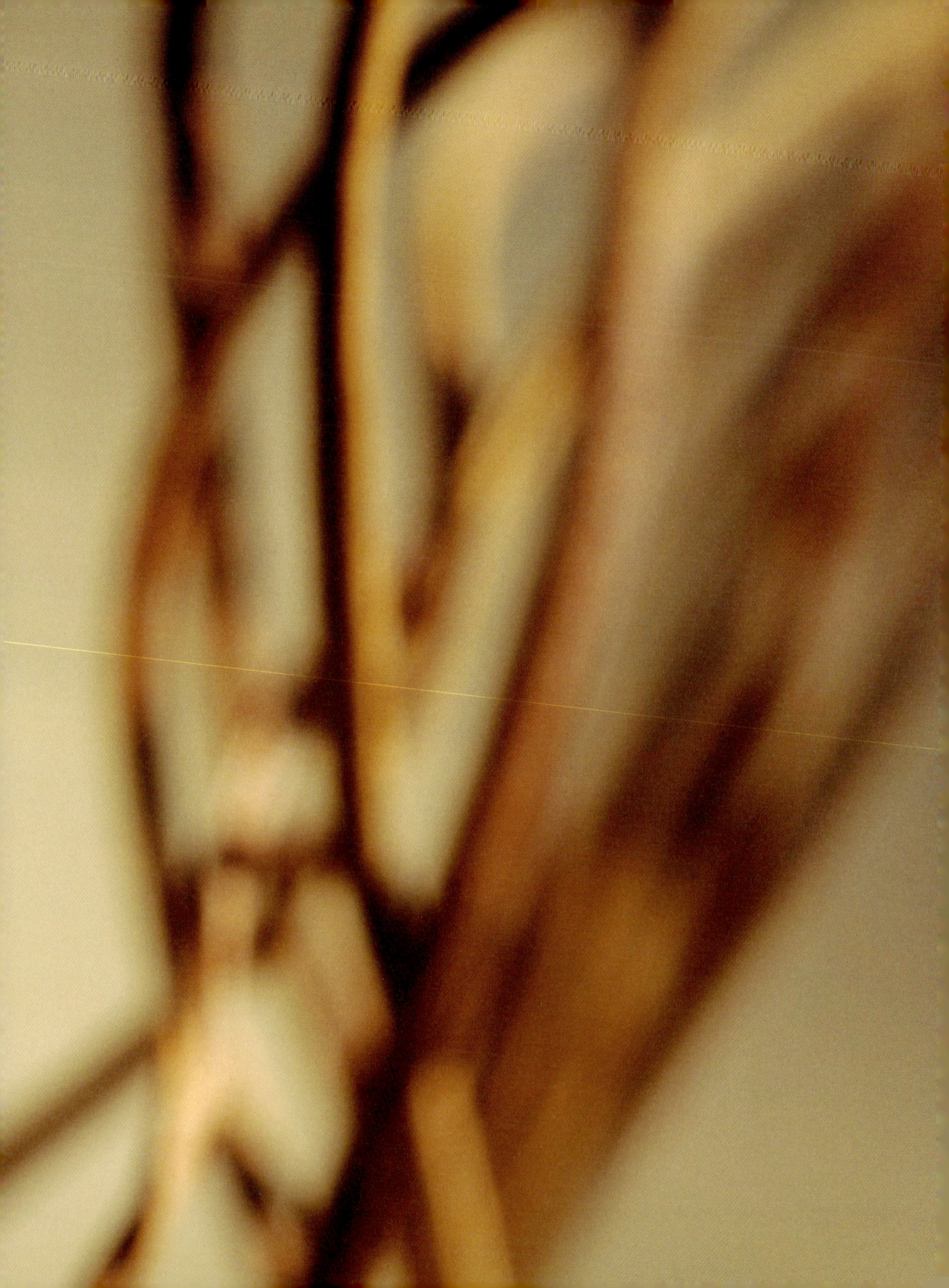

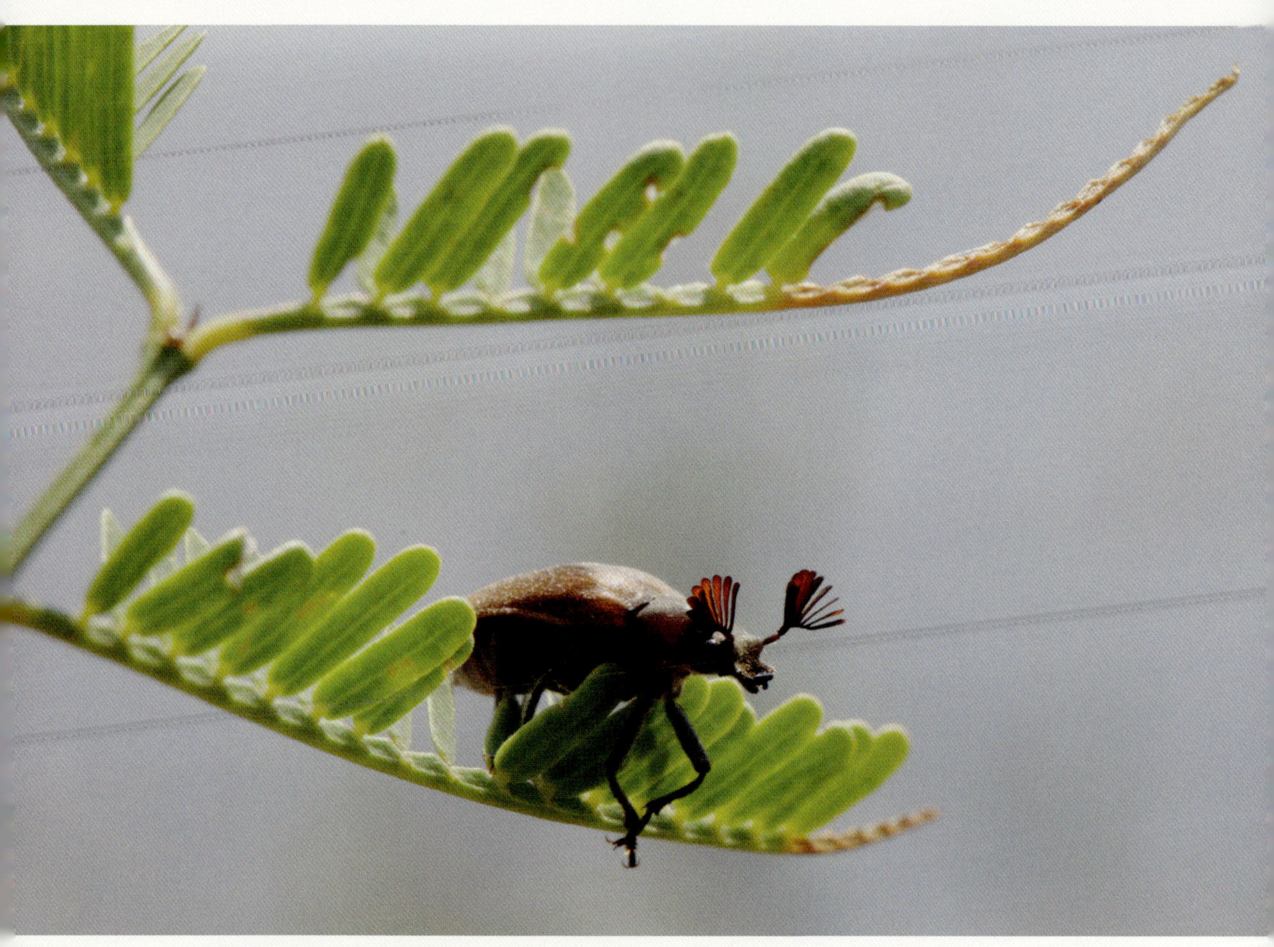

LESS IS
MORE

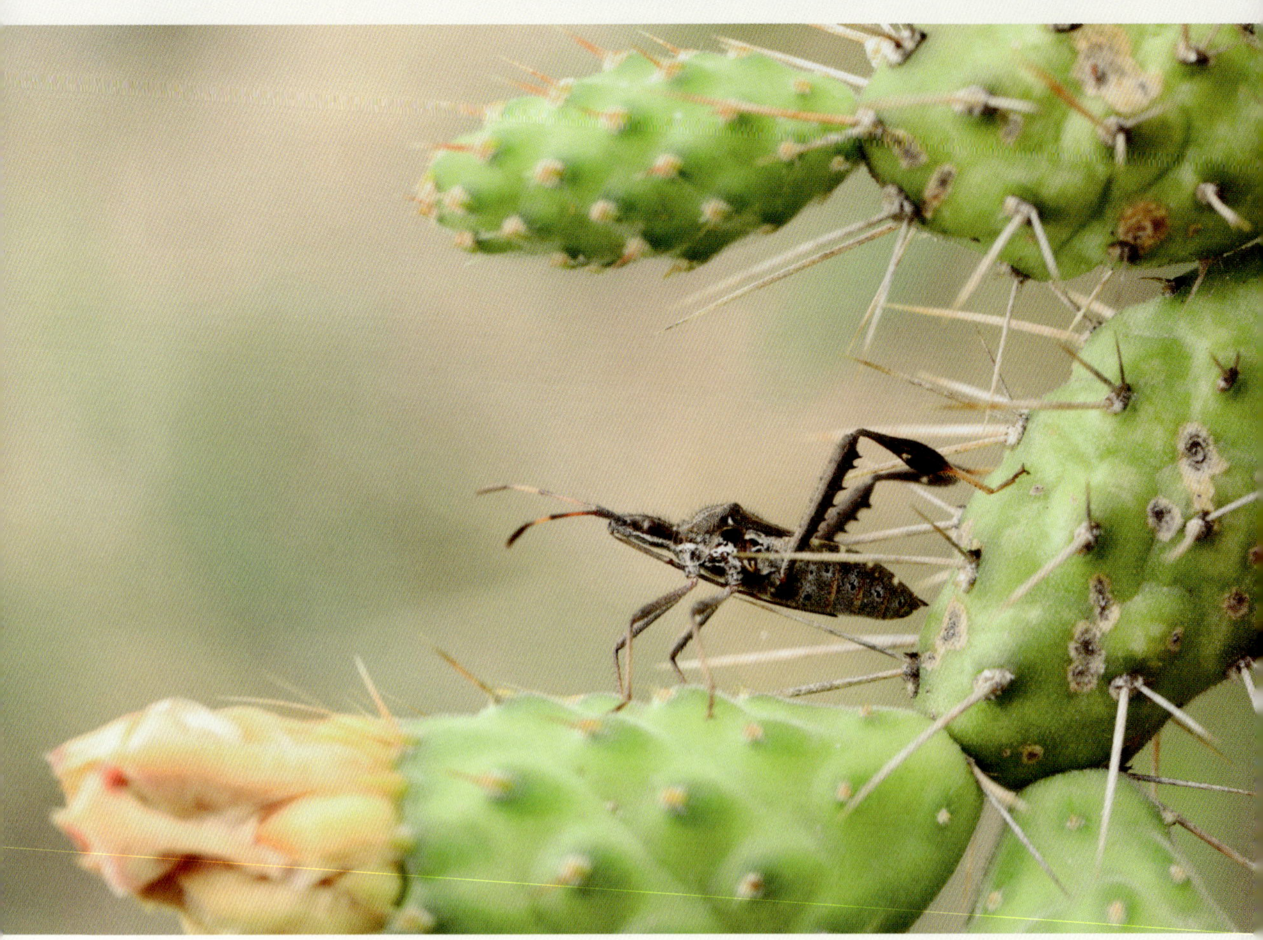

As the days slide into weeks, my attention shifts from death to life, even though the land remains largely bare. I learn anew the age-old wisdom: less is often more. There are days when I do not see a single living creature during my hours of observation. It is precisely this scarcity that makes the discovery of a new species or plant so special. Finding a single insect or flower amid the dirt, stones, and thorns can feel even more precious, I discover for the first time, than witnessing a whole field teeming with life.

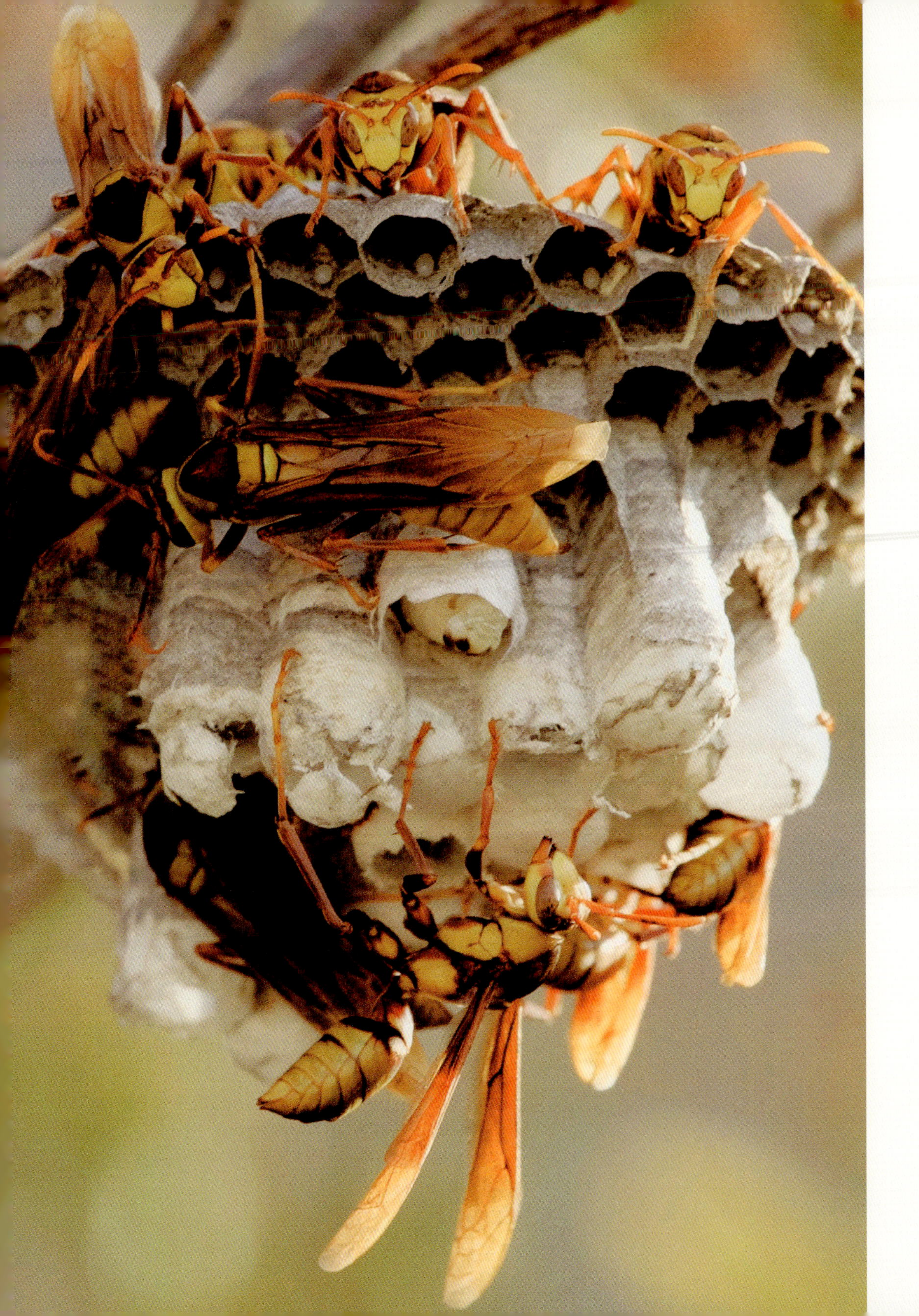

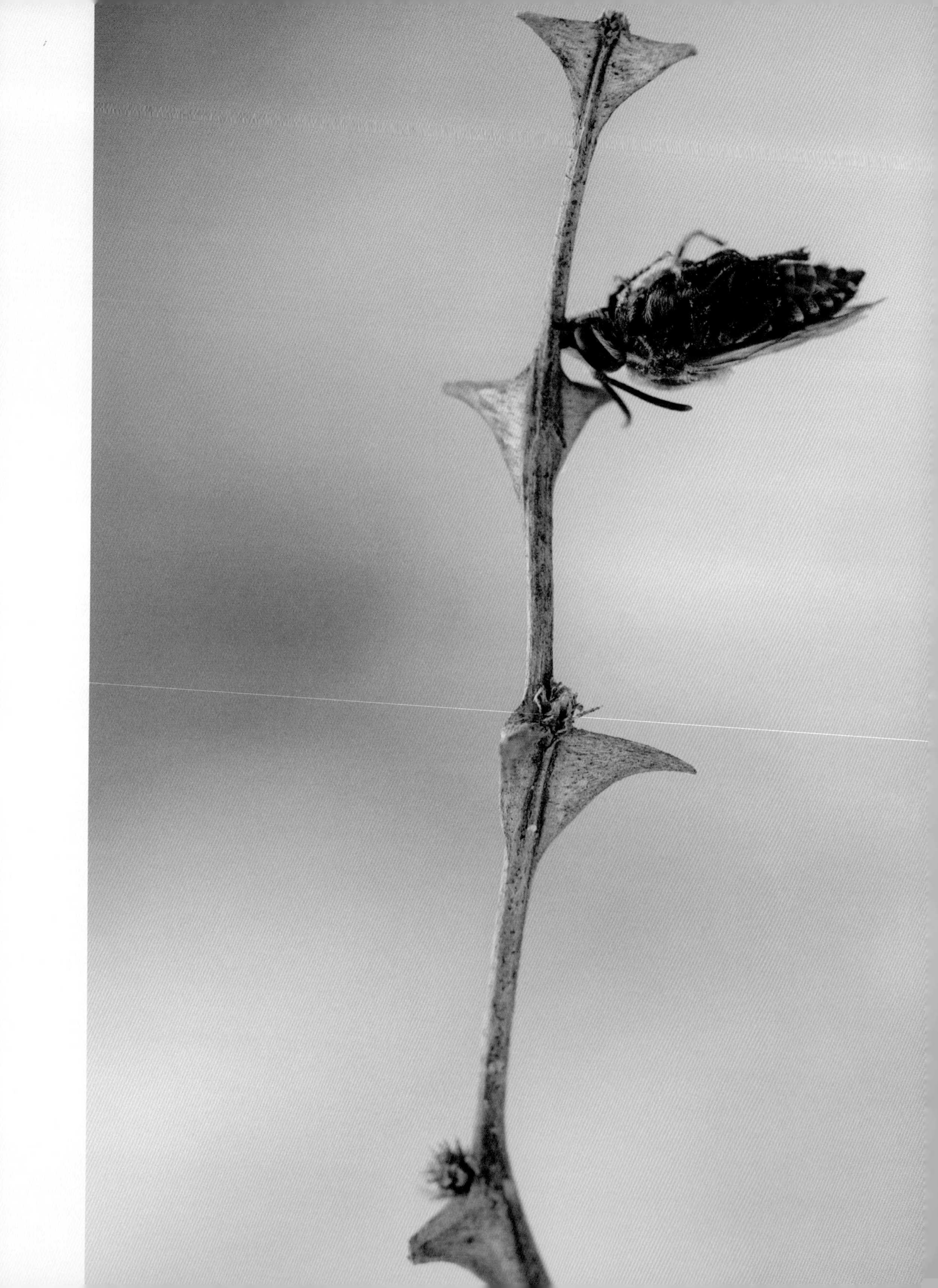

Before Mitla, before lockdown, I would not have given a moment's notice to a lone insect sitting on a leaf. But here, having chosen to slow down and look more closely, each creature I encounter reveals a fascinating glimpse into the ever-present cornucopia of life. Each appears to have its very own personality (though I suspect this is a figment of my imagination). I discover insects sleeping upside down while clasping the stalk of a plant, hornets watching me warily as they guard their nest, and bees and flies covered in pollen. I am particularly enchanted by one small creature with fan-like eyebrows, sitting on a leaf with its legs crossed as if pausing to rest from the day's hardships. I sit on the ground for several minutes, also with legs crossed, simply enjoying its quiet company.

Like many of the insect species I encounter, I see this particular one only once during the fourteen weeks that I walk this land. In sharp contrast, one species seems to be everywhere, all the time and all at once: ants. While the other creatures I see seem to operate on their own, the ants work as a community and with ruthless efficiency—I watch as entire bushes

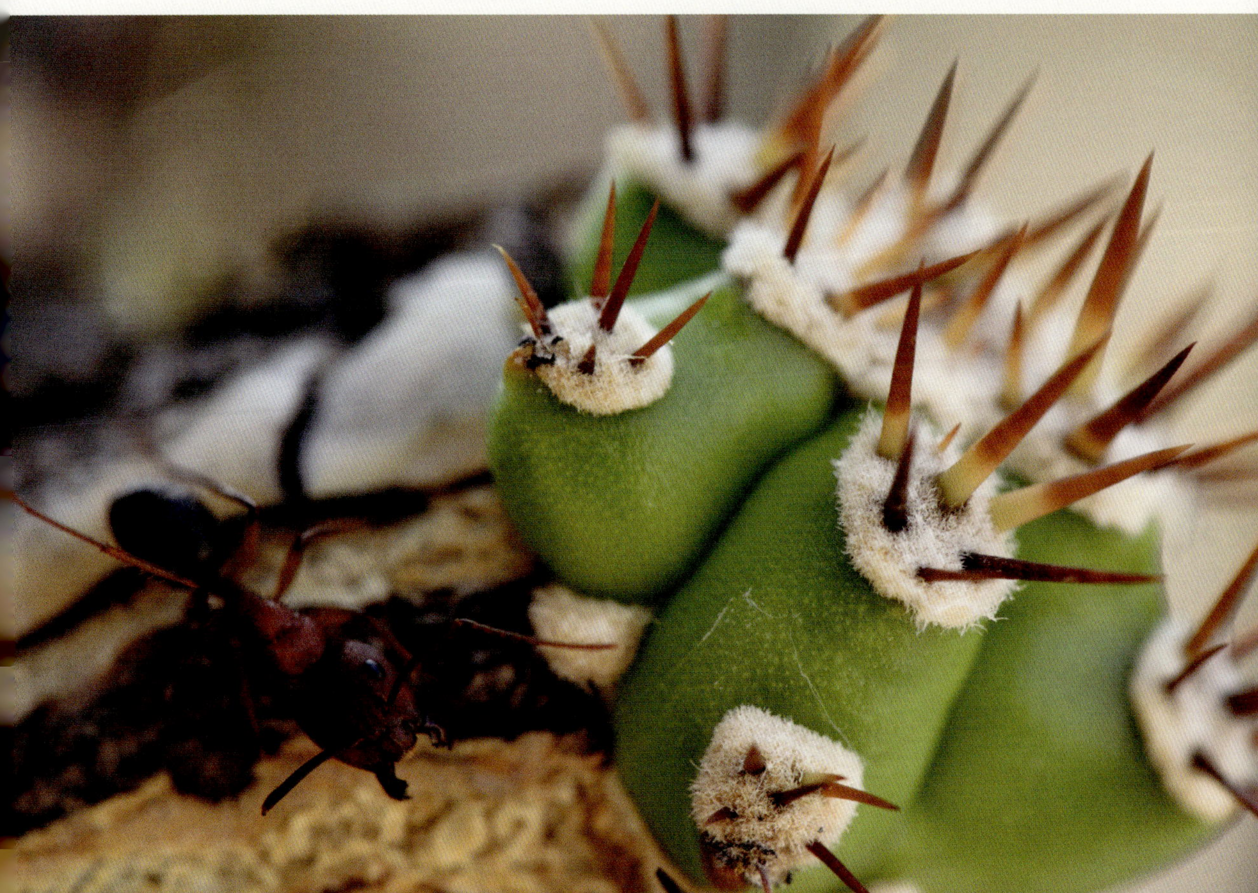

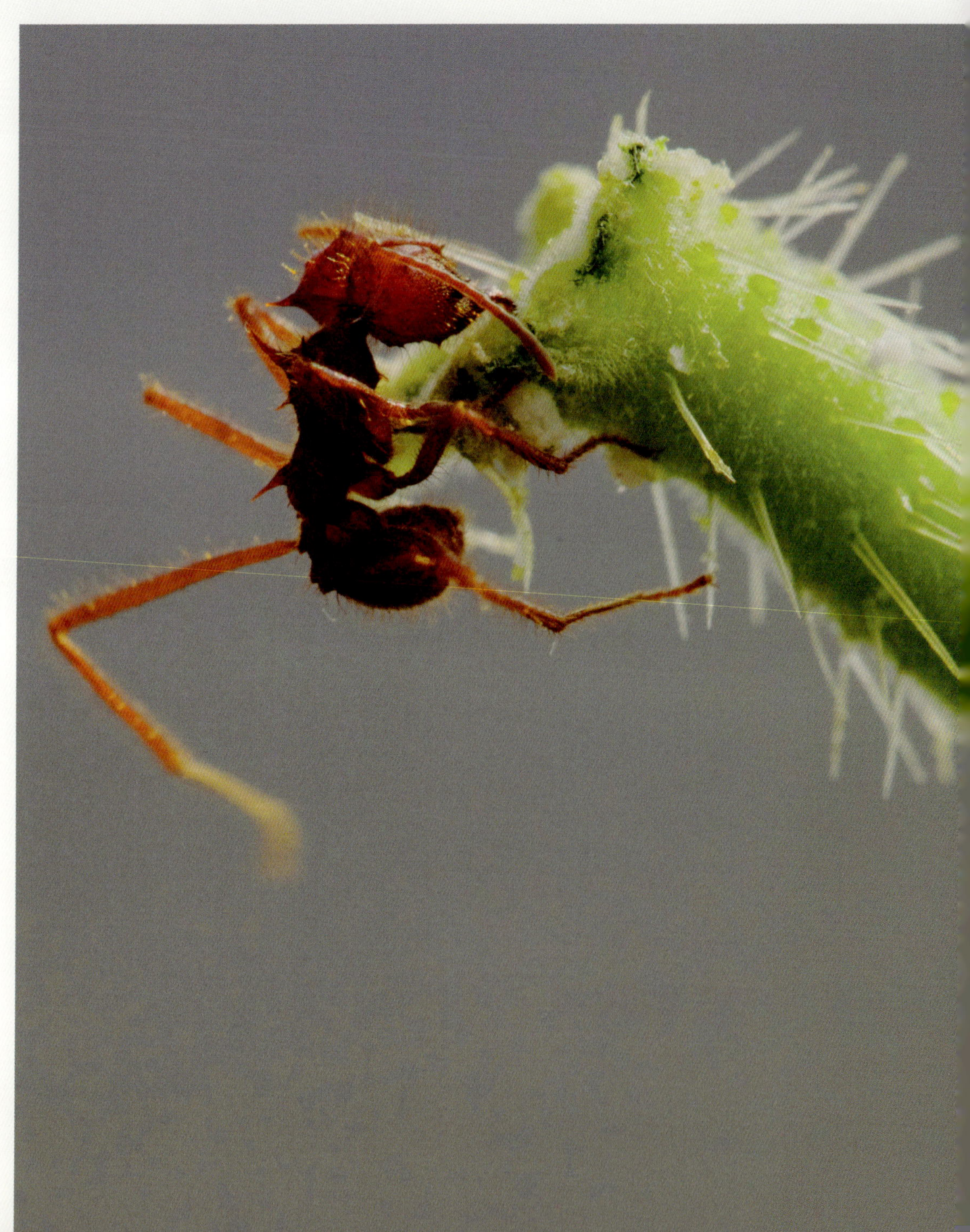

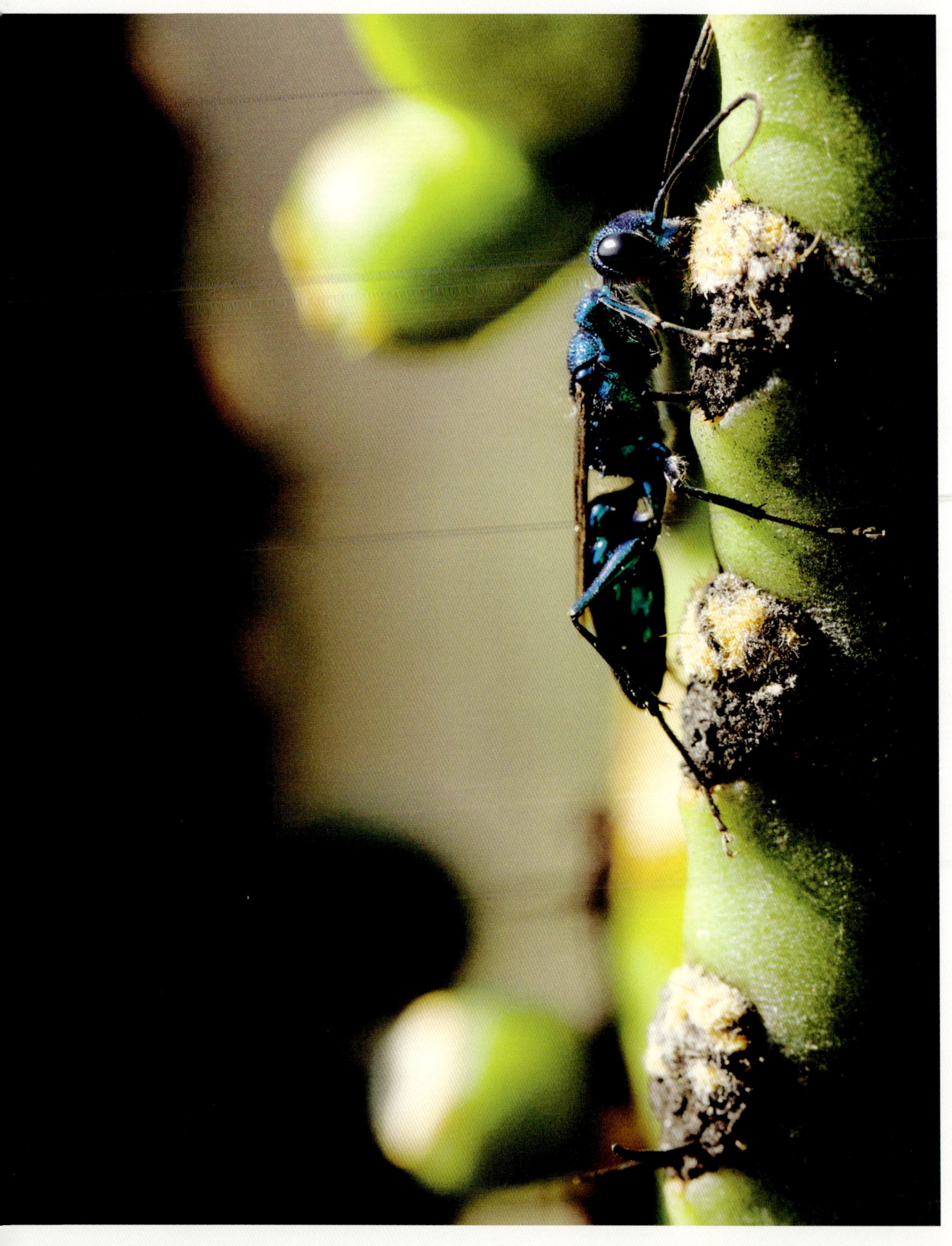

are stripped within a matter of hours, the leaves carried back to sprawling underground nests.

In the often merciless heat of the day, the sight of even a single insect serves as a quiet reminder that even in times of great stress, life continues to assert itself. Unexpected, extraordinary flashes of insect color—iridescent greens and metallic blues—pierce the muted palette of the scrubland, offering moments of joy and wonder.

In my youth, I often associated abundance with a carefree, even careless attitude. If I had too much of something, such as a particular food, I started to take it for granted—I lost my appreciation for it. Over time, as I have become more attuned to mindful consumption, I have experienced that letting go of craving and embracing scarcity allows me to more deeply cherish and savor what I already have. In Mitla, this capacity unfolds with new depth. Finding such joy in simply spotting a single insect, I am reminded that abundance is a state of mind— by releasing expectations and shifting my attention to the present moment, happiness arises naturally.

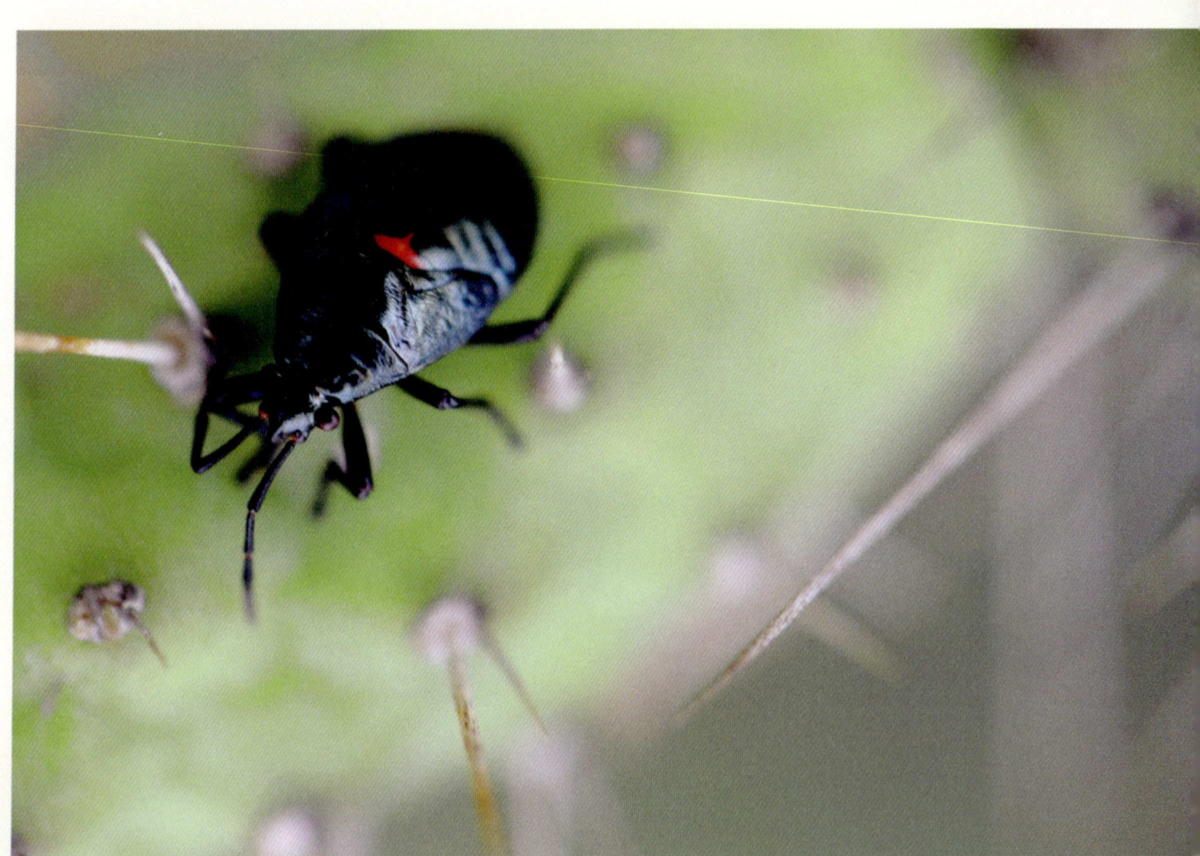

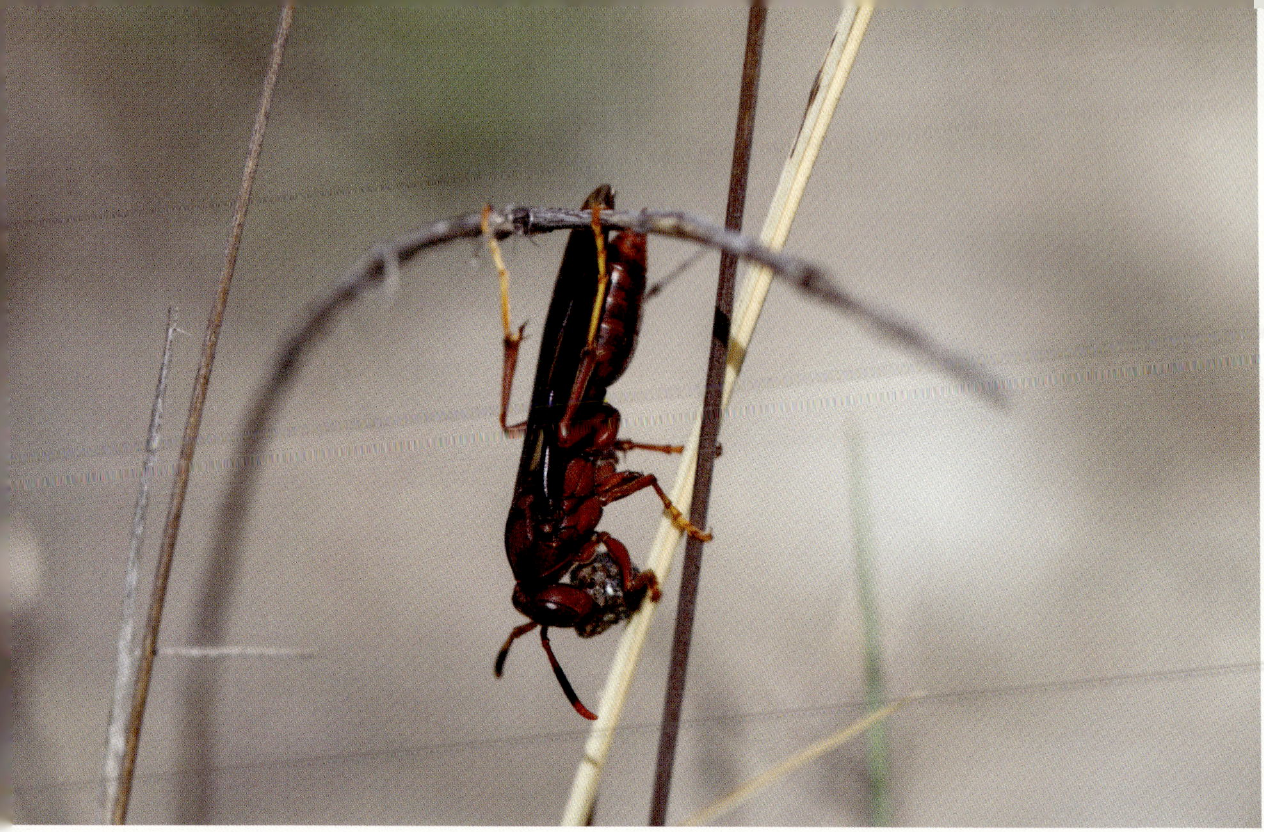

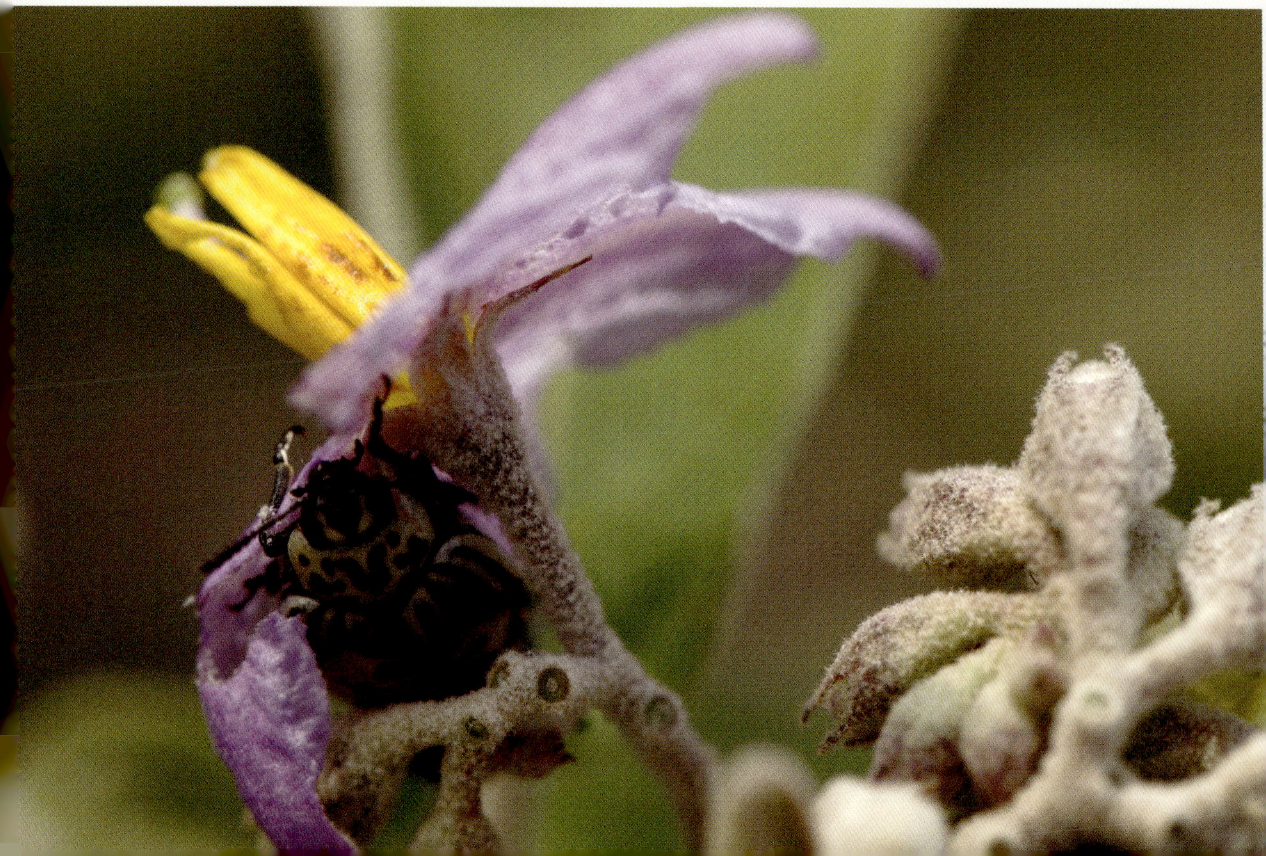

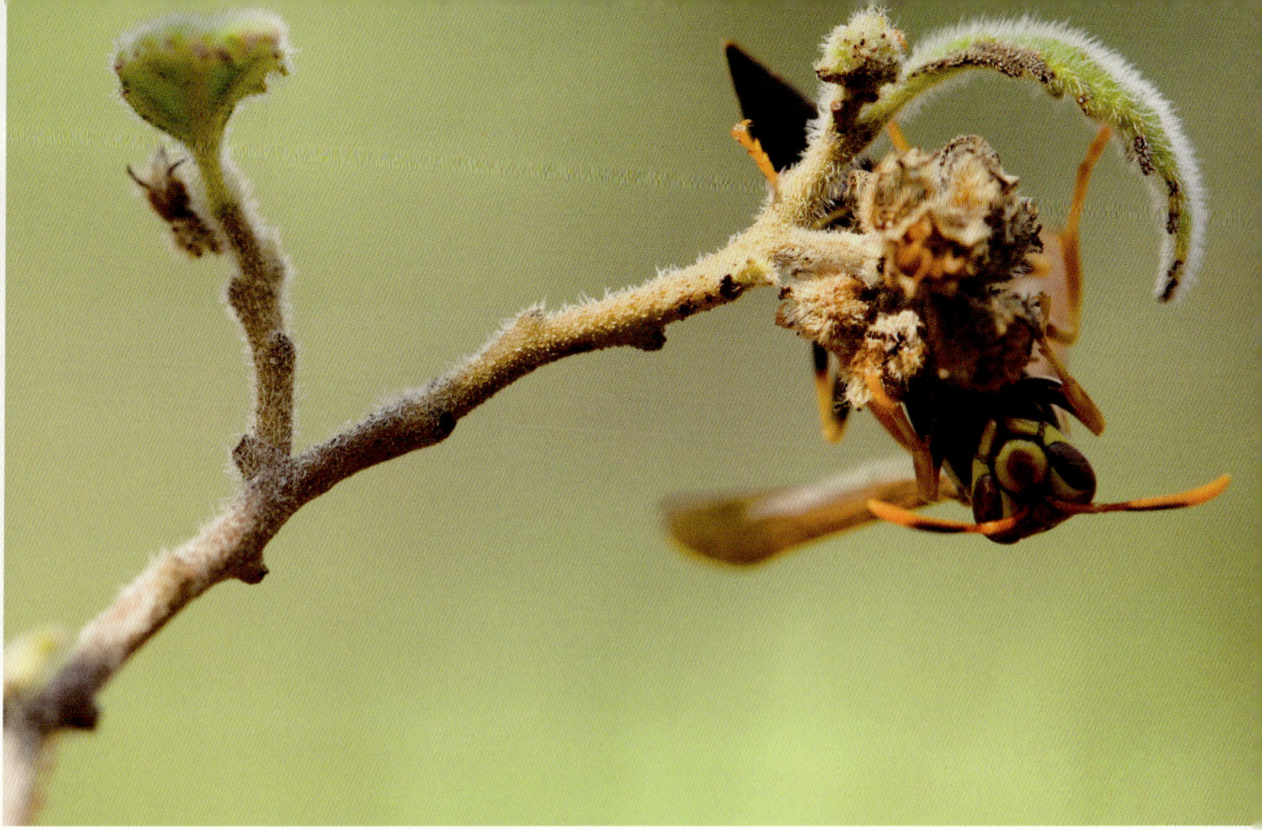

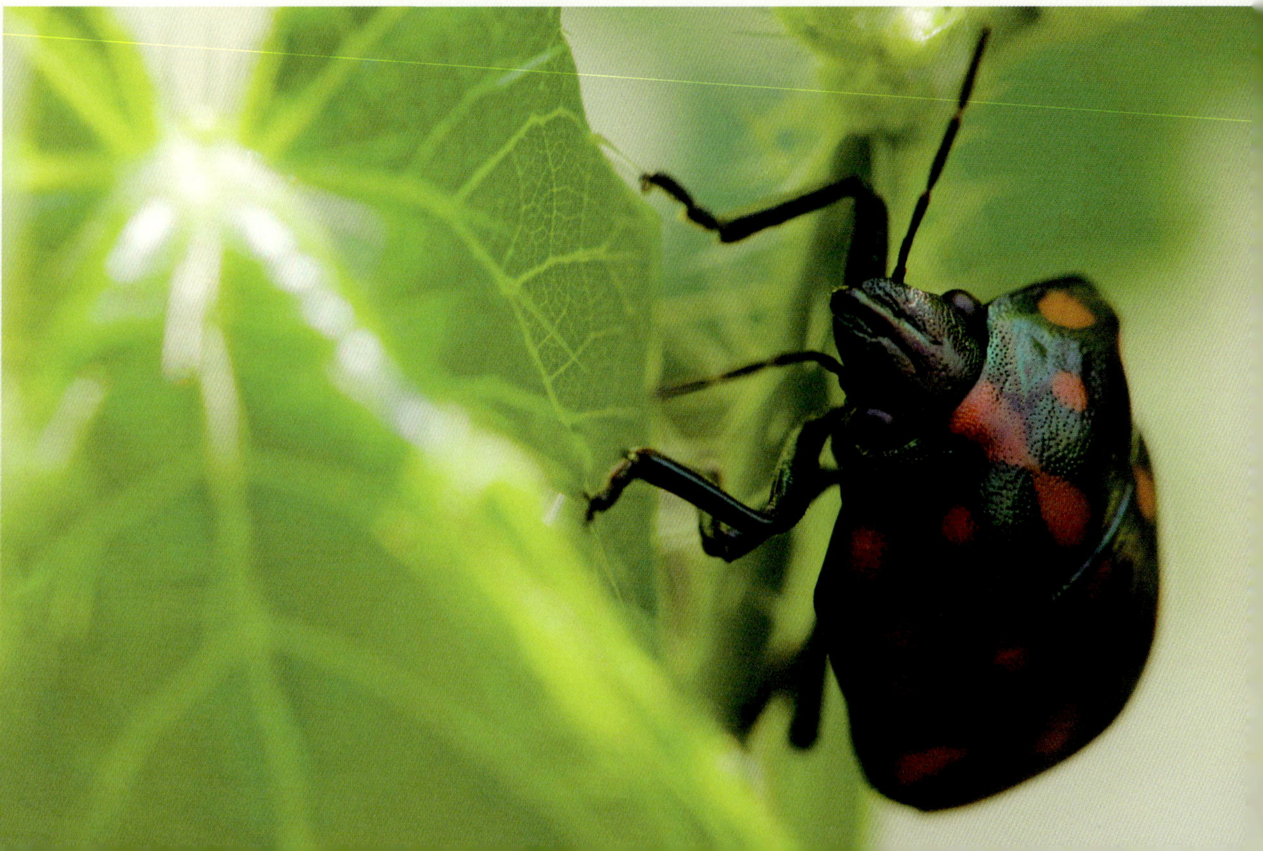

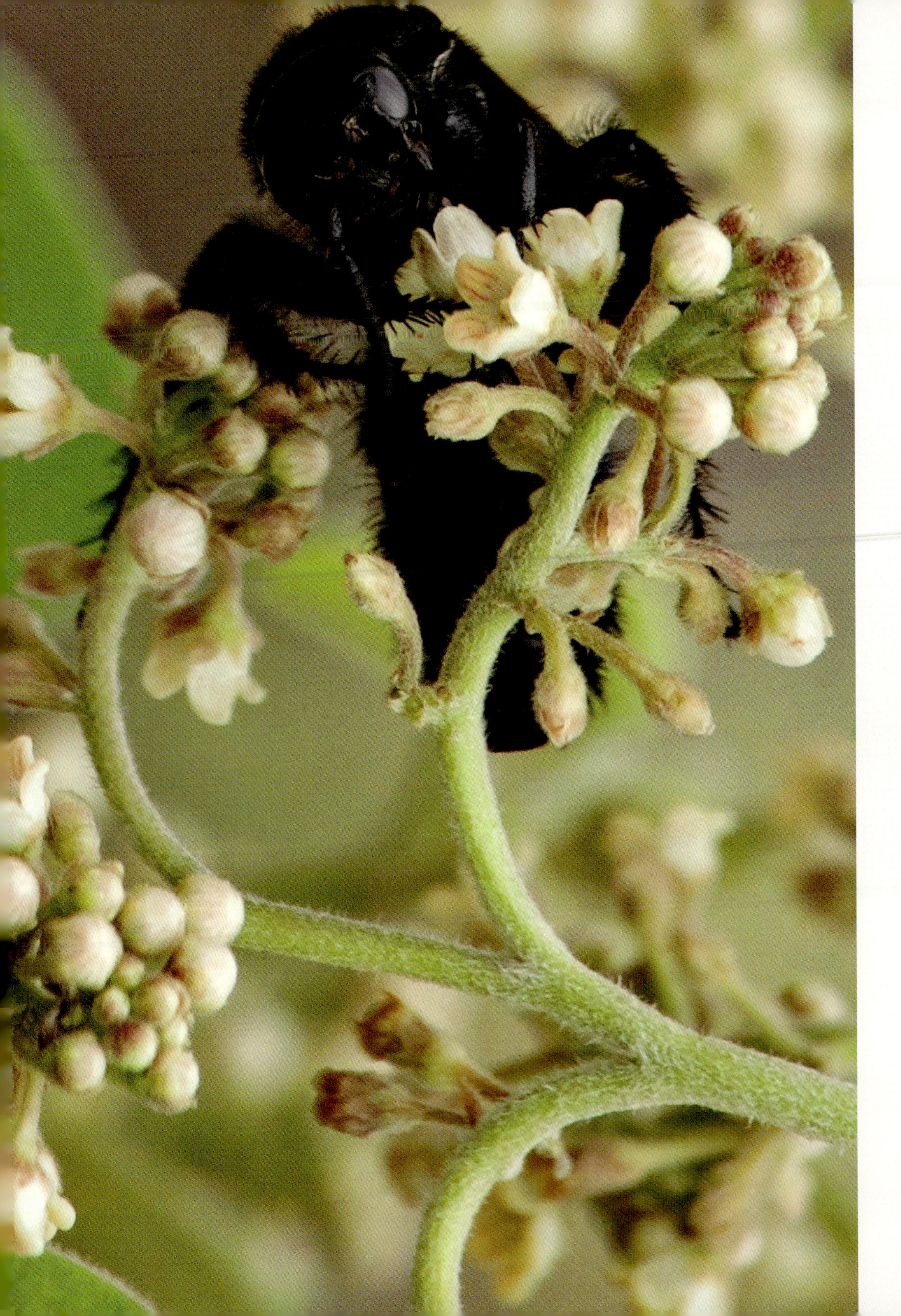

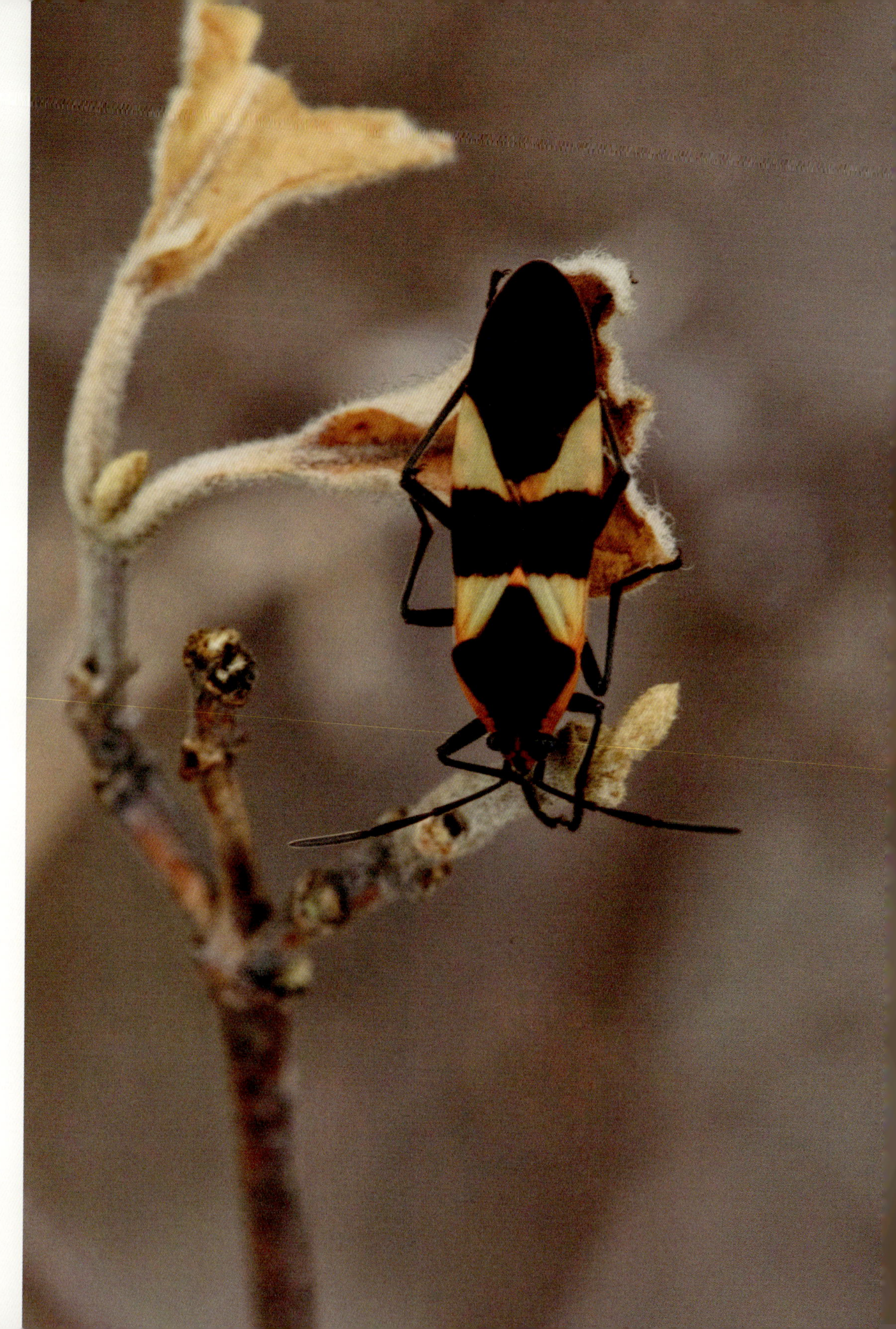

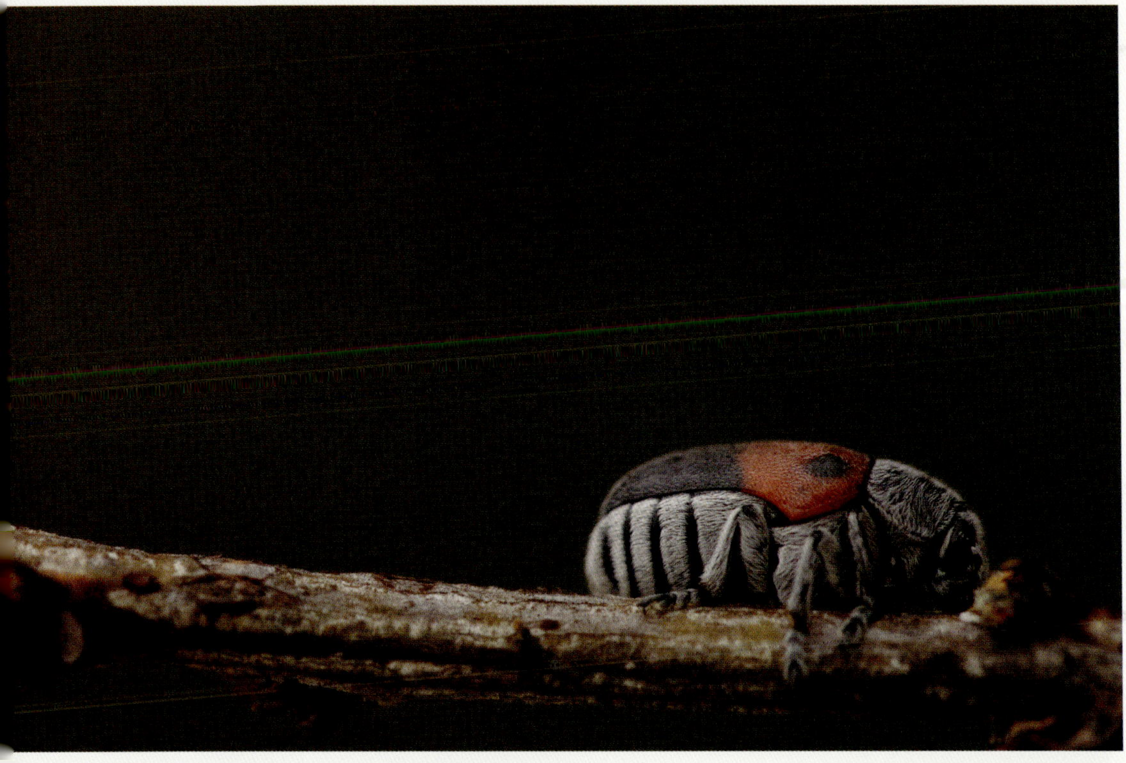

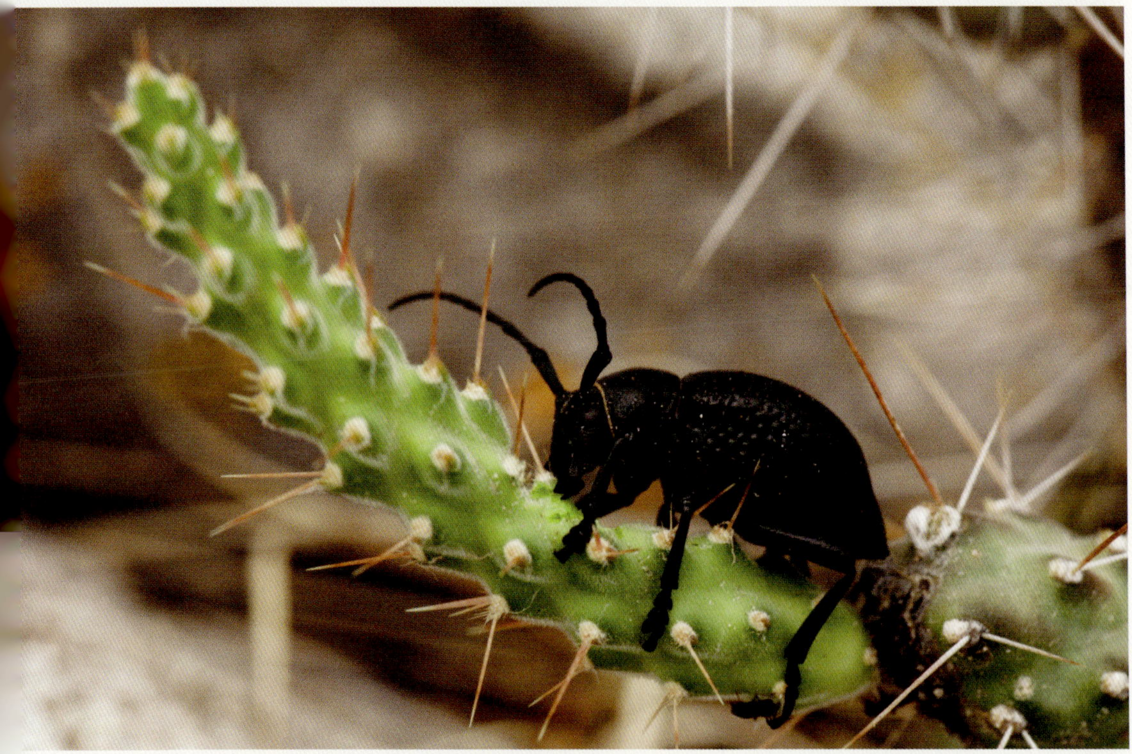

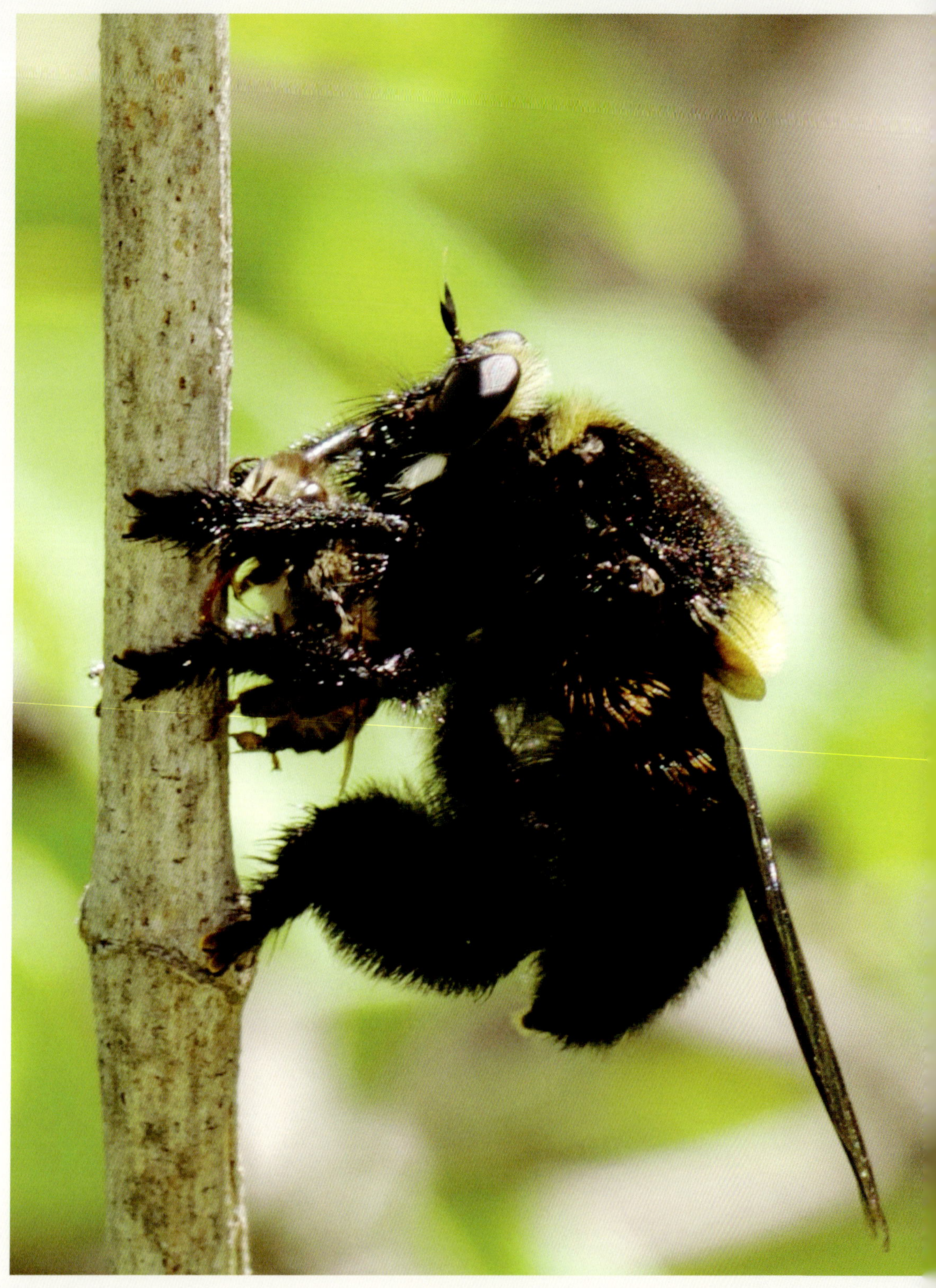

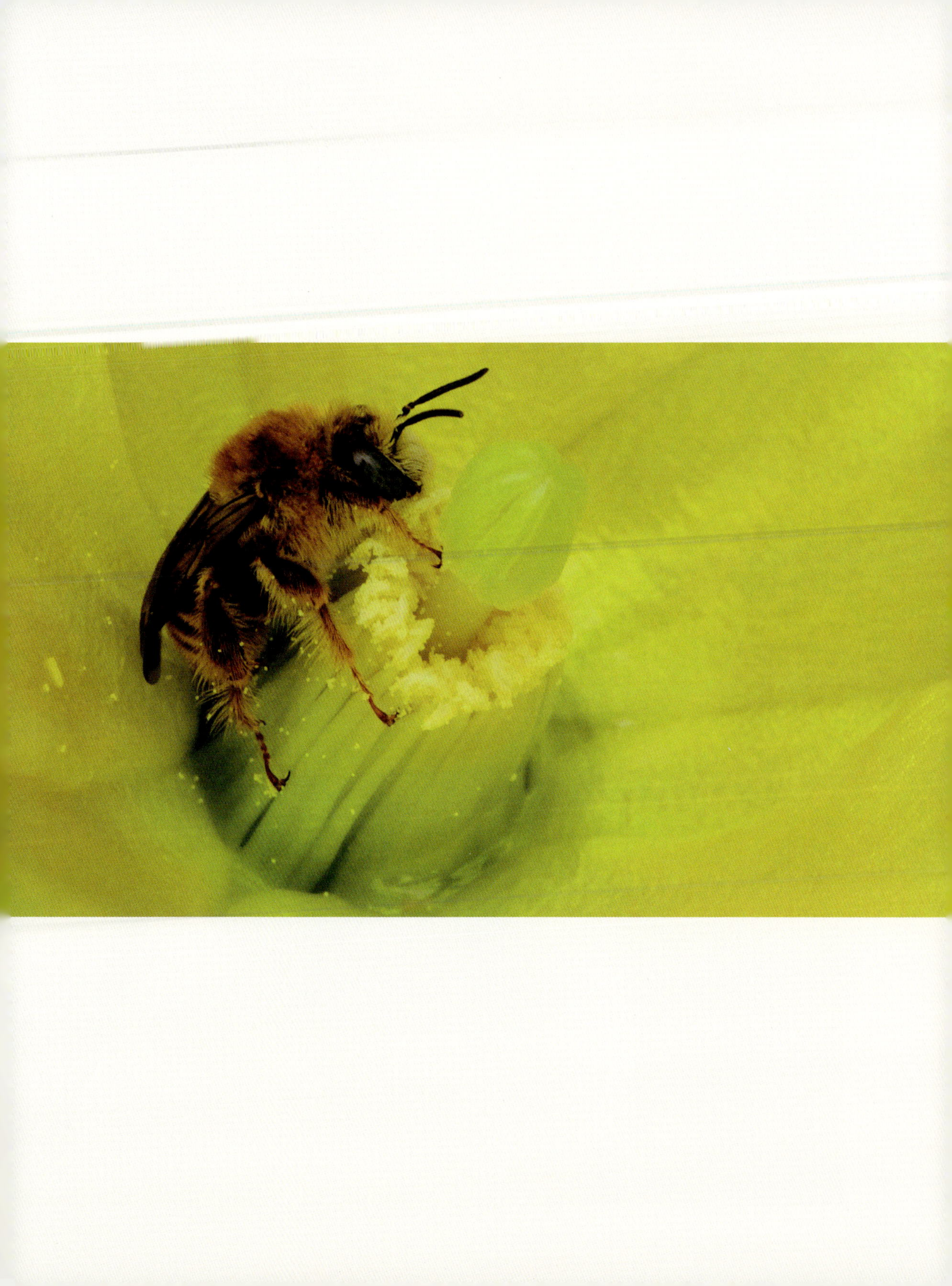

"Non-craving is an opportunity to take time to sit down and figure out what true happiness really is. We discover that we already have more than enough conditions to be happy, right here in the present moment. Letting go helps us disentangle ourselves from suffering and transform and release painful feelings."

THICH NHAT HANH
The Art of Living

FAITH

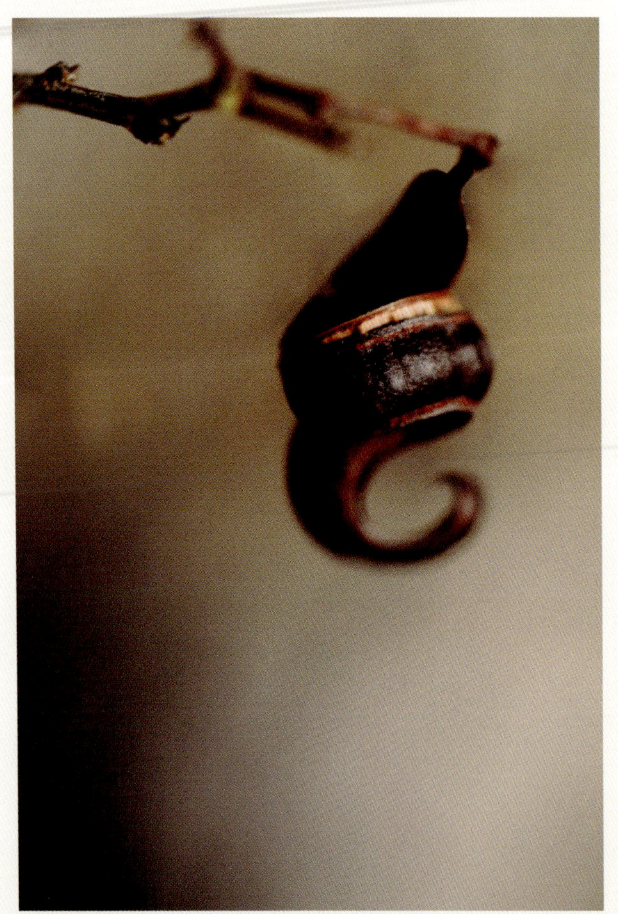

Individual seeds and seed pods clinging to dried-up plants connect me to a deep faith: even amid so much uncertainty—about the pandemic in particular as well as the broader risks of civilizational and ecological collapse—life will continue in one form or another. These seeds carry the legacy of the plants they come from forward. They contain all the knowledge they need to grow into their fullness when

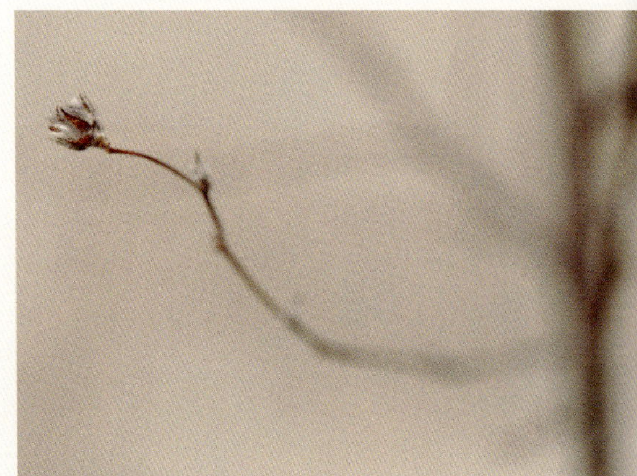

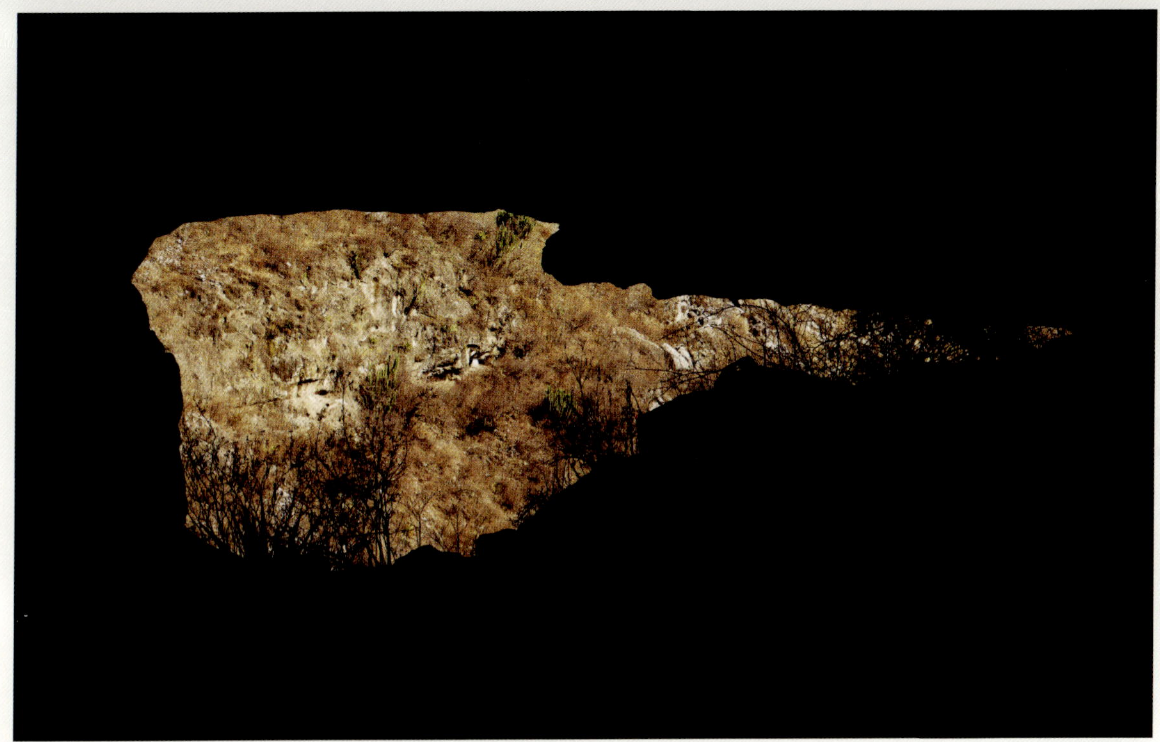

the right conditions arise. This way of seeing time as a vast unfolding arc rather than through the lens of a single human lifespan creates a sense of spaciousness and quiet calm in me.

This understanding of deep time is etched into my mind when, one day, I am able to walk to nearby prehistoric caves. Though now empty, I learn that 10,000-year-old squash seeds, the earliest known evidence of domesticated plants on the continent, were discovered in one of these caves. Corn cob fragments from the same cave are the earliest documented evidence of domesticated maize, a key link in the rise of Mesoamerican civilizations.

I am reminded of an article I once read about a 2,000-year-old seed that germinated after being recovered from the rubble of King Herod's pleasure palace in the Judean desert. Scientists have grown plants from seeds that were more than 30,000 years old, buried by squirrels in the Russian permafrost. Life finds a way.

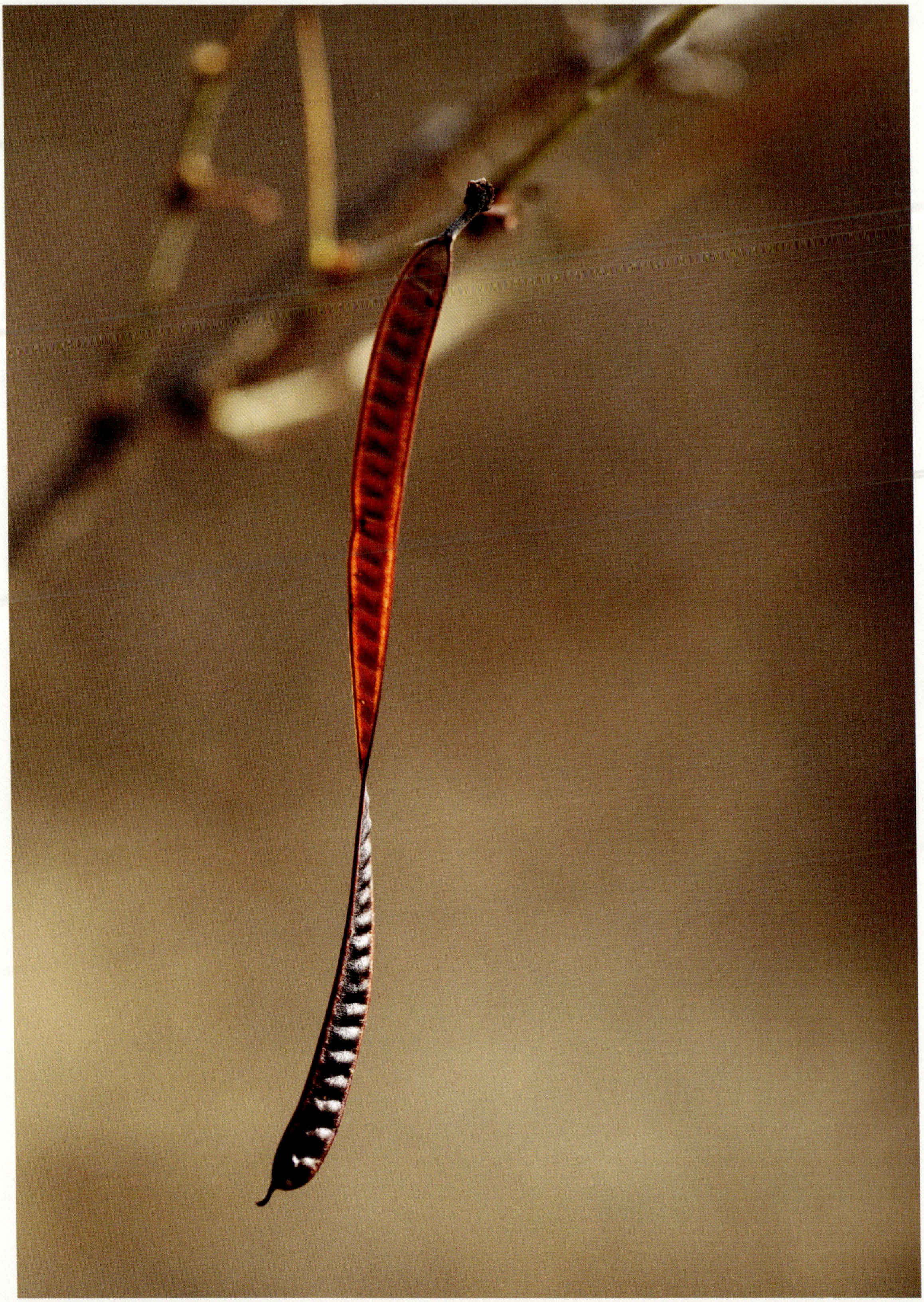

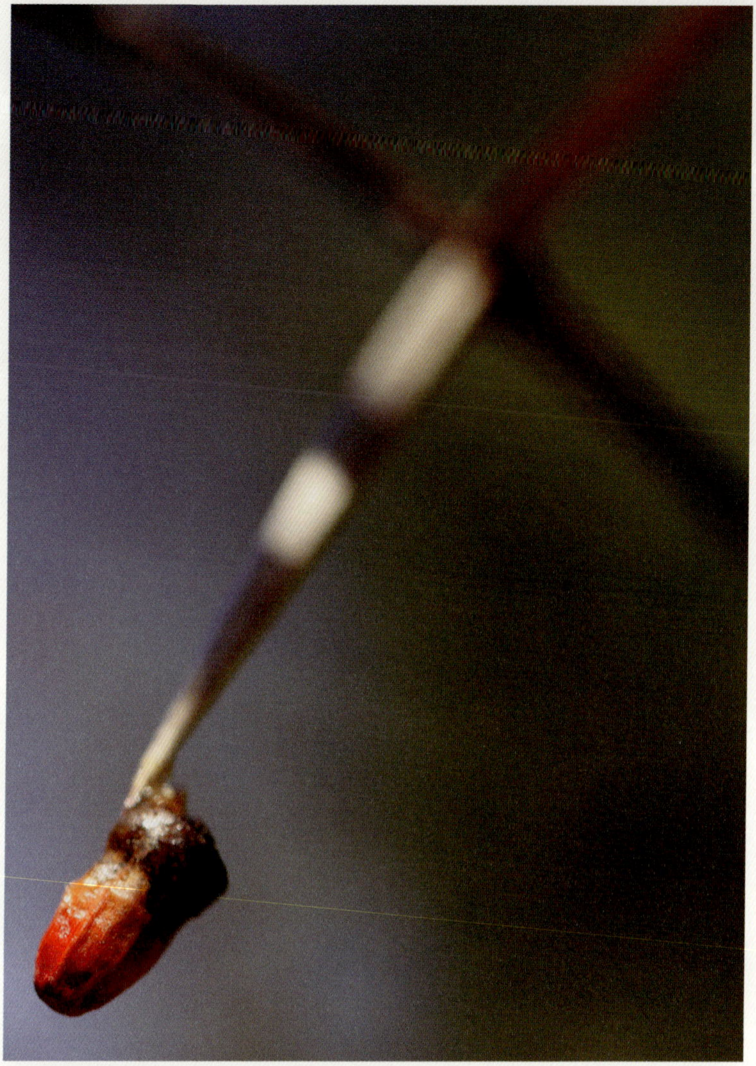

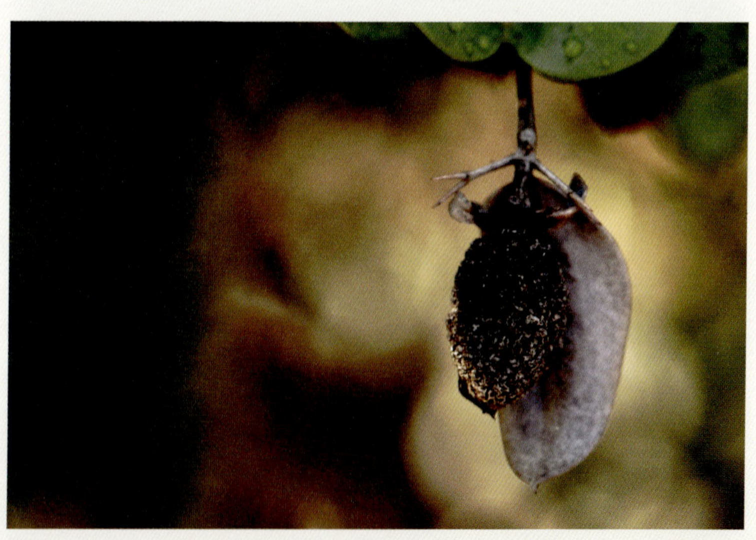

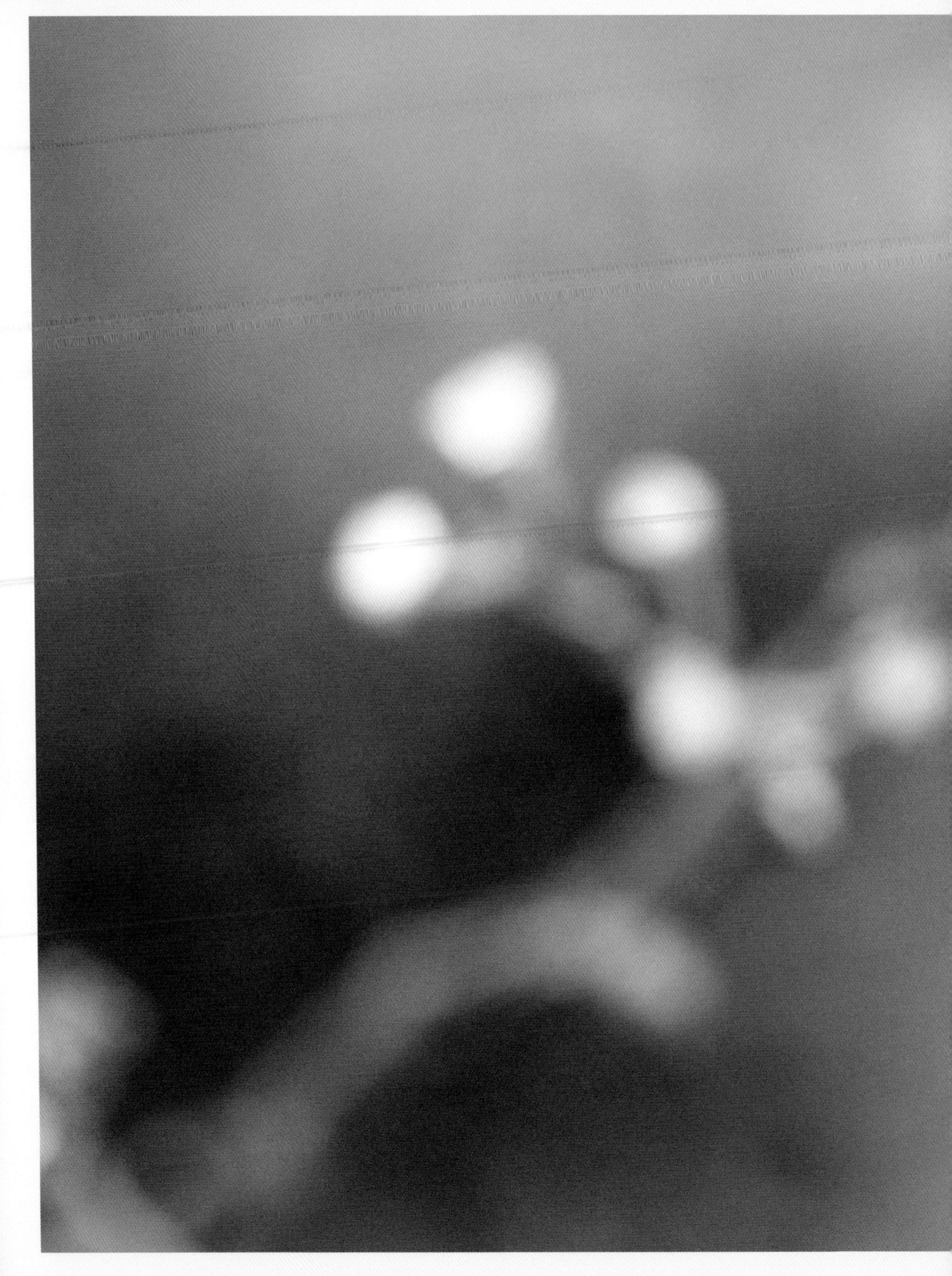

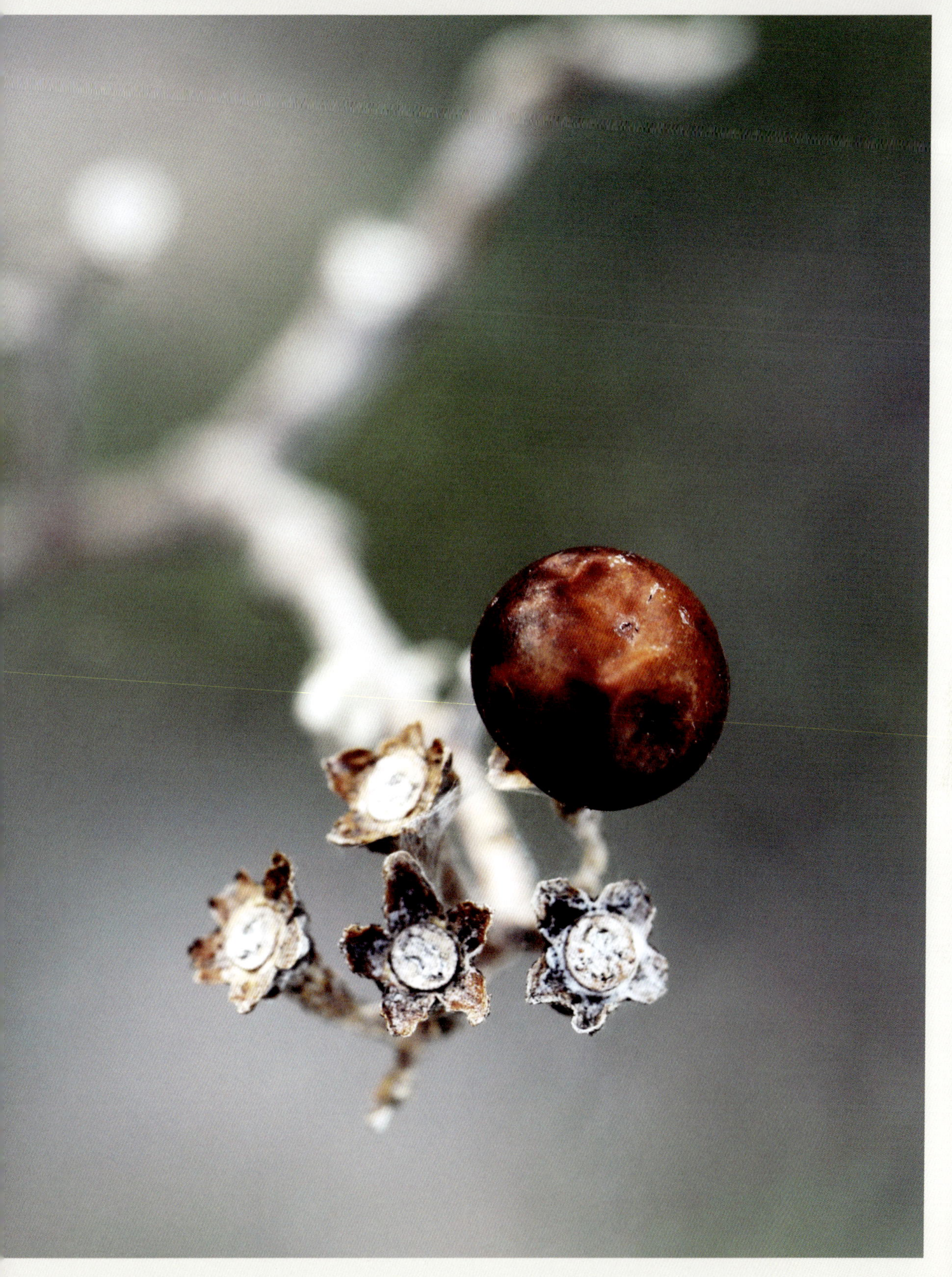

REVERENCE

My embedded scientific materialist outlook on life often leaves little space for sacred reverence. Most of the time, I see life through an intellectual lens. I have been awestruck by nature many times, but usually in spectacular circumstances —standing atop a high mountain peak, for example. That sense of wonder has rarely extended to more everyday experiences.

In Mitla, this begins to change. In particular, I start to feel animated by the same sunrise that used to fill me with foreboding over the coming heat. The first rays of the sun usually crest the mountains after I have been hiking for around an hour. Rather than turning around, I stop and stand in the stillness. I feel the light and warmth enter me to my core, like tea leaves suffusing a glass of hot water. I open my arms to the sky and allow it all in.

For a few short minutes, I stand in quiet wonder as the earth is bathed in a golden halo, bringing incomparable beauty to the most ordinary objects, things I know will appear drab after the sun rises higher into the sky—a leaf, a tiny piece of bark, a droplet of sap. Spider webs shimmer with all the colors of the rainbow and some arachnids take on a translucent glow.

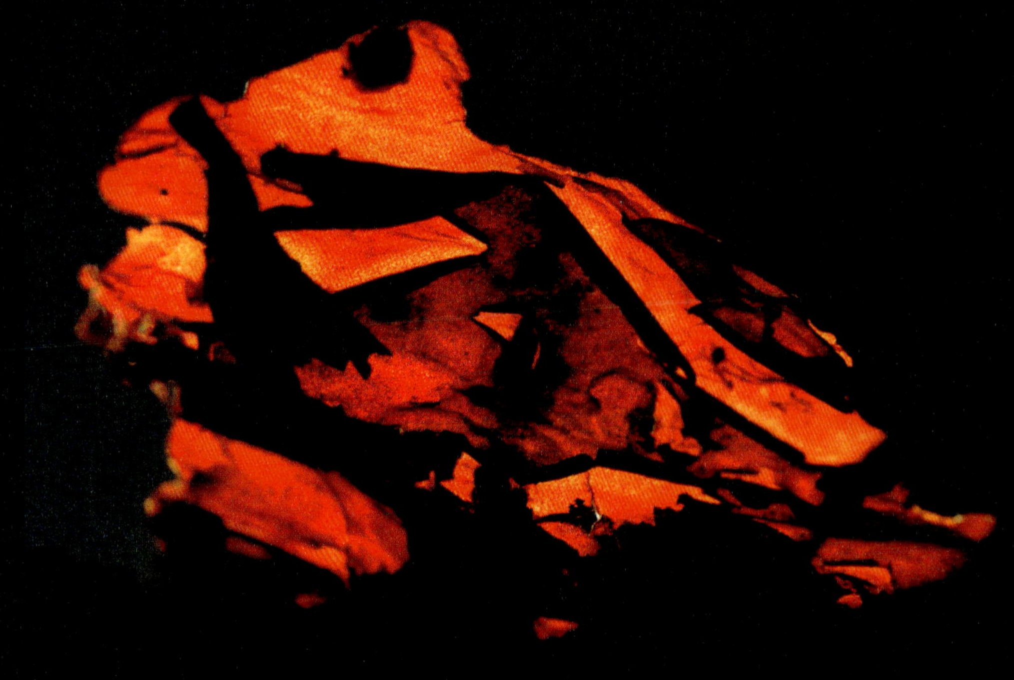

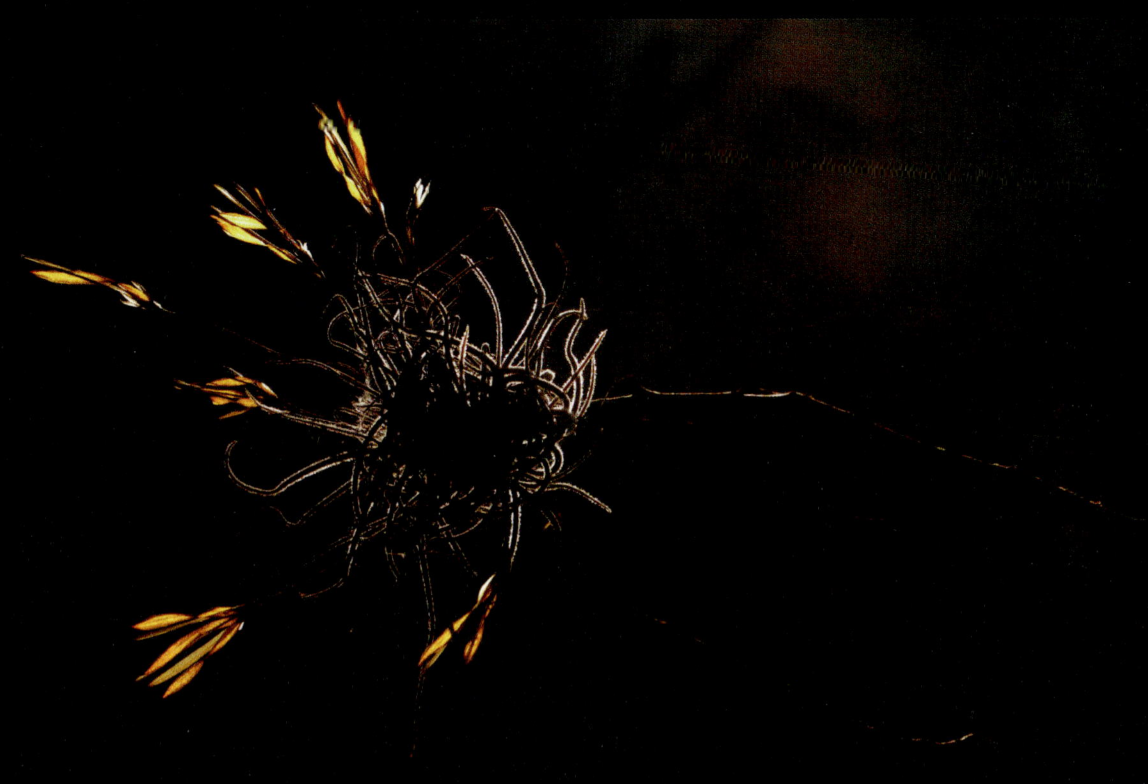

As the weeks pass, the land feels more alive, though I know it is I who have changed. A greater intimacy is taking root. I now greet individual plants and bushes I pass regularly, as if acknowledging friends on the path. I am reminded of the words of American naturalist John Muir, who said that the "clearest way into the Universe is through a forest wilderness," and also reflected that "when we try to pick out anything by itself, we find it hitched to everything else in the Universe." These words now feel less like an abstract truth and more like something I am beginning to live.

As I continue to learn about the local cultures, iterations of ways of being that reach back thousands of years, new depths unfold. In local Zapotec stories, the first beings—the ancients—lived before the creation of the sun. The ancients built stone temples in the dark. When the sun first rose, they went underground and transformed into stone idols. A new world was then fashioned by the gods in the light. In that world, everything was animated by spirits; people made offerings and prayed to plants.

Hearing this story, something stirs in me—a recognition, perhaps, that this reverence for the unseen and elemental is not foreign, but echoes places where the spirit of gratitude still moves among us. In my experience of Western society, we have largely lost our deep connection and reverence for the non-human world. Broadening my lens beyond my own blood lineages, I can see, in the past and in the present, ways in which these connections were and are a natural way of seeing and knowing.

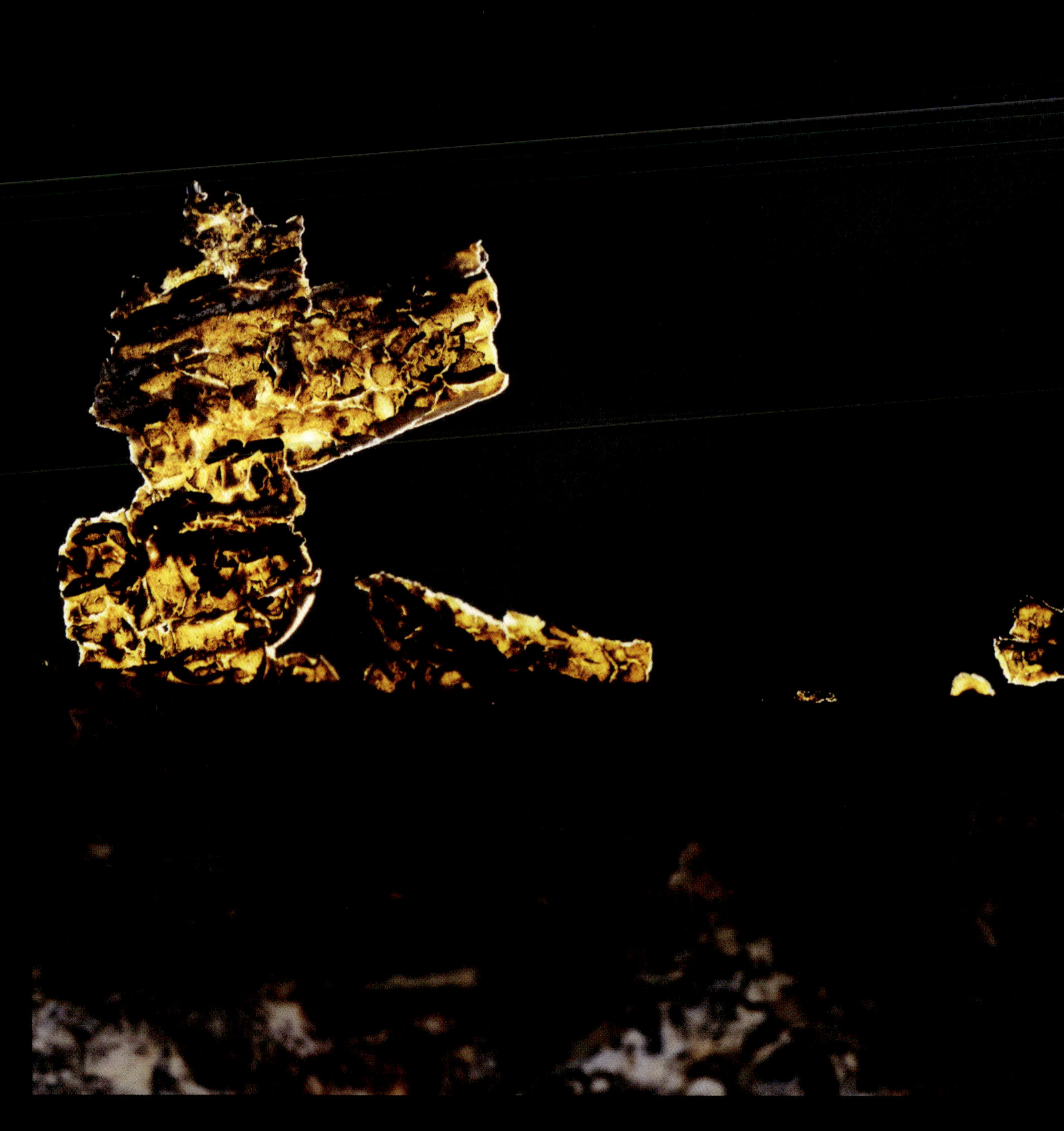

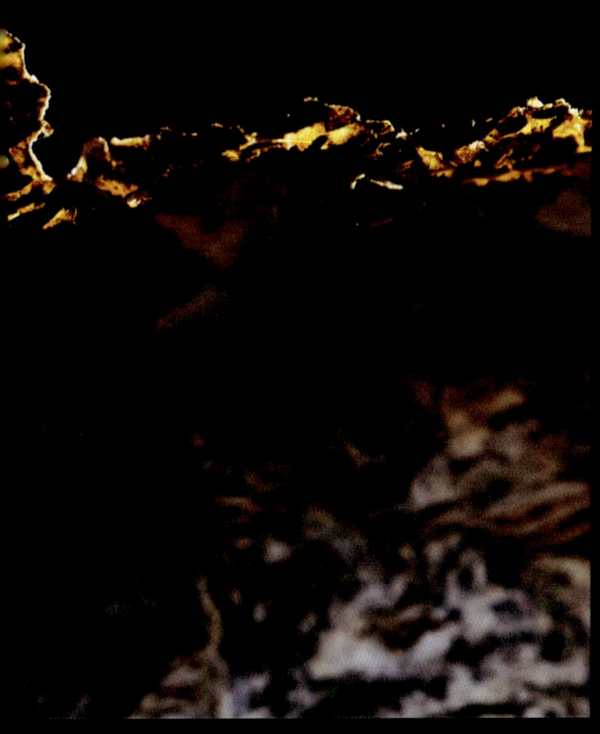

The reverence of the Zapotec culture is not so very different from the teachings within the Plum Village Zen tradition I am familiar with, a tradition where monastics and lay practitioners regularly express gratitude and humility—not just to spiritual and blood ancestors, but also to Gaia and the Sun.

In Plum Village, one of the common ceremonies is the practice of Touching the Earth. We perform a series of full body bows in recognition of our interbeing with all of nature. Touching the earth, we surrender to Gaia and show our appreciation for the sun. When I first encountered this practice, I felt awkward prostrating myself to Mother Nature, but even more so when I got on my hands and knees to express reverence to the sun. This, of course, is precisely the point: we must actively break our narrow Western views and venerate the more-than-human to understand that we are not separate, and to embody this knowing.

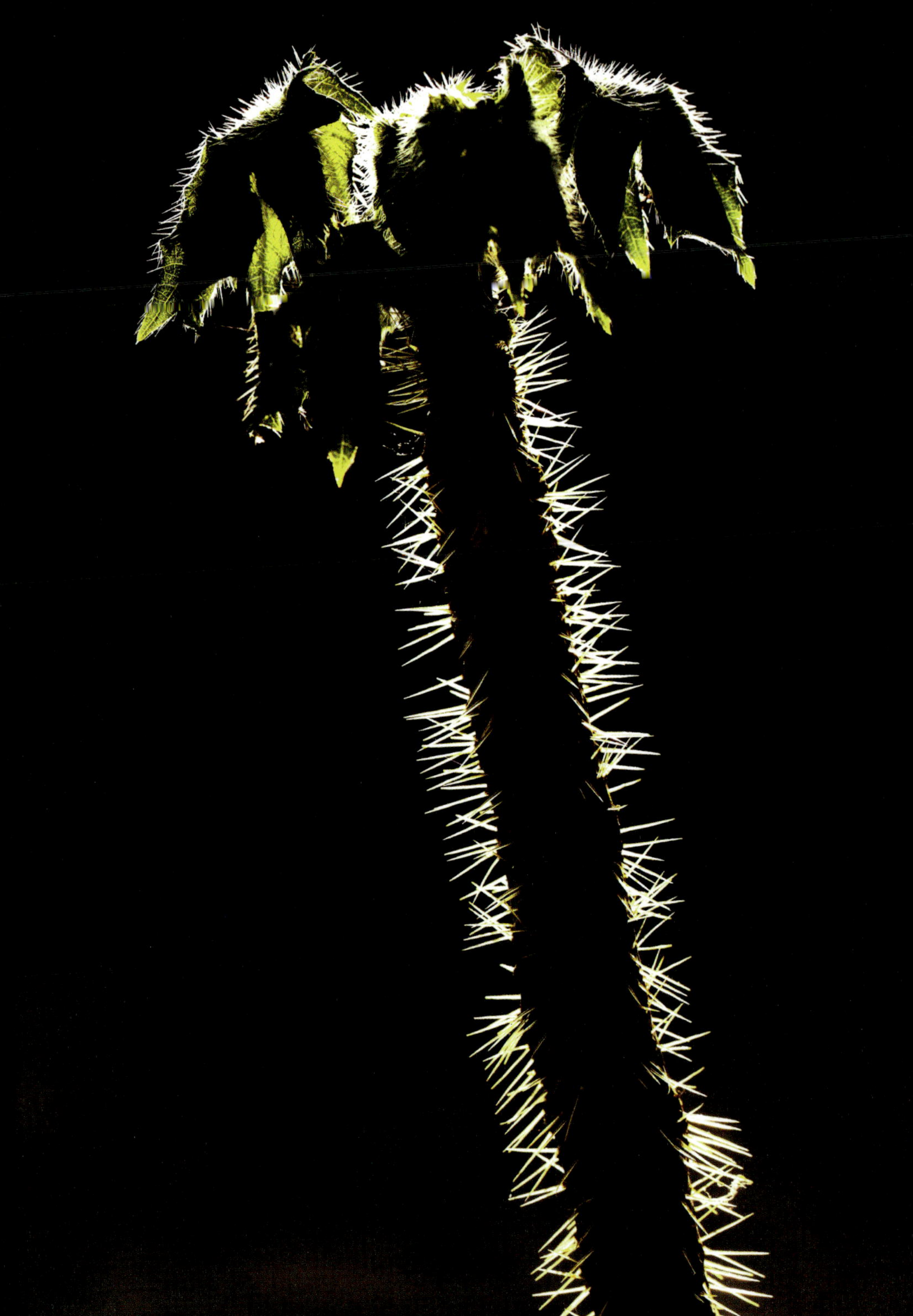

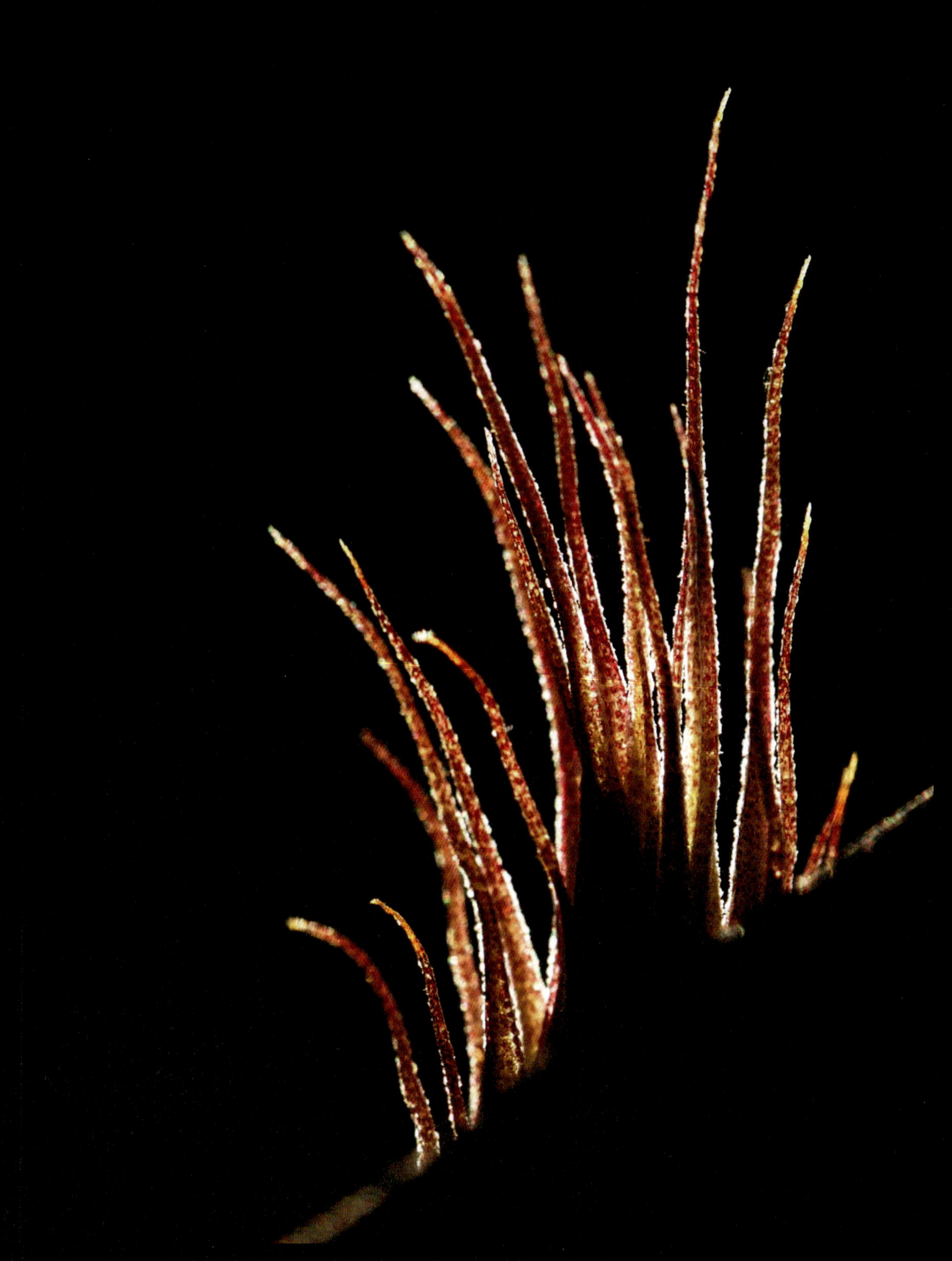

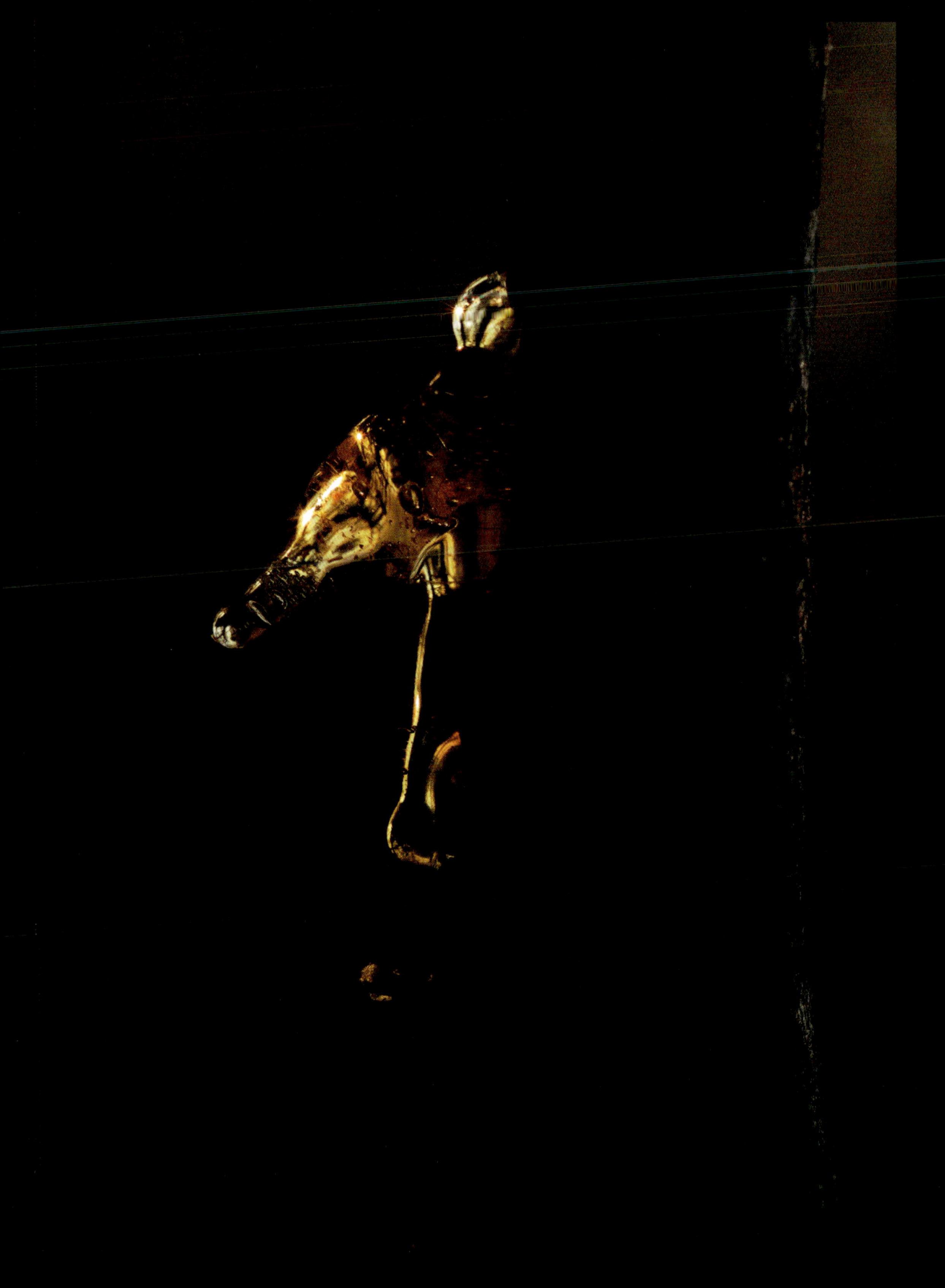

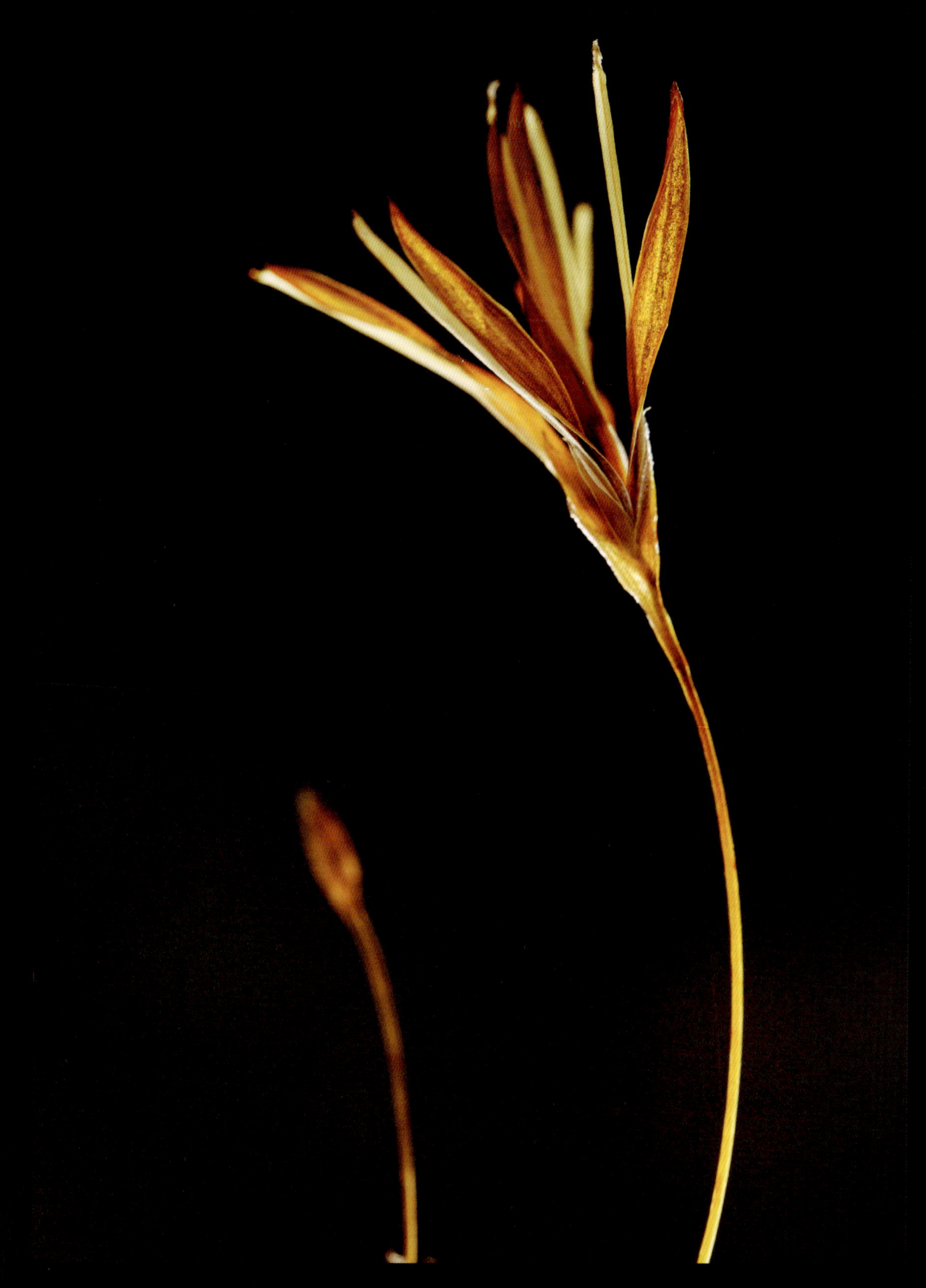

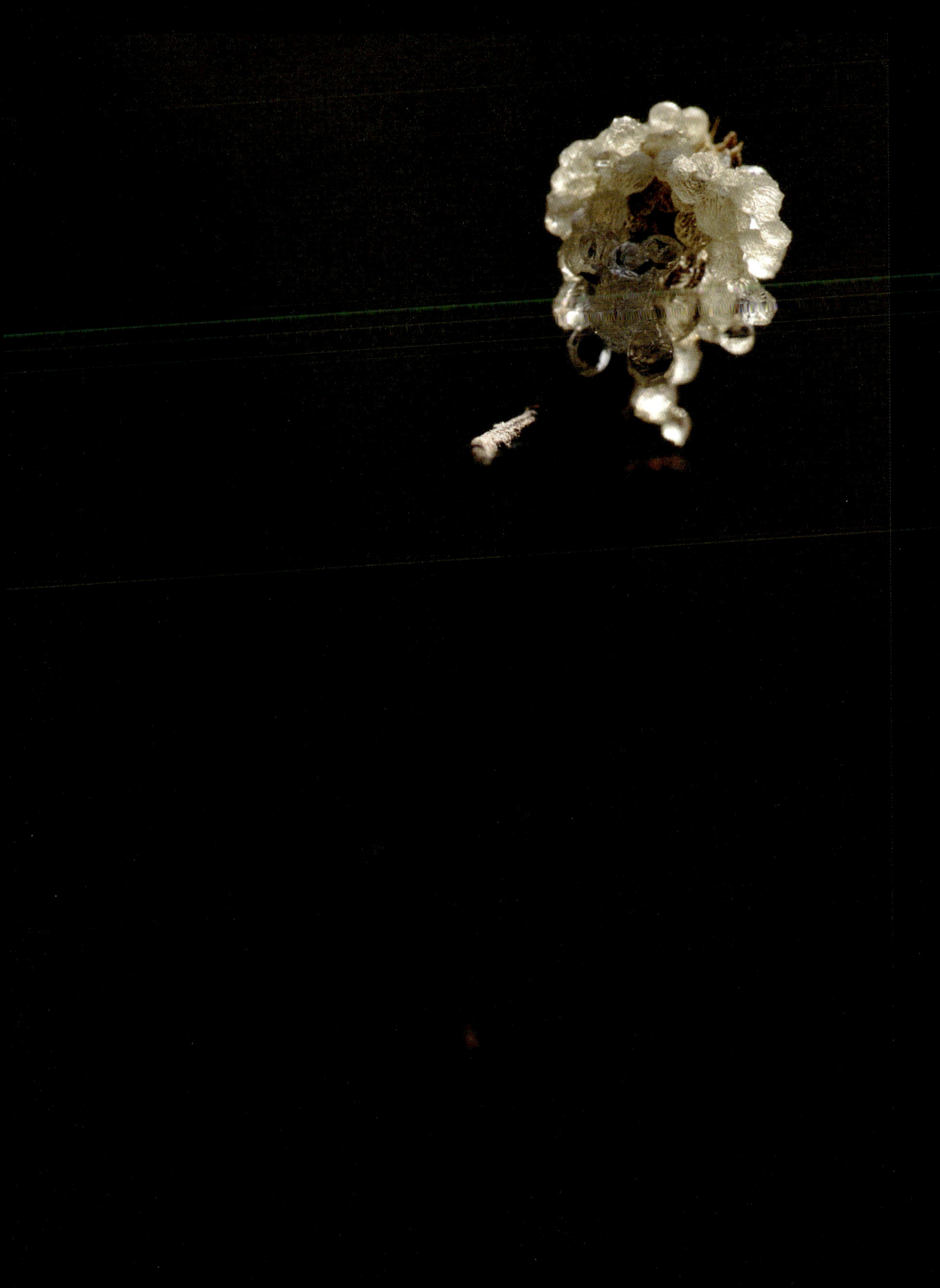

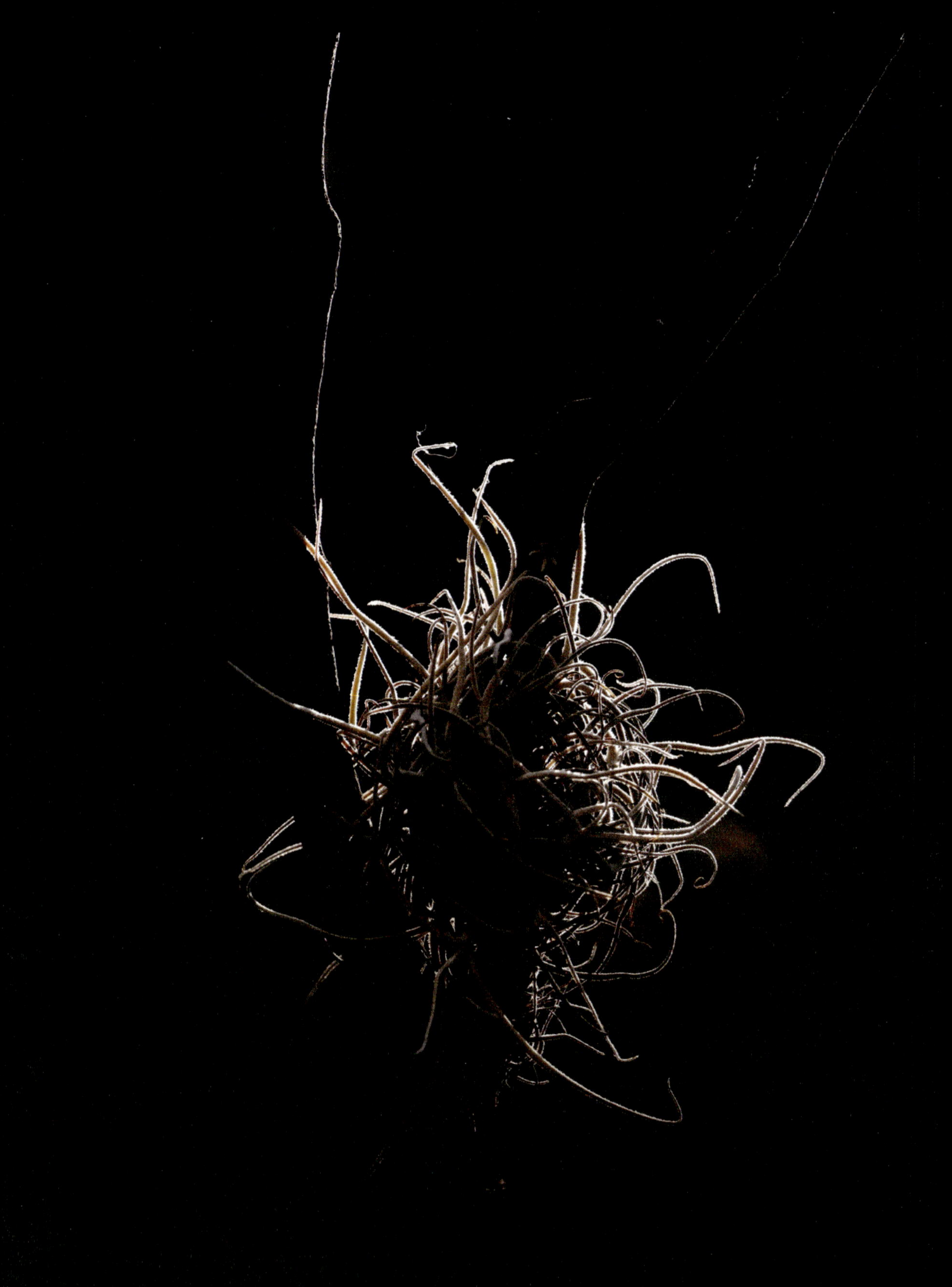

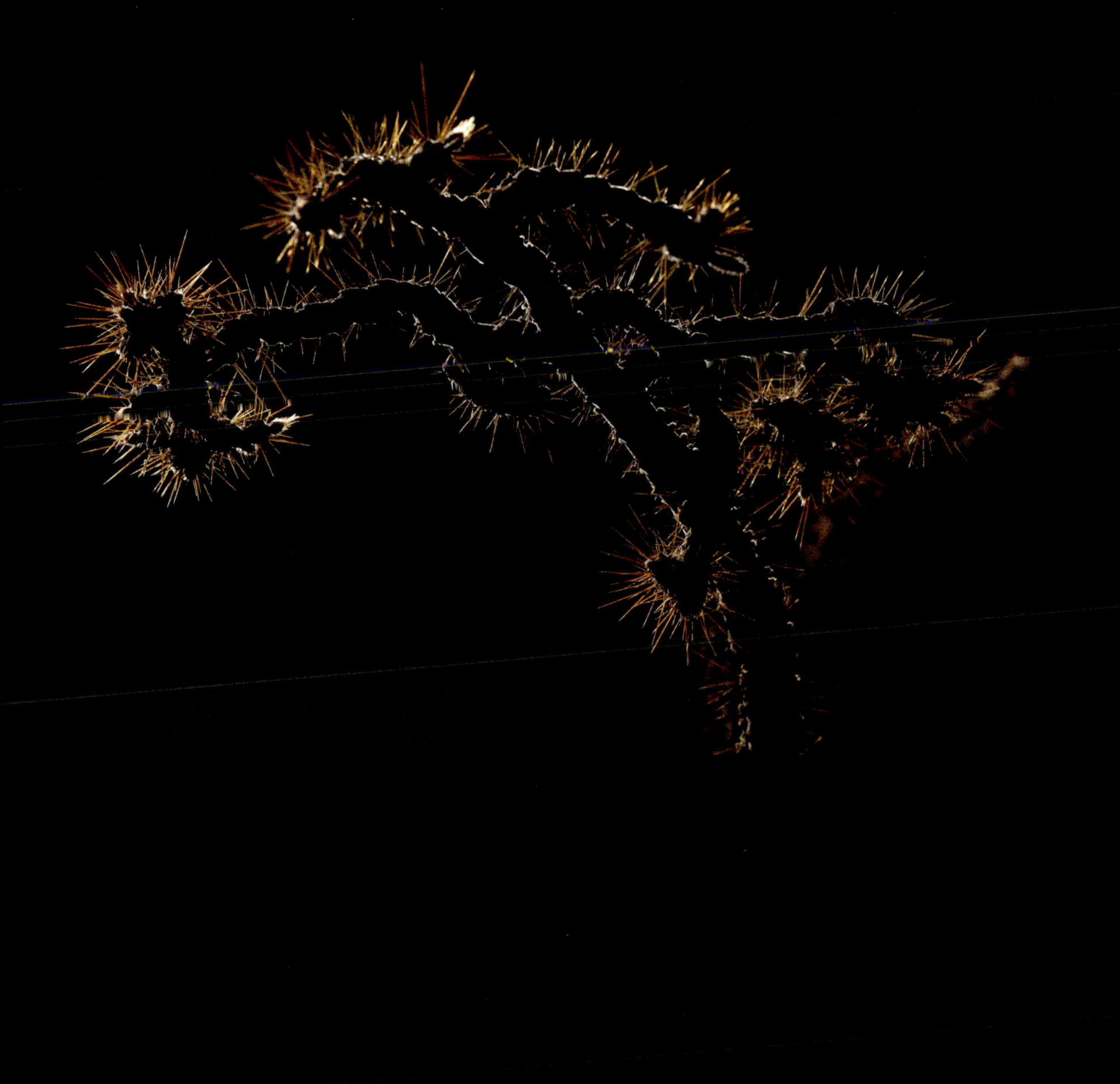

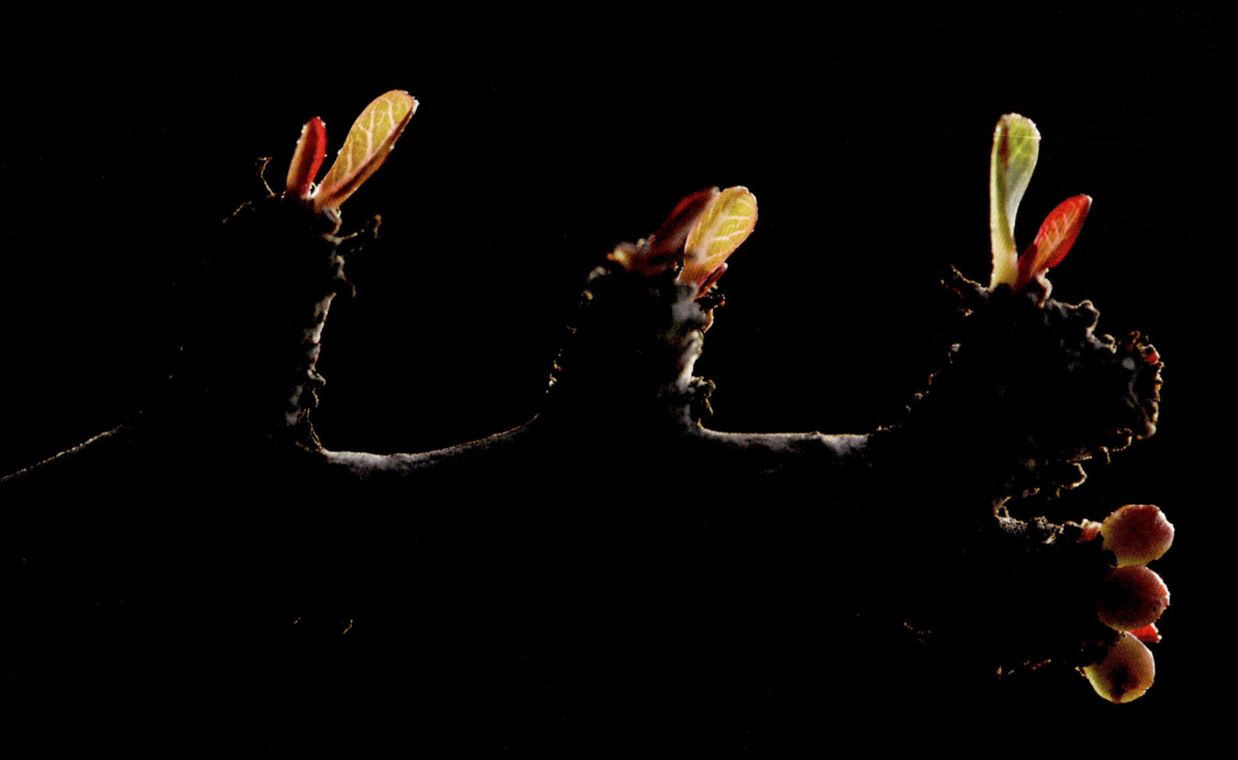

HEALTHY
BOUNDARIES

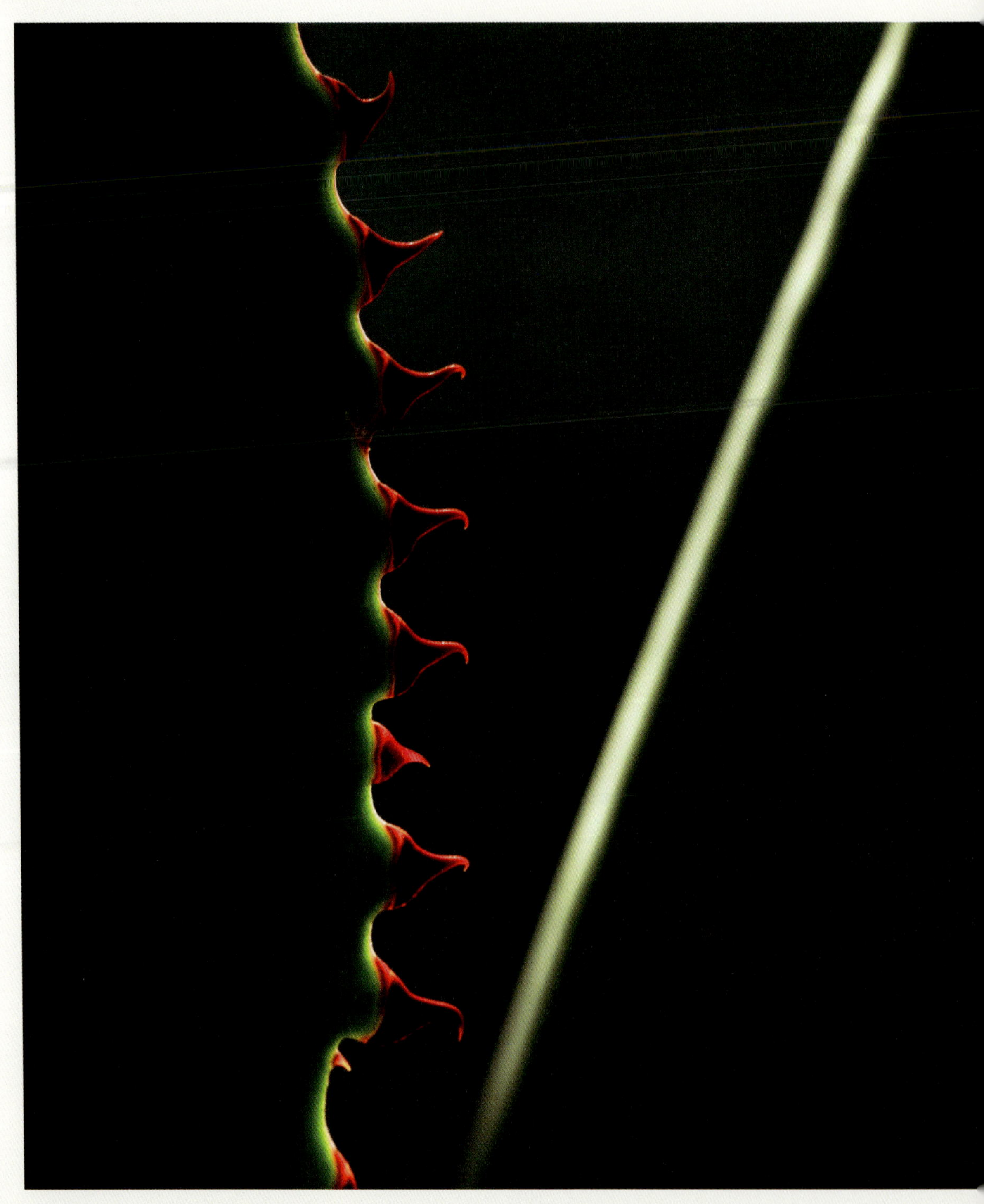

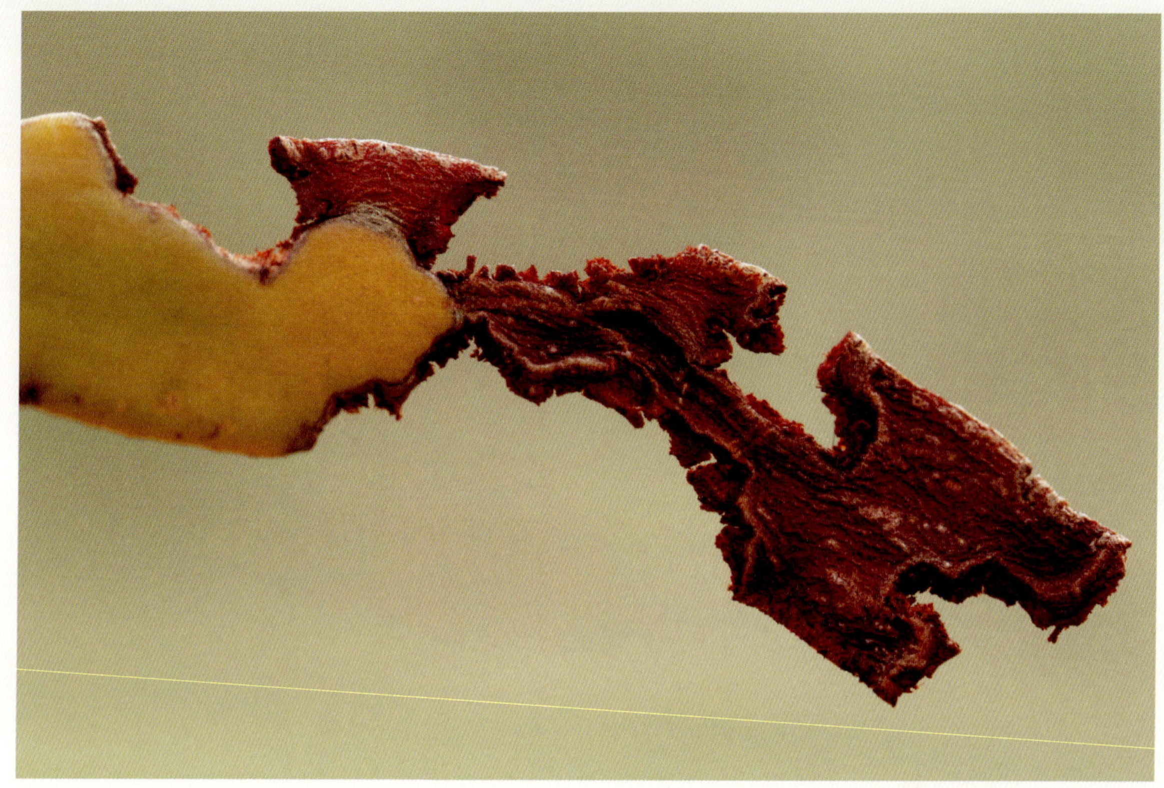

The cacti that pervade the landscape remind
me of a story the Buddha told about a cow who
had lost its skin. Without this protective layer,
the cow became an easy target for countless
flesh-eating insects and got an infection.

Like the cow, cacti rely on their outer defenses.
Without their thick skin and formidable spikes,
cacti would likewise quickly be devoured for
the water and nutrients they contain within.
Yet their defenses are not impregnable. I watch
insects crawl between cactus spikes, searching
for a way into the succulent interior. Birds, too,
gorge on prickly pear cacti fruits until their

chests are stained bright red. Though the cacti
lose their fruit, the birds help to spread seeds
far and wide, thereby improving the cacti's
ability to survive as a species.

I am not so very different from a cactus. I
too have developed ways to protect myself
from past hurts and future fears. We all need
healthy boundaries to preserve our life force.
Despite my best efforts, sometimes someone
finds a way through my defenses, and I can
suffer greatly. But like the prickly pear, I can
also benefit from the presence of others—
for example when someone is able to break
through and motivate me to face an emotional
wound. If I stay present and engaged, this
reckoning inevitably supports healing and
change, even if the process at times feels slow
and painstaking. While my defenses can make
me appear somewhat prickly at times, I hope
others can see beyond the surface and into my
softer and more tender side, the side I spent
my early years protecting for fear it would not
survive attack.

Developing compassion for ourselves is a core
Zen teaching. Compassion gives us permission
to recognize that we are already enough and
allows us to gently let go of outdated childhood
survival strategies that hold us back. It is
equally important to go beyond our surface
perceptions and be compassionate with
those who needle us. When someone pushes
our buttons, we can recognize that they are
touching an old wound within us. Rather
than blame the other person, we can see how
their presence can be a true service—a signal
pointing to the inner healing work we are still
called to undertake.

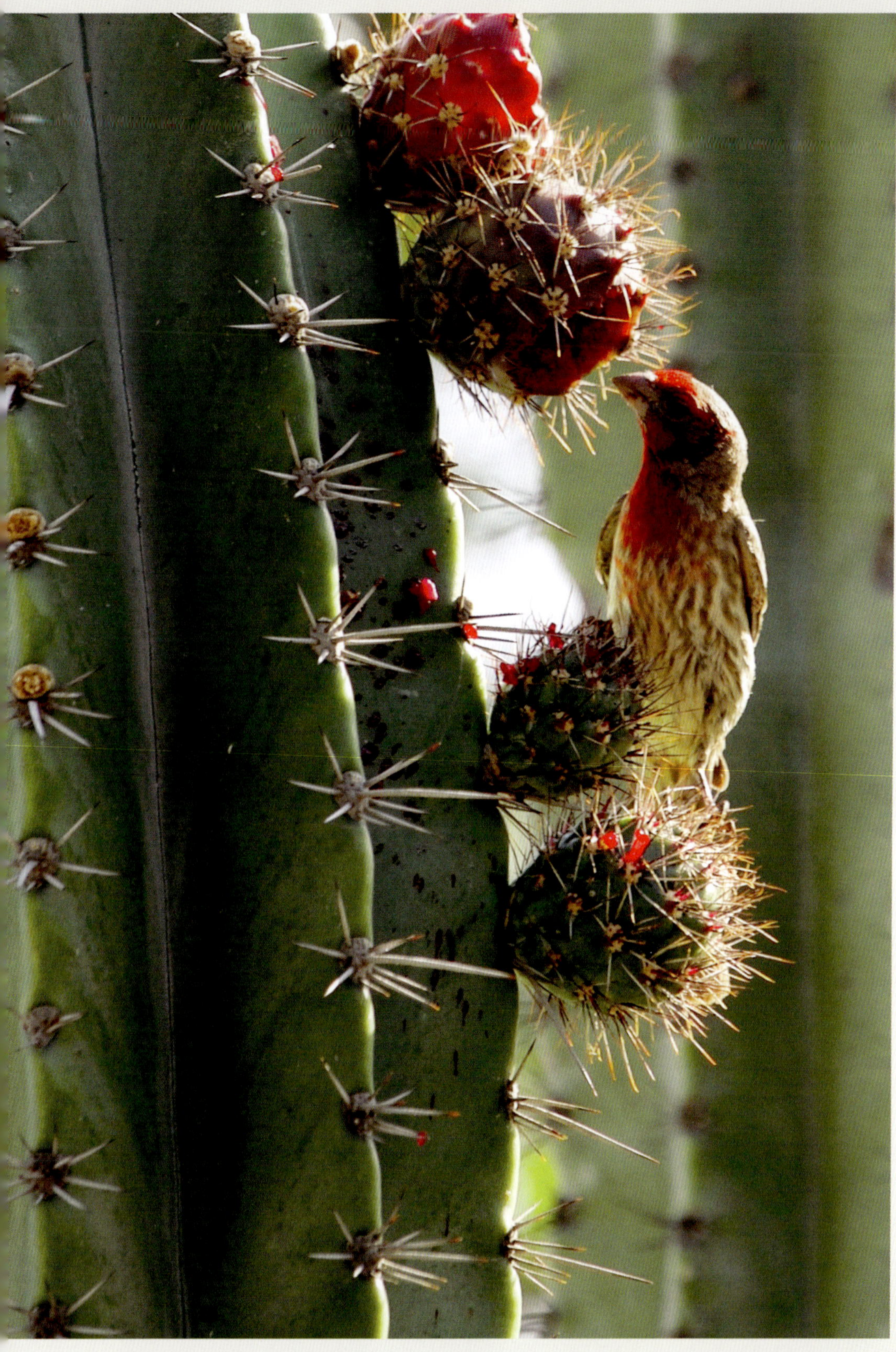

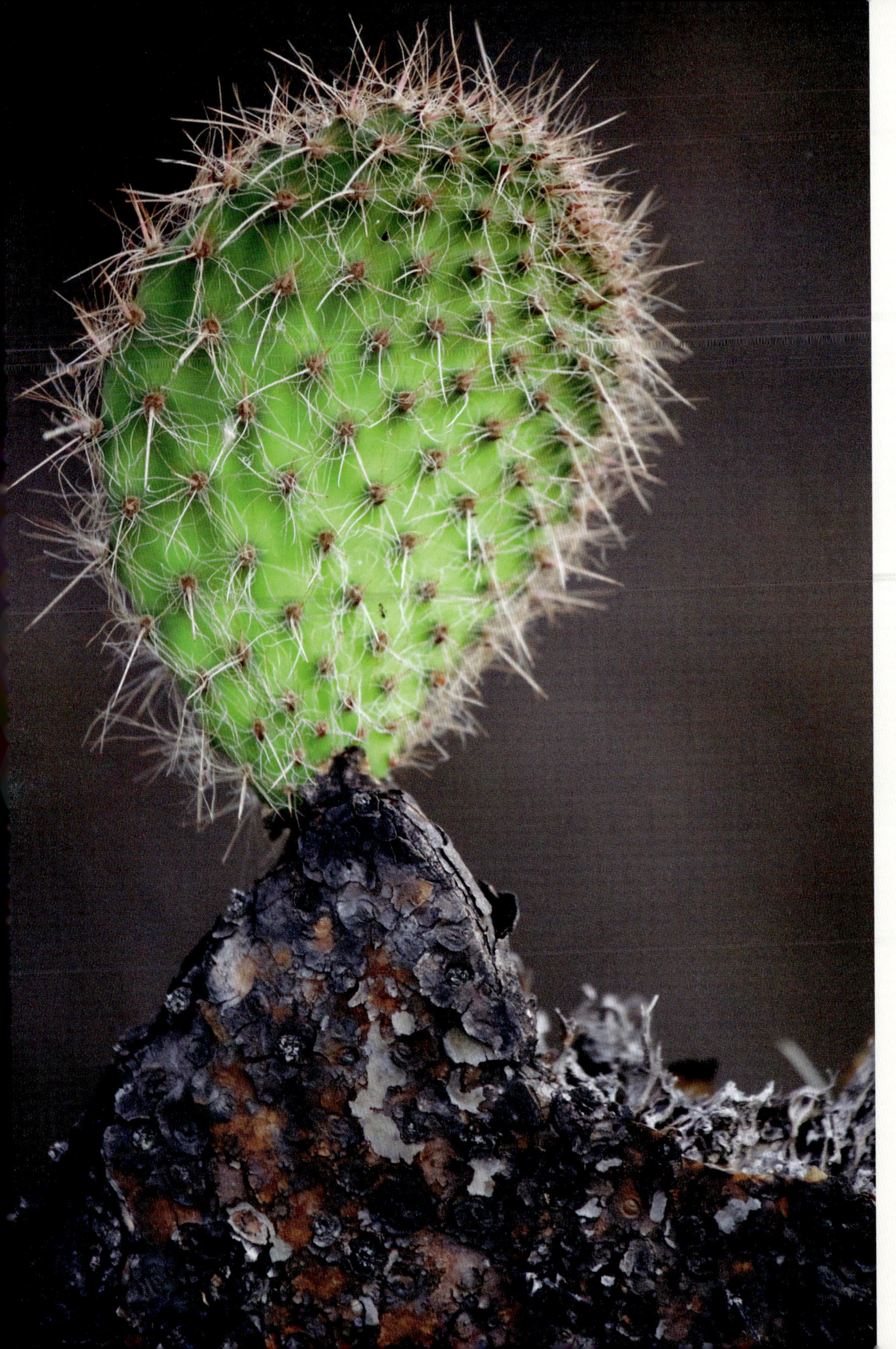

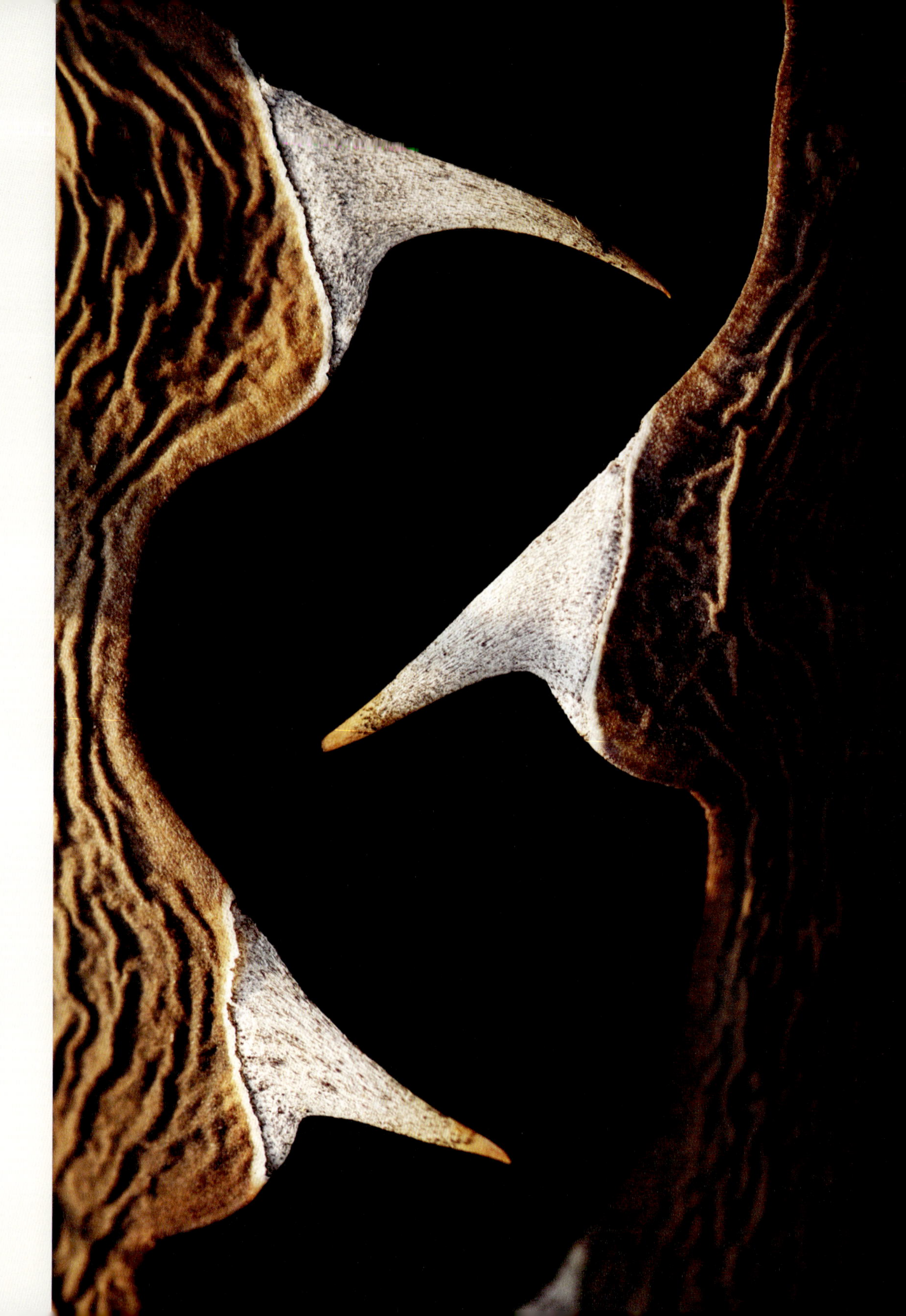

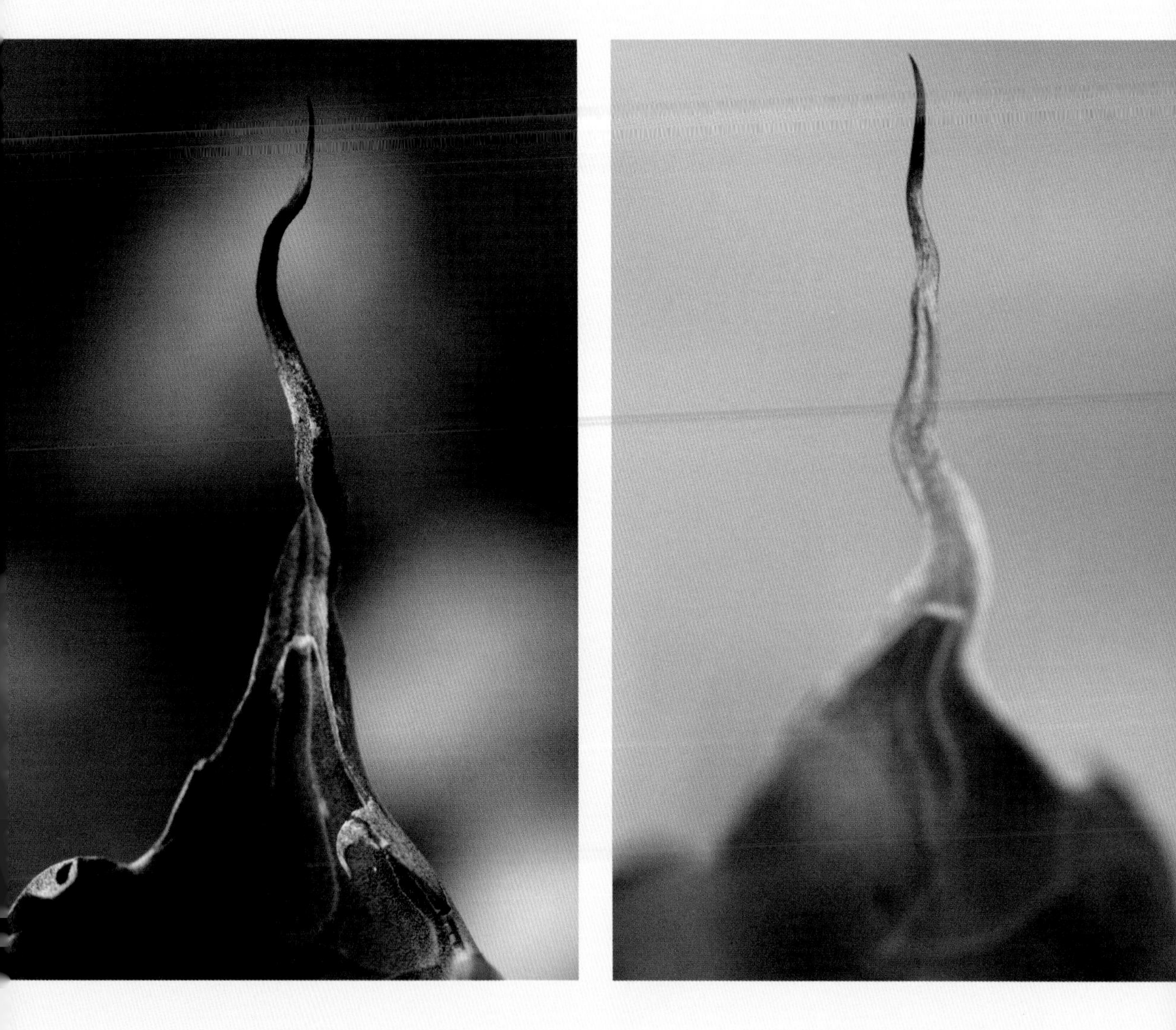

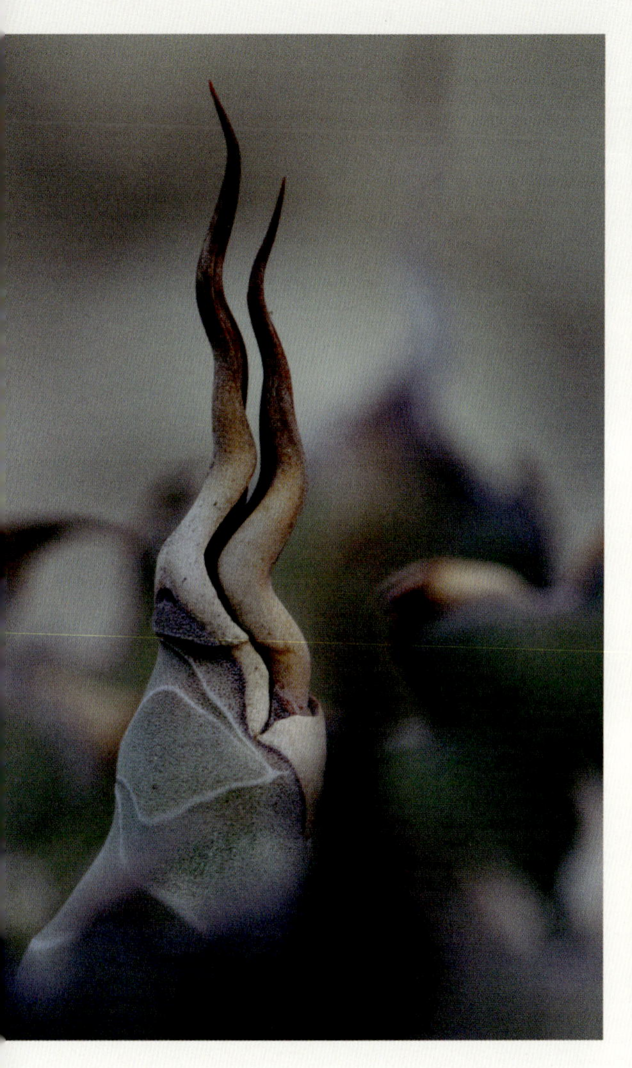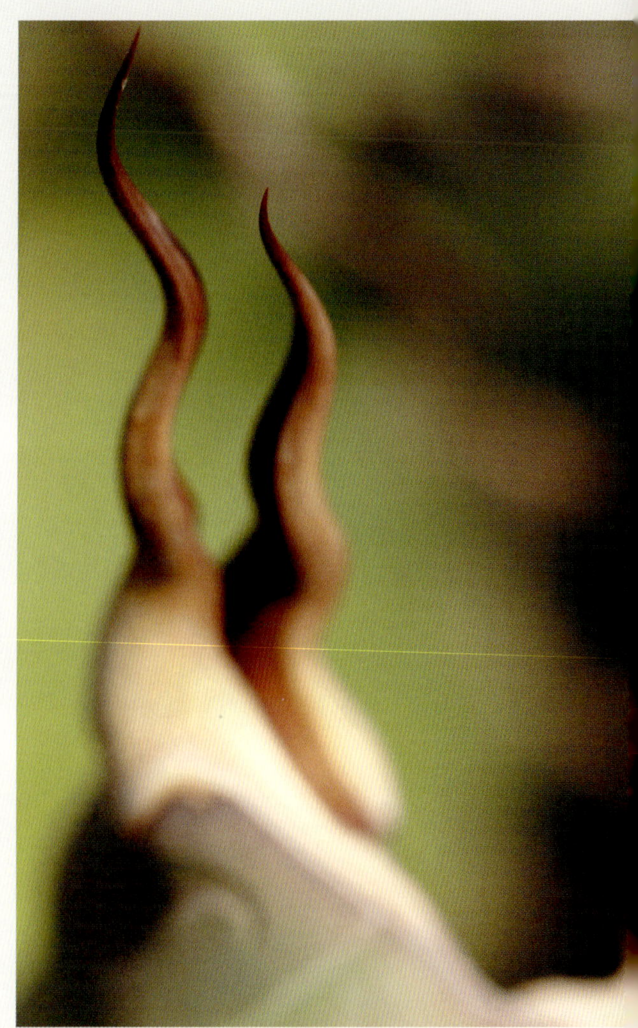

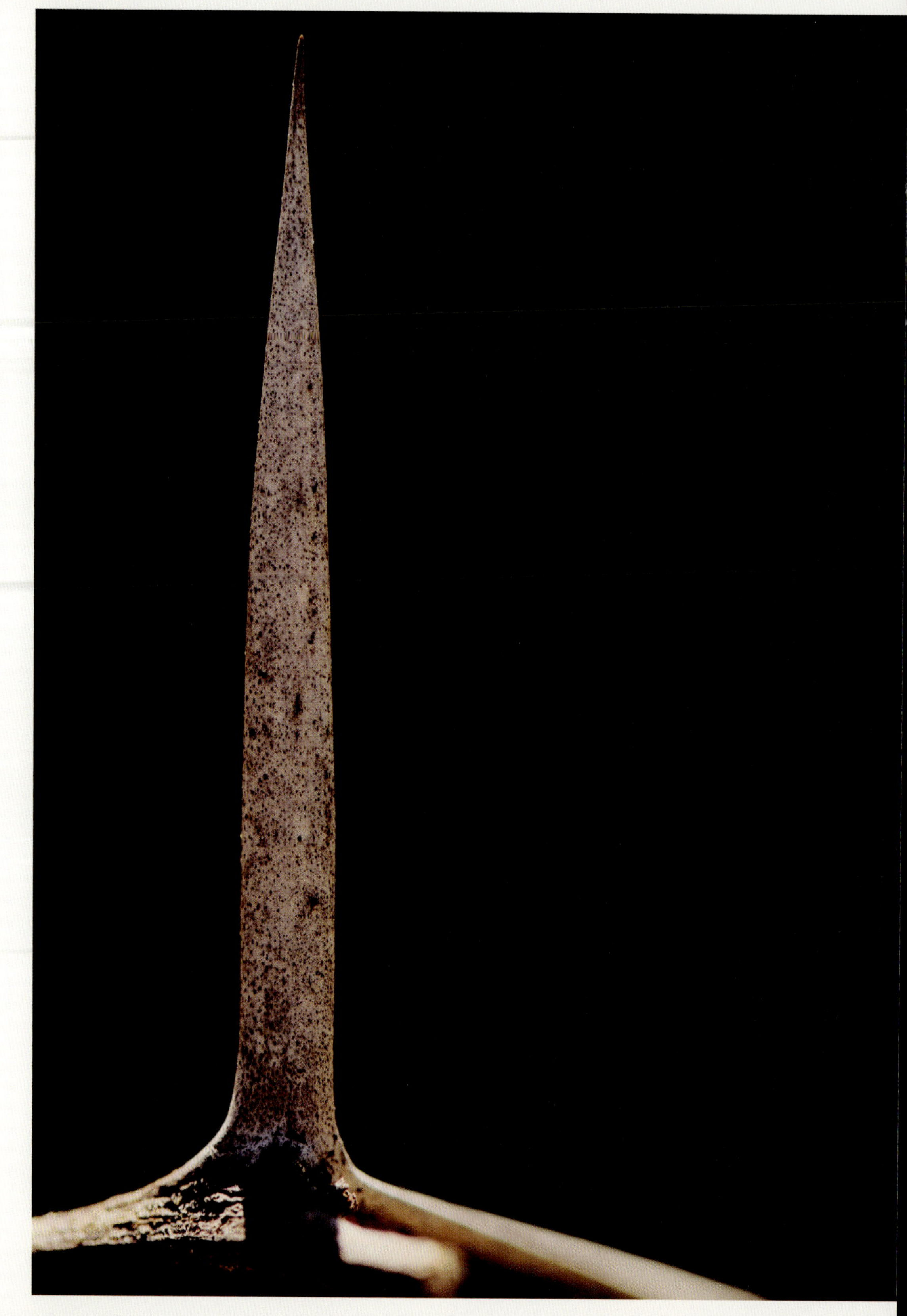

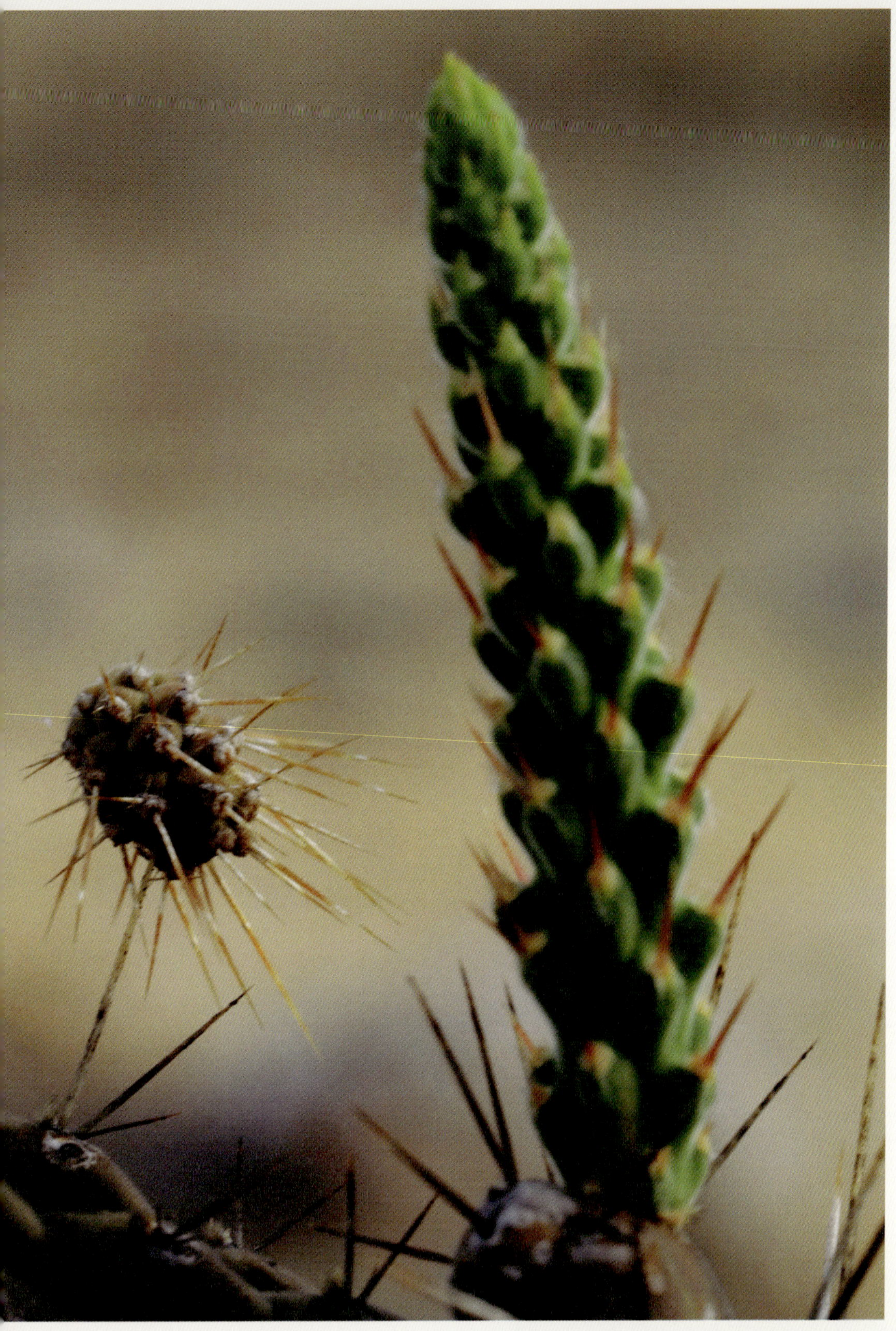

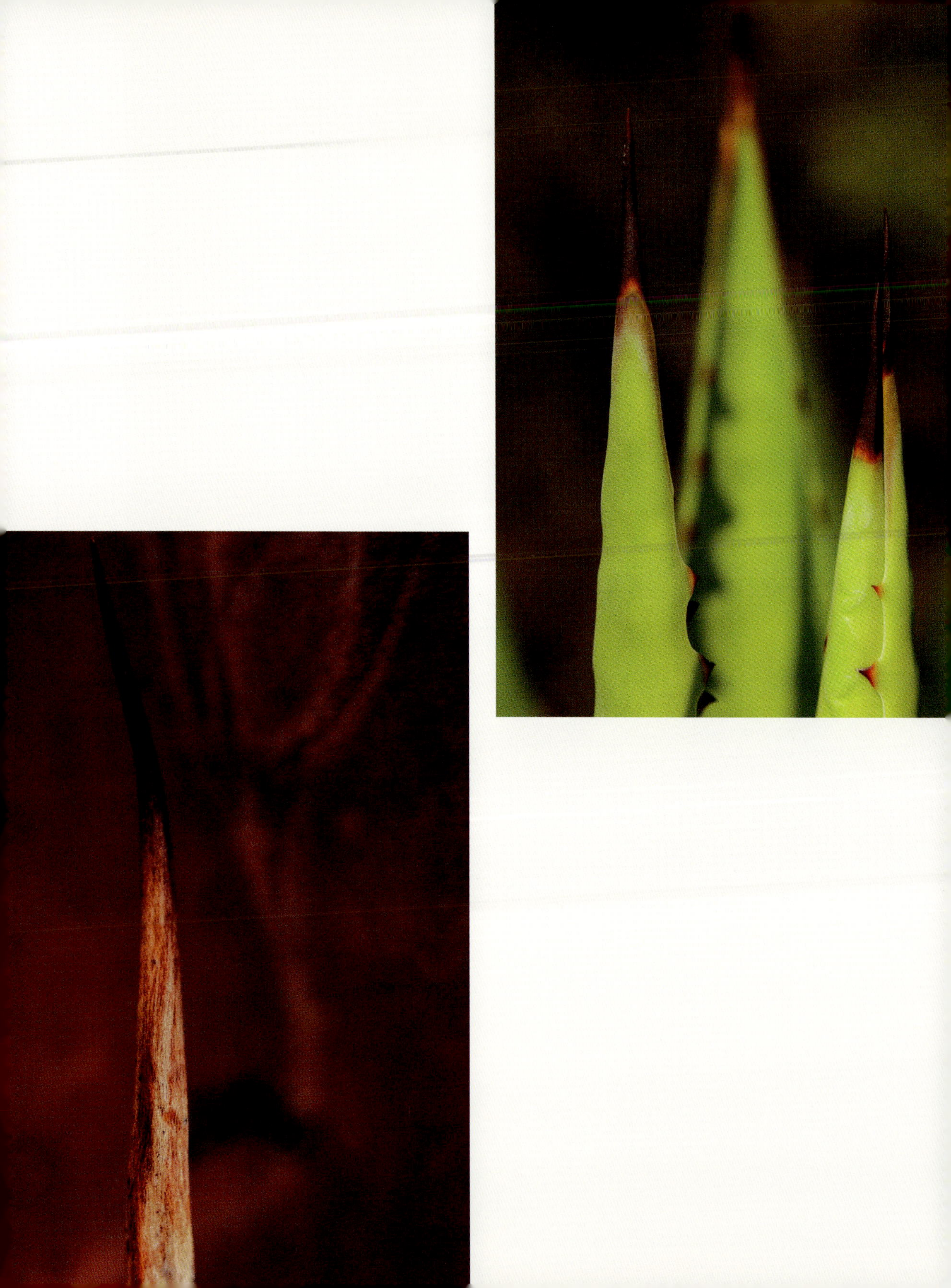

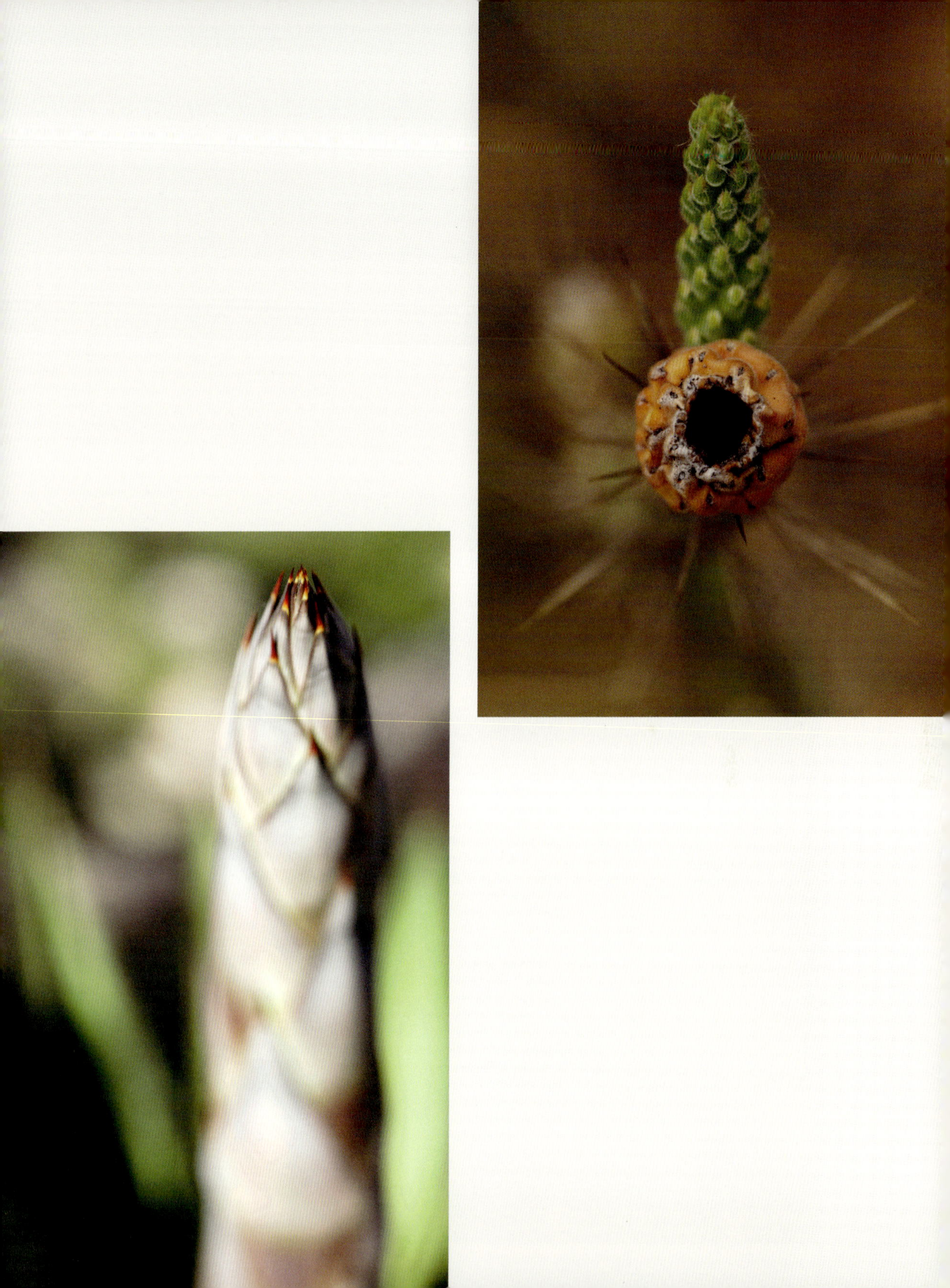

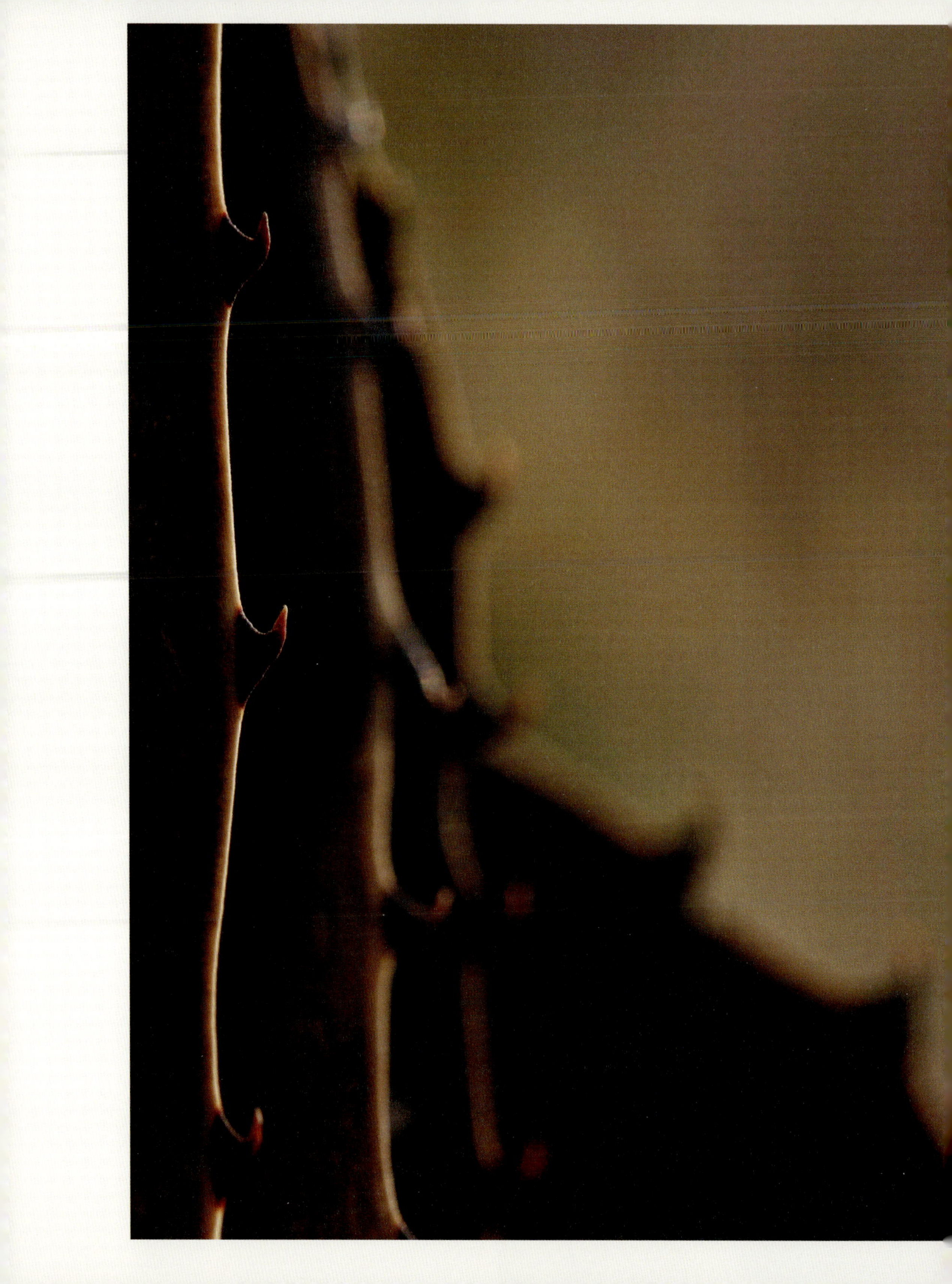

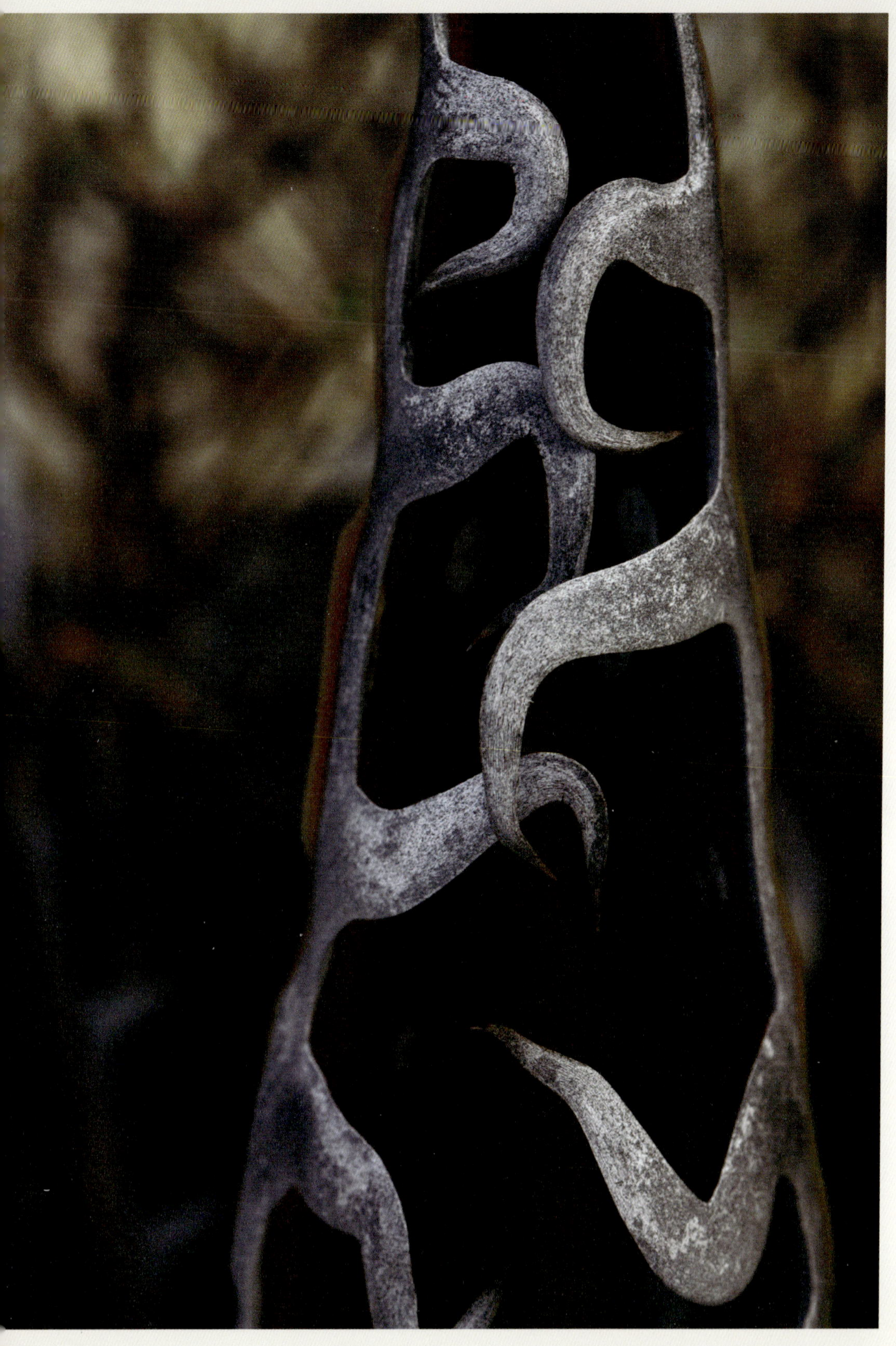

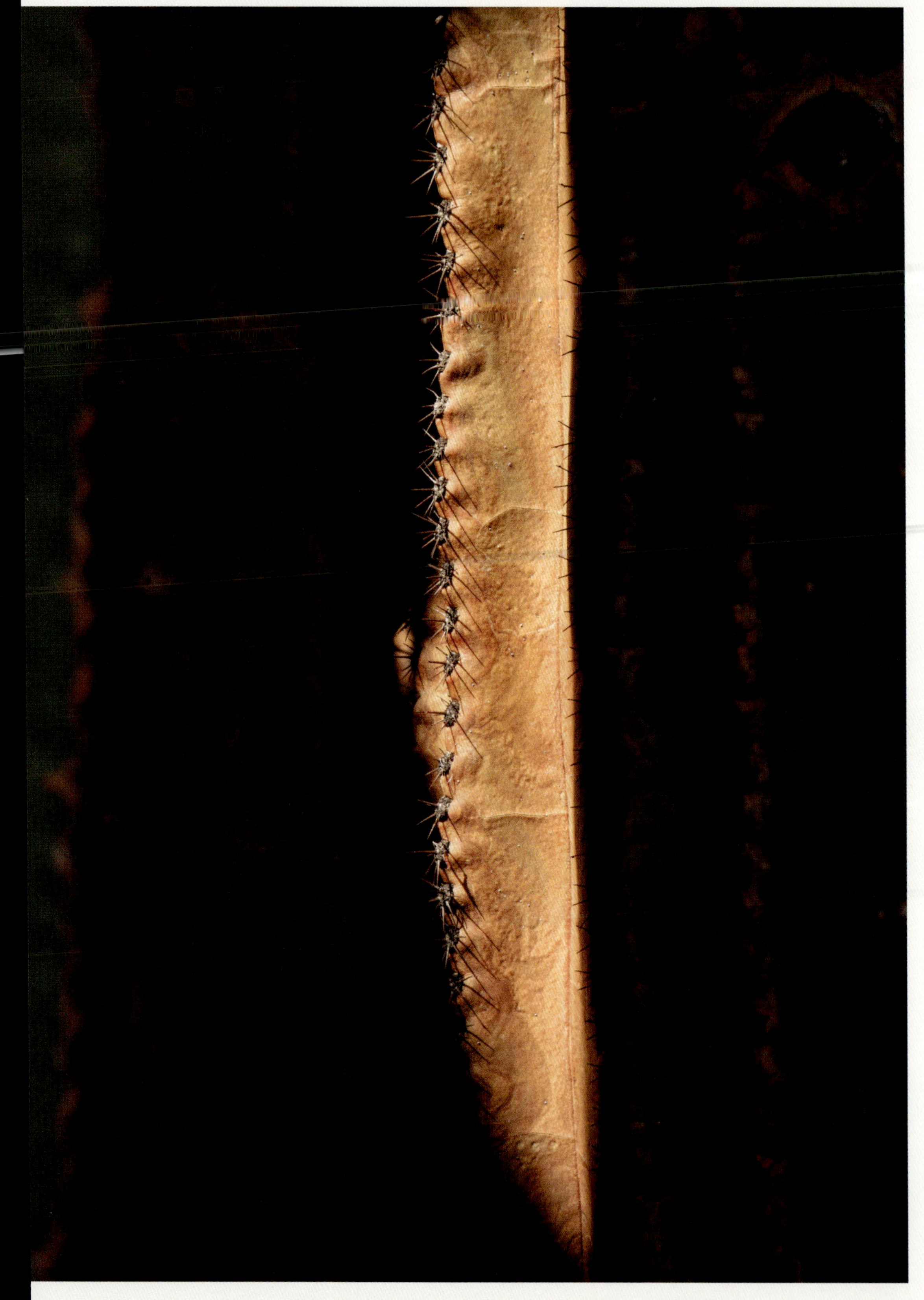

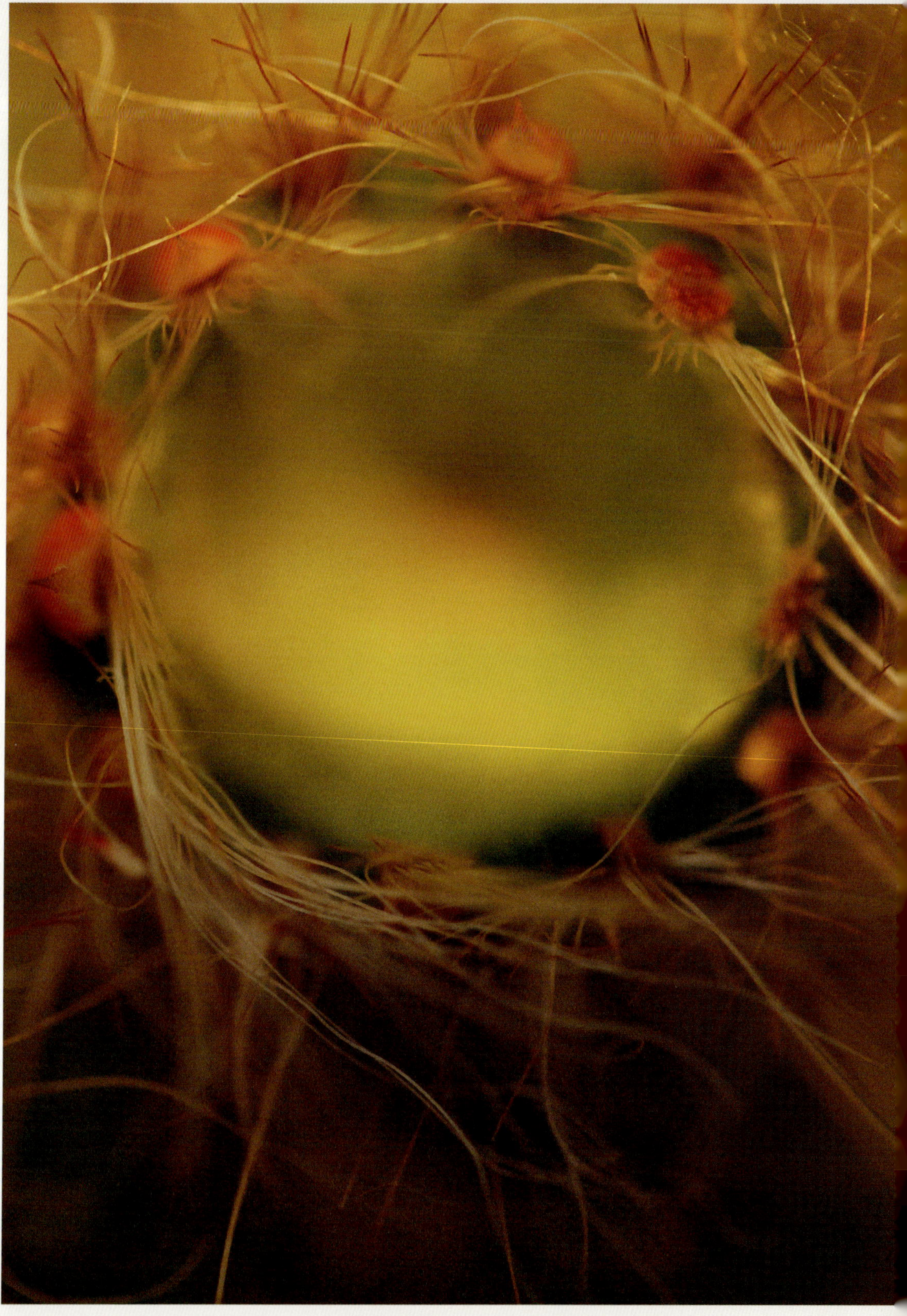

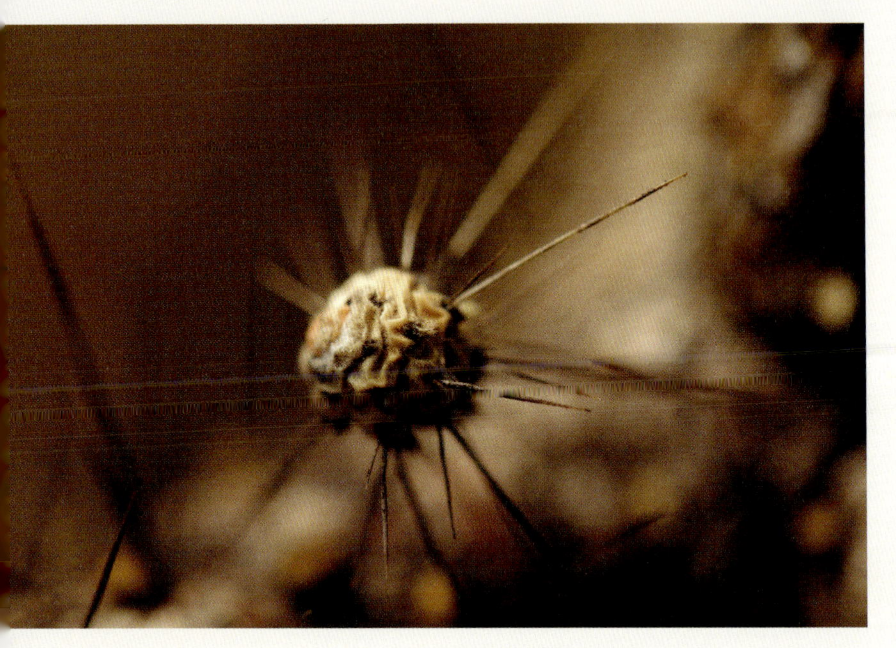

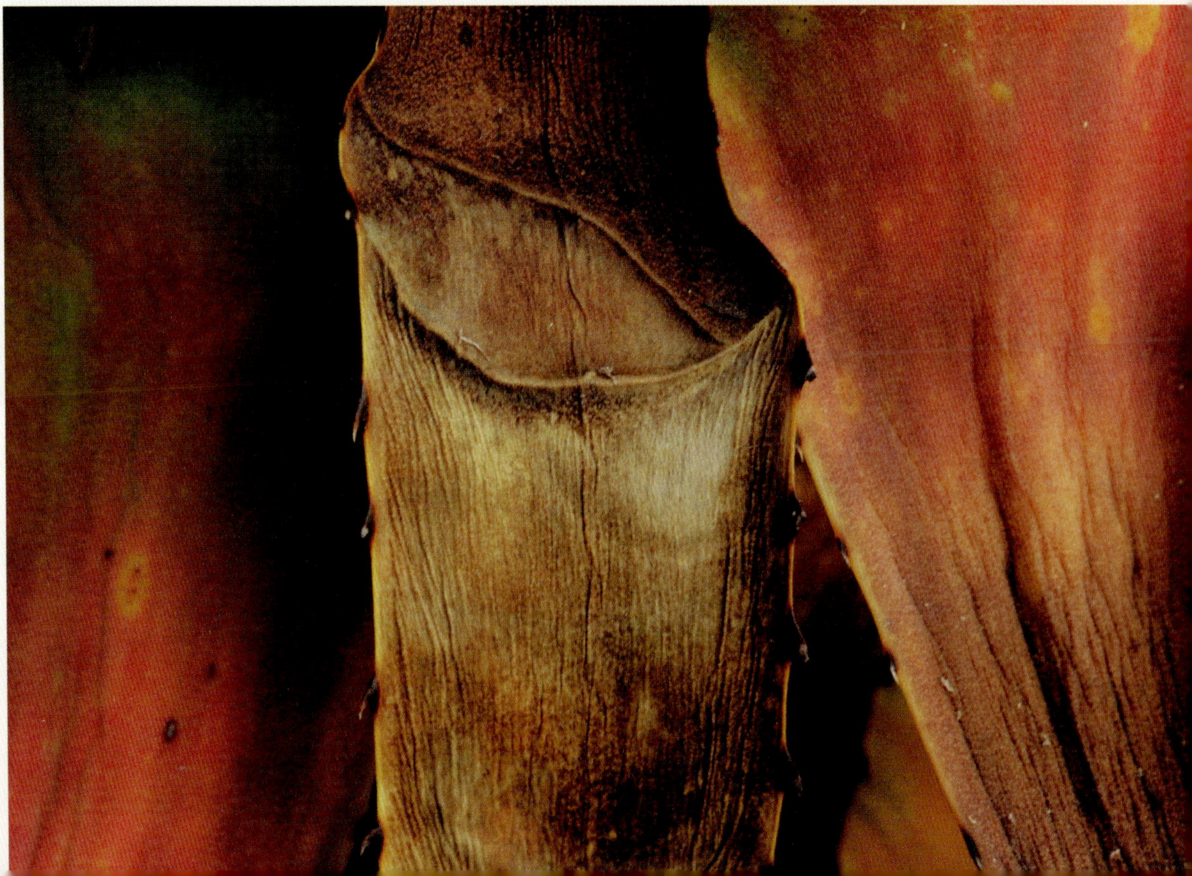

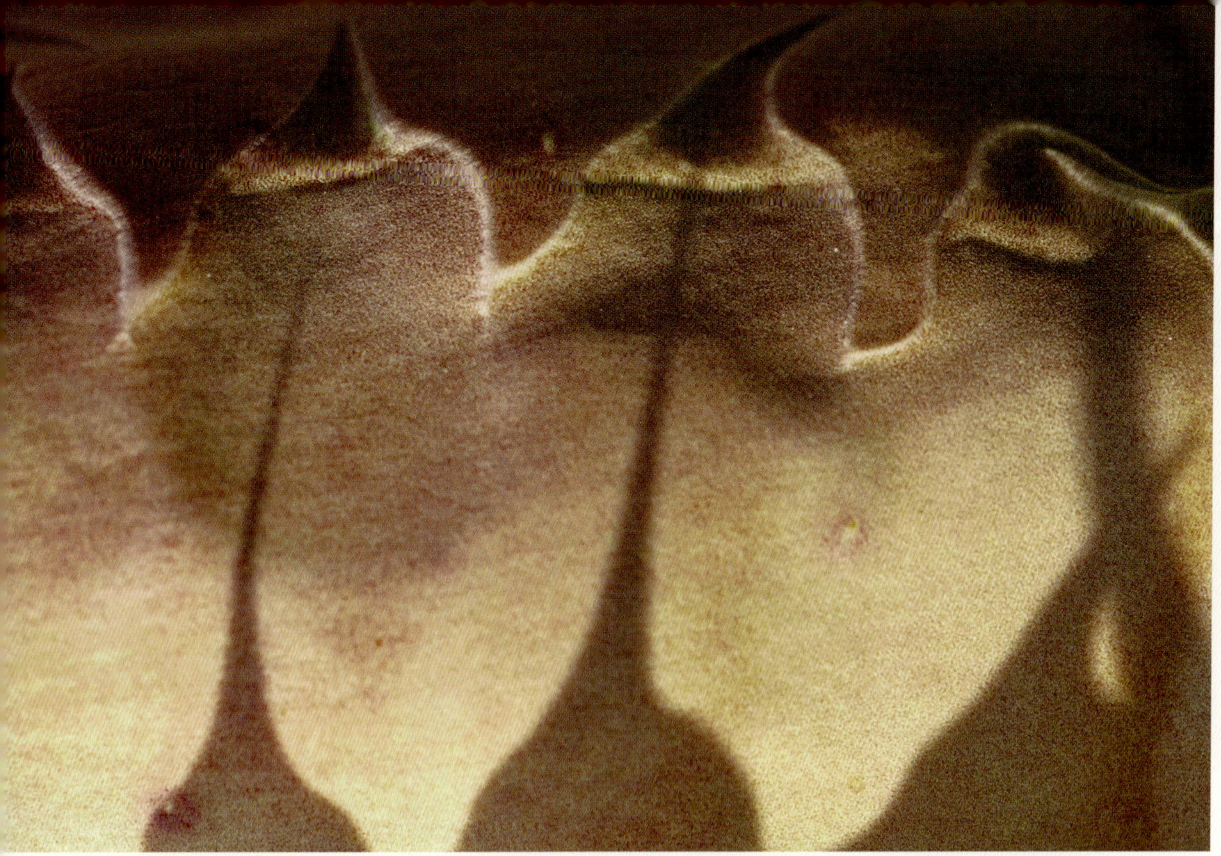

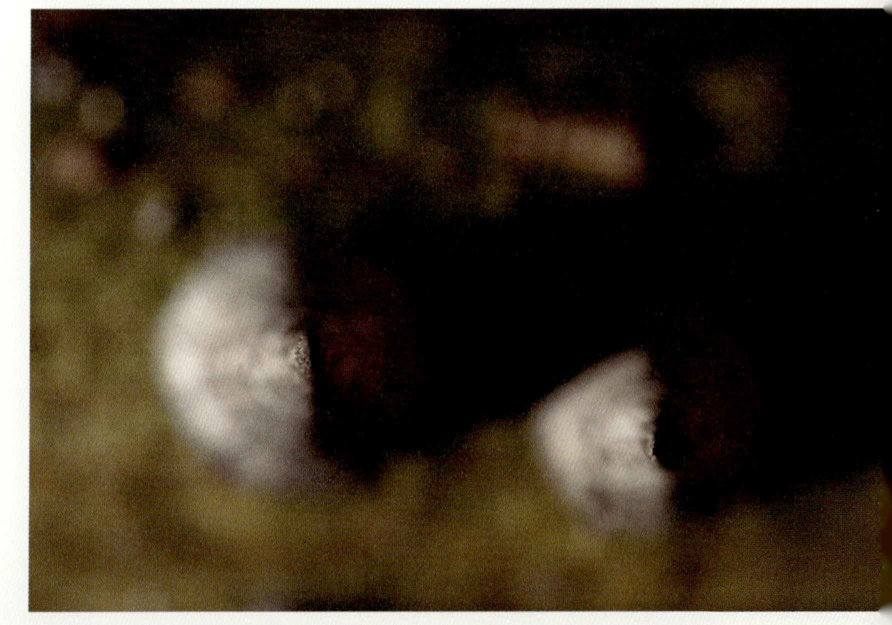

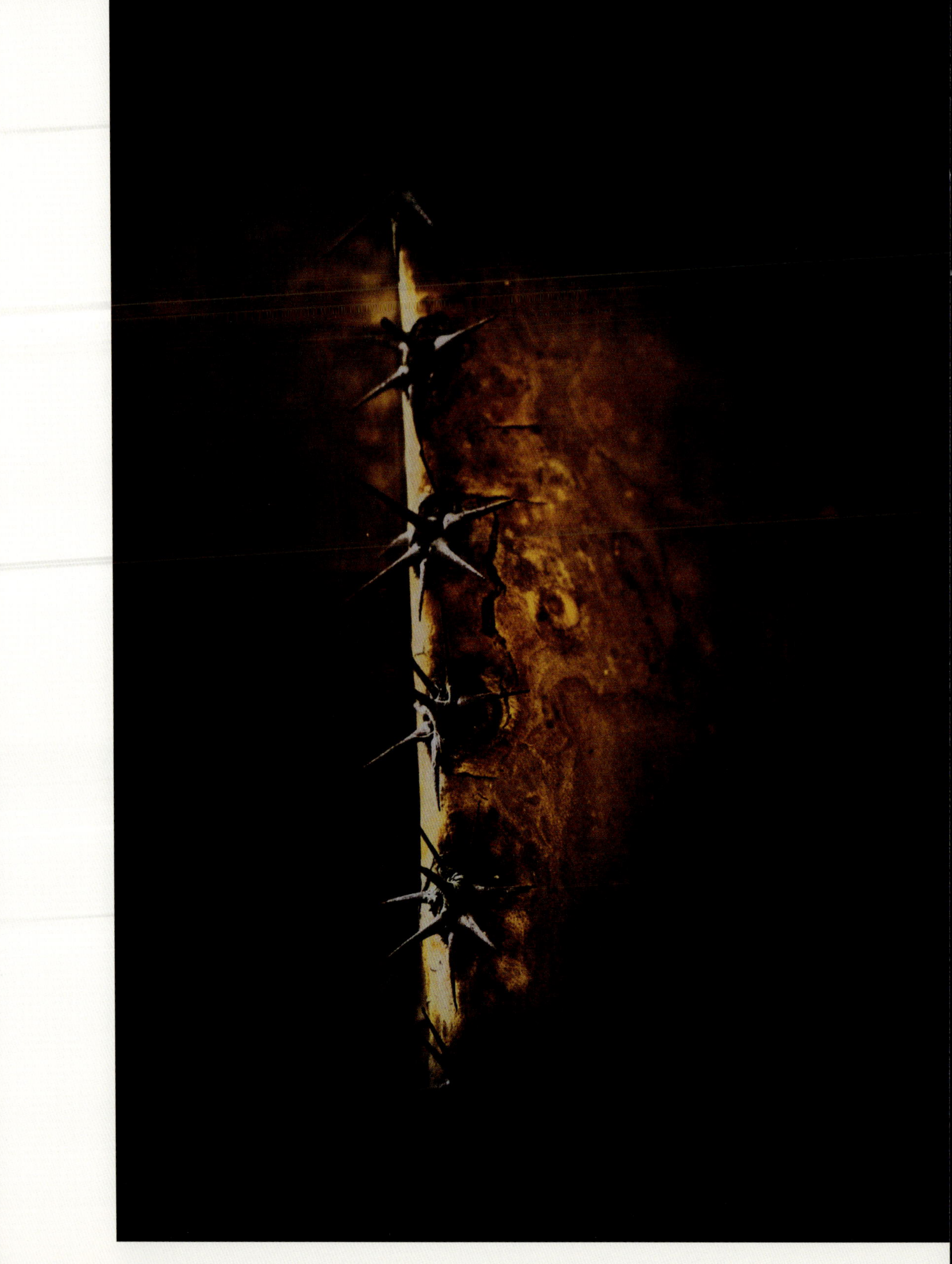

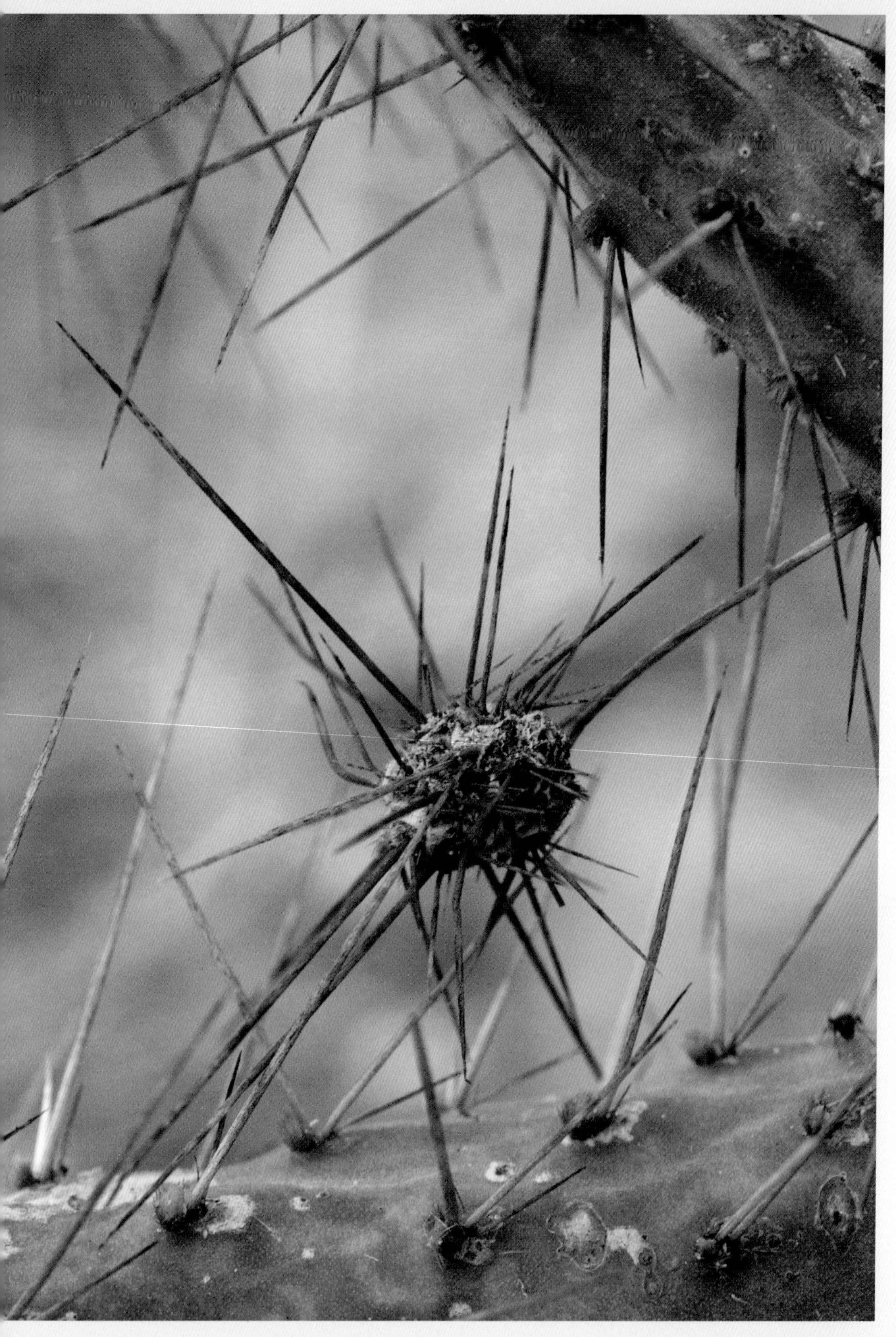

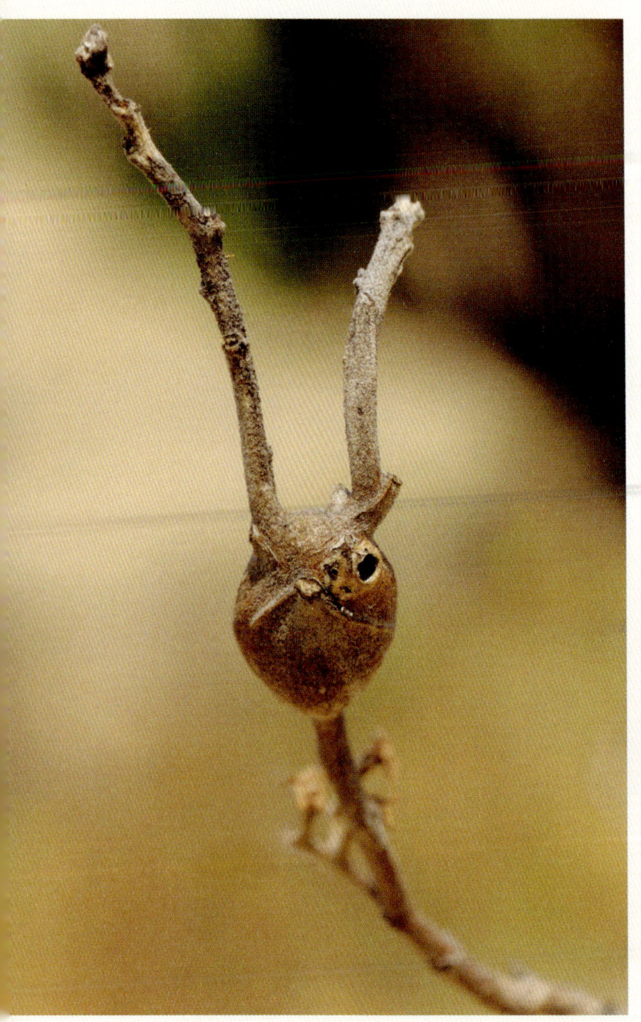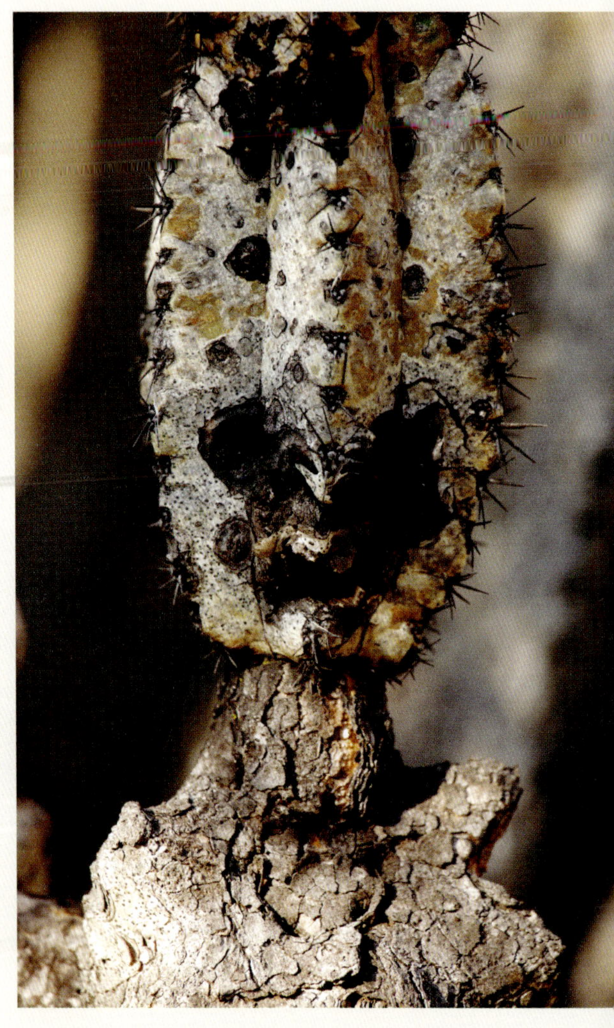

THE MIRACLE
OF LIFE

Sometimes we find it easier to connect to animals and plants when we imbue them with human traits. While this homocentric approach can limit true connection to the natural world (clouding our perception with the desire to see things in our own image), it can also bring joy—just think of the last

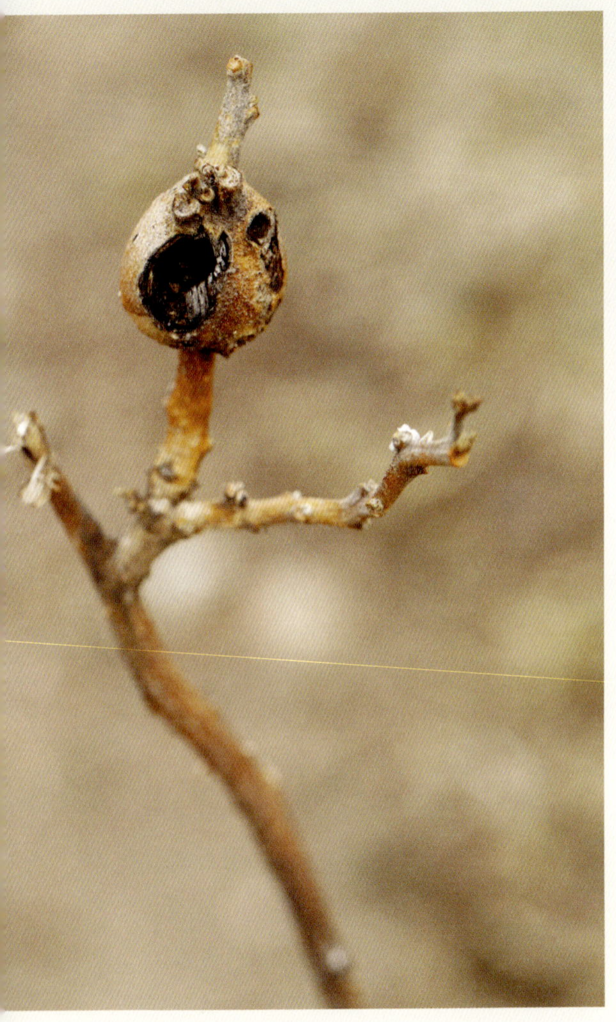

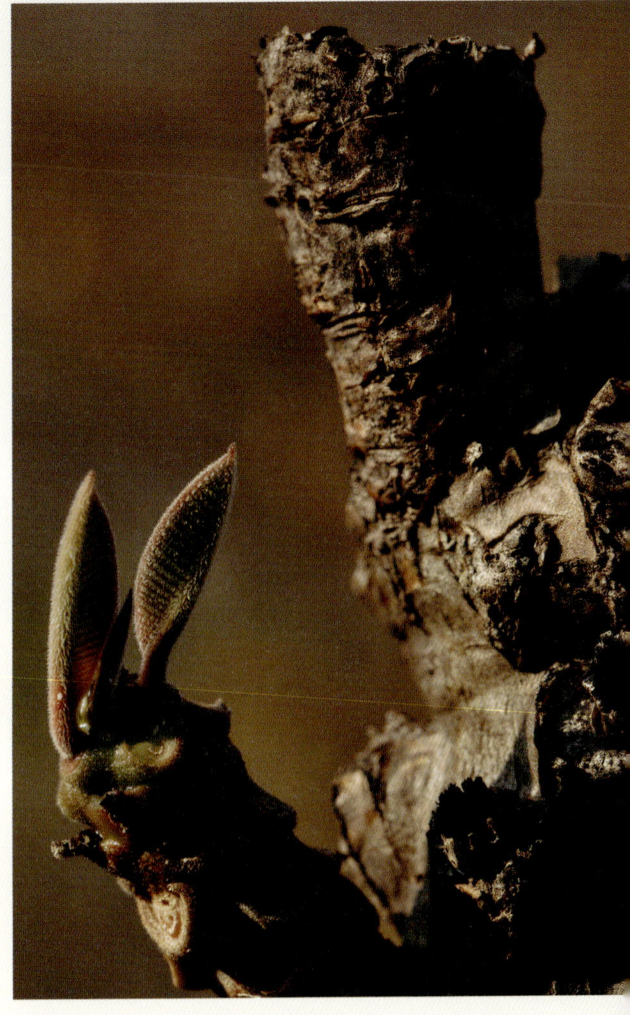

time you noticed a dog looking and behaving just like their owner, or a cloud that looked remarkably like an animal.

As the weeks in Mitla pass, my imagination grows more vivid. I begin to see cacti and other plants as fictional characters—perhaps a protector of the underworld, a desert warrior, or a Greek god. The most expressive examples I come across are twigs and small branches that insects have bored into to lay their eggs. Many remind me of great art works such as Edvard Munch's *The Scream* or famous characters from plays and films.

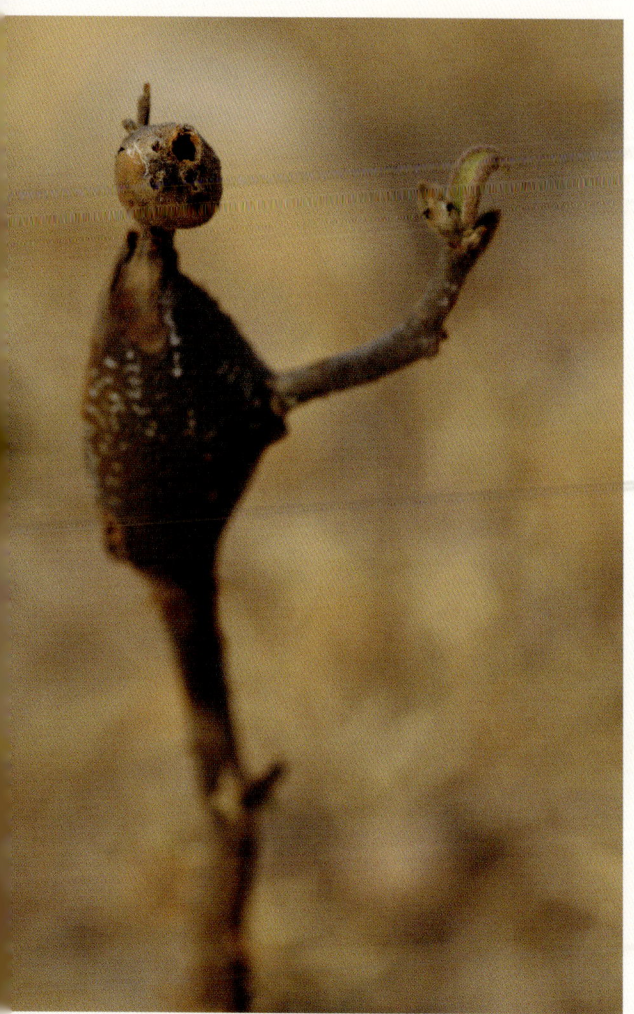

At one point, I even find one that resembles Shakespeare's Hamlet holding Yorick's skull, as if ready to deliver his famous monologue.

Where be your gibes now?
your gambols? your songs?
your flashes of merriment,
that were wont to set the table on a roar?
Not one now, to mock your own grinning?
Quite chap-fallen?

Shakespeare reminds us to cherish life because we inevitably face the bleak reality of death. Here, in Mitla, I gradually find beauty within my own feelings of loss; and through that beauty, I find hope. I take refuge in my walks, which become daily affirmations: *life finds a way.*

These moments echo Thay's challenge to all his students to see that the miracle of life is not to be able to walk on water, but to walk on the earth—an invitation to dwell deeply in the present moment and feel truly alive. "Imagine you and I are two astronauts," he says. "We have landed on the moon, and we find that we cannot return to earth. What would you and I think of, other than going back to our dear green planet and walking side by side, in peace and without worries? Only when confronted with death do we know the precious value of our steps on this green planet."

What is alive will one day perish, and what perishes will one day live. I am certain nearly all the twigs I have seen, even the one that reminds me of Hamlet, are dead. But on closer inspection, I notice that right where I had imagined Yorick's skull, a tiny new leaf is forming. The shock of realization feels like a small miracle.

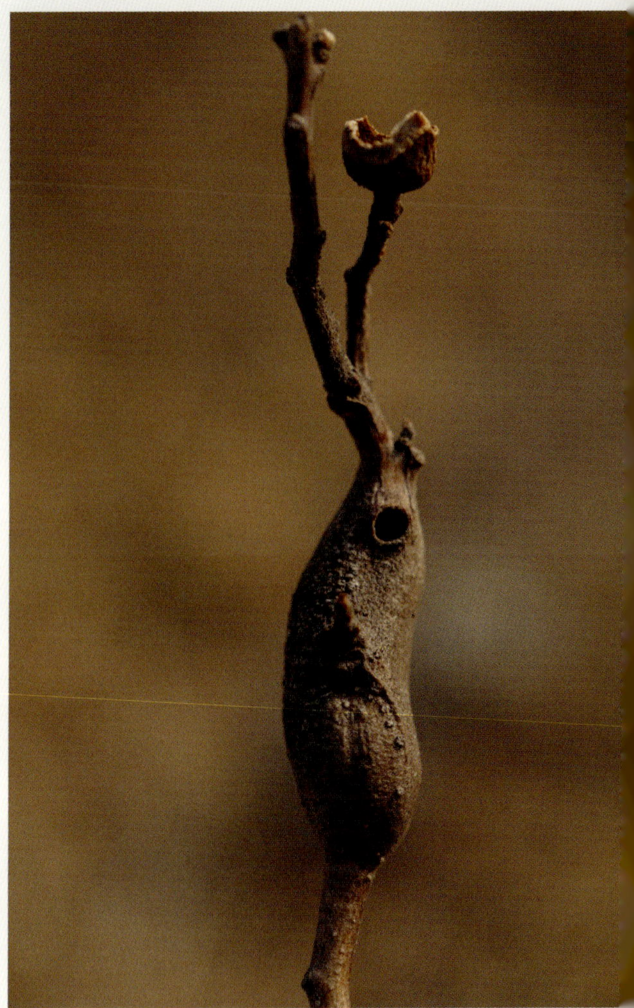

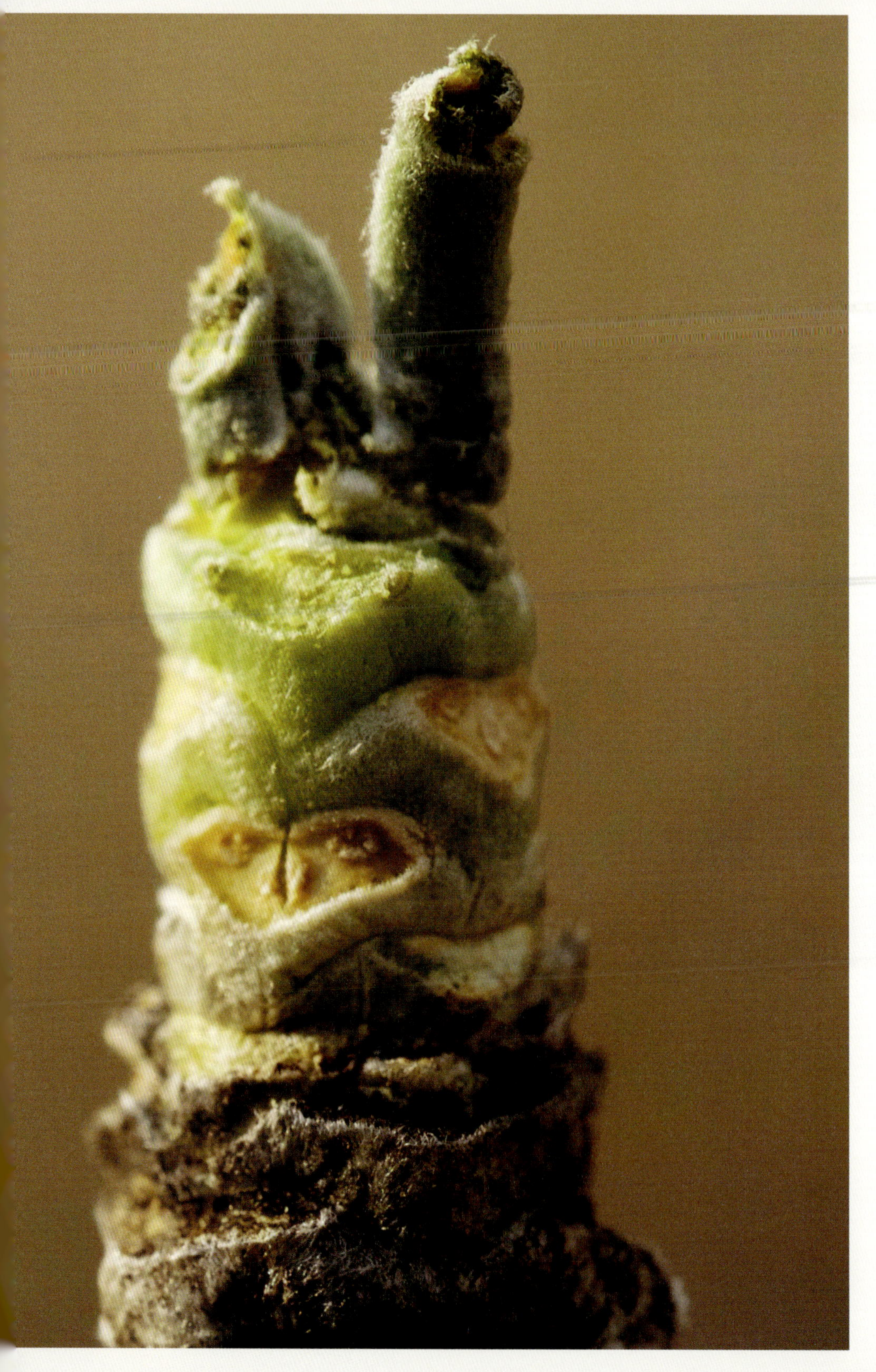

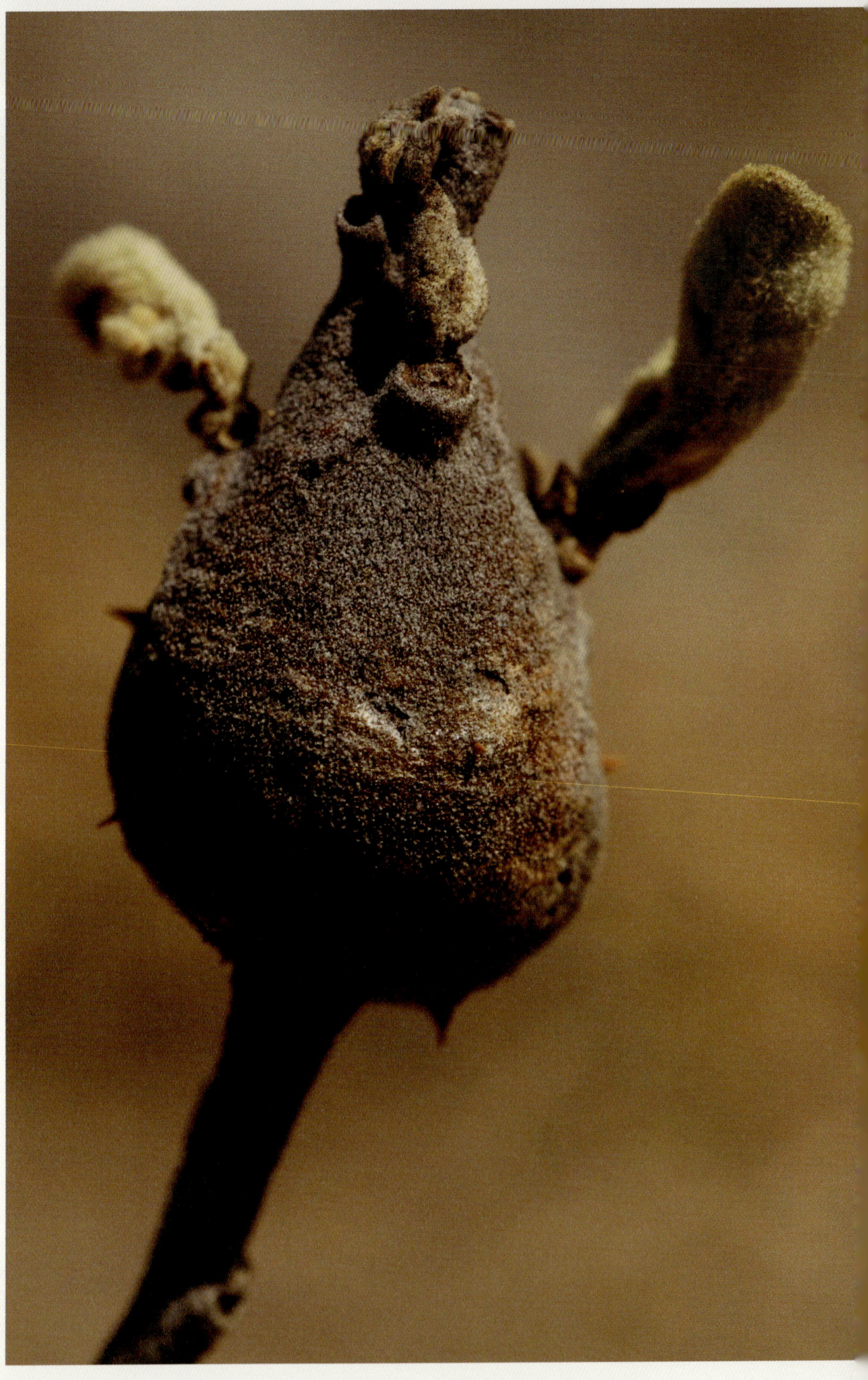

PART 3

RENEWAL

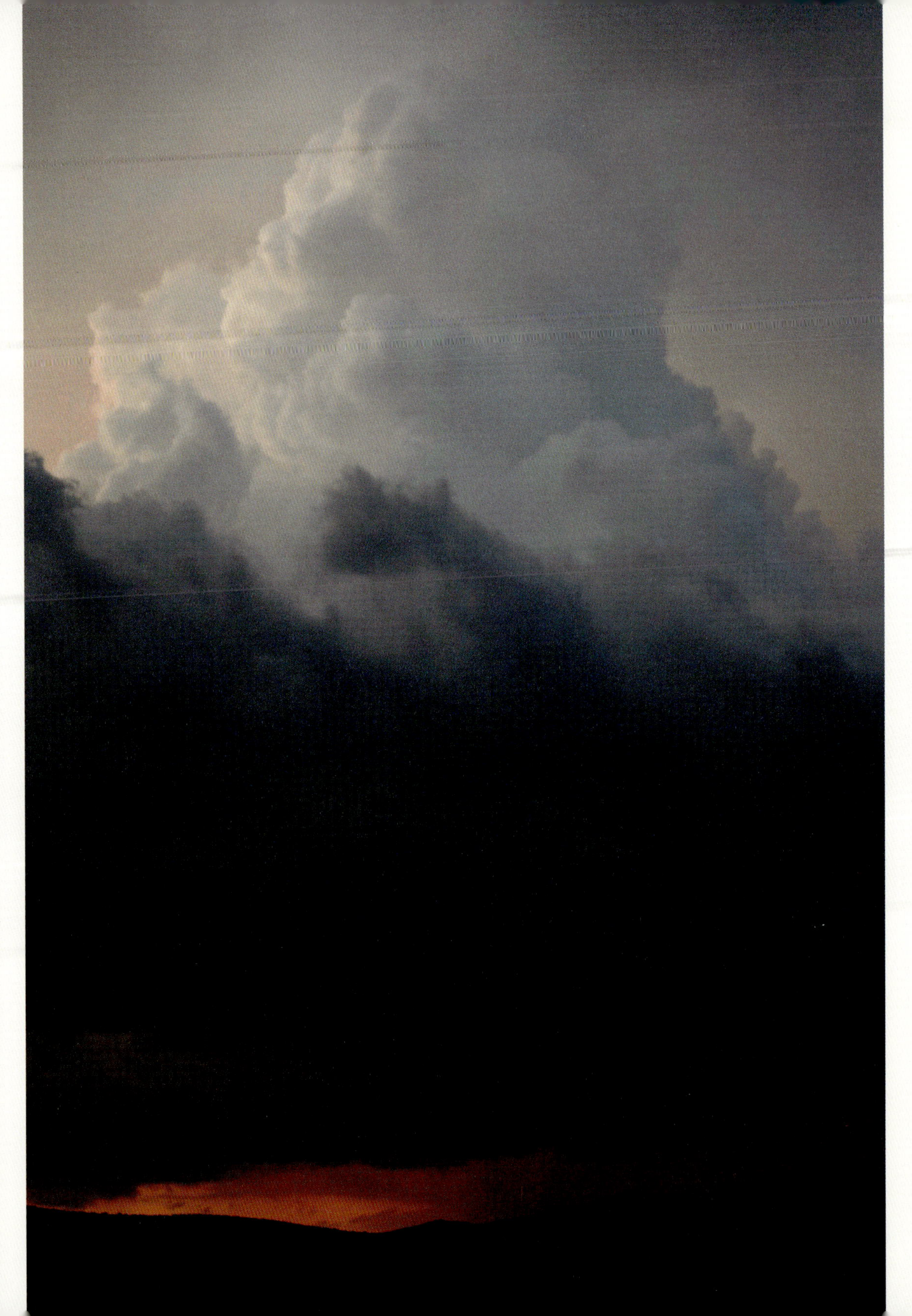

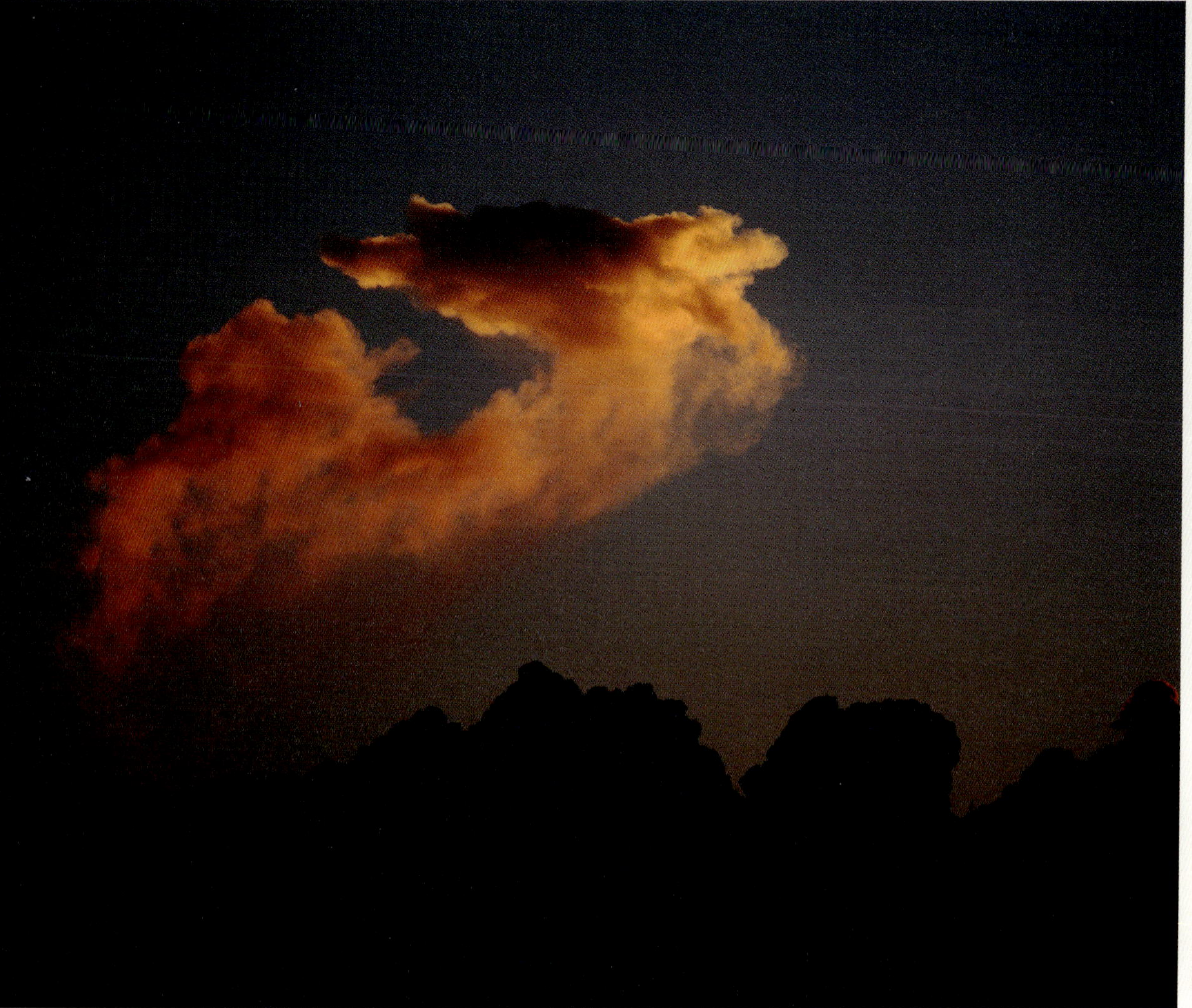

IMPERMANENCE

I keep referring to the land I walk through as a desert. Paul, our host at Casa Lyobaa, gently corrects me each time. He insists that once the rains come, the land will transform into a green paradise. I nod politely, but find it hard to believe him.

Then, two months after our arrival, everything shifts before my eyes.

The cloudless and windless sky transforms into a boiling cauldron. Dramatic cloud formations, the likes of which I have never seen, form at breakneck speed, accompanied by howling winds and distant thunder claps that reverberate across the landscape. Soon life-giving rain starts to fall. As the Zen teaching goes, "Thanks to impermanence, life itself is possible." If nothing ever changed, no seeds would germinate, no food would grow, no babies would be born, and we would remain stuck in the same patterns of behavior.

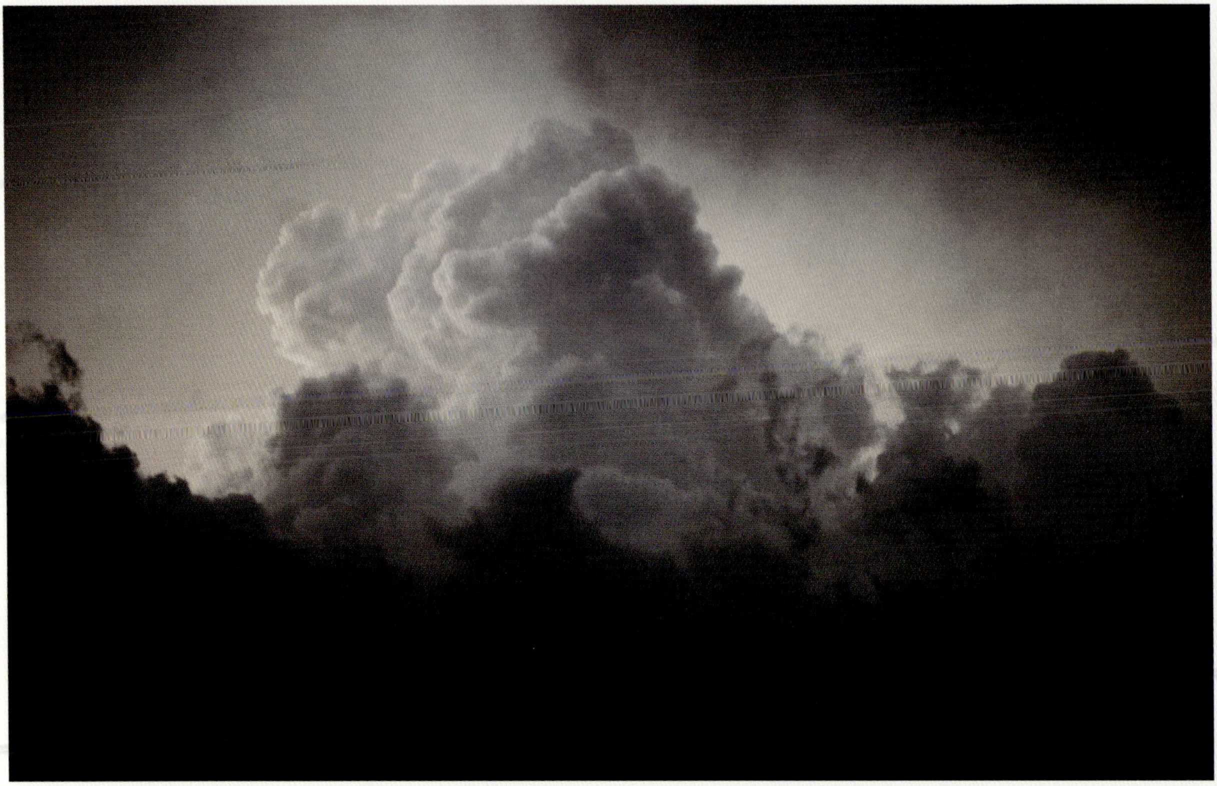

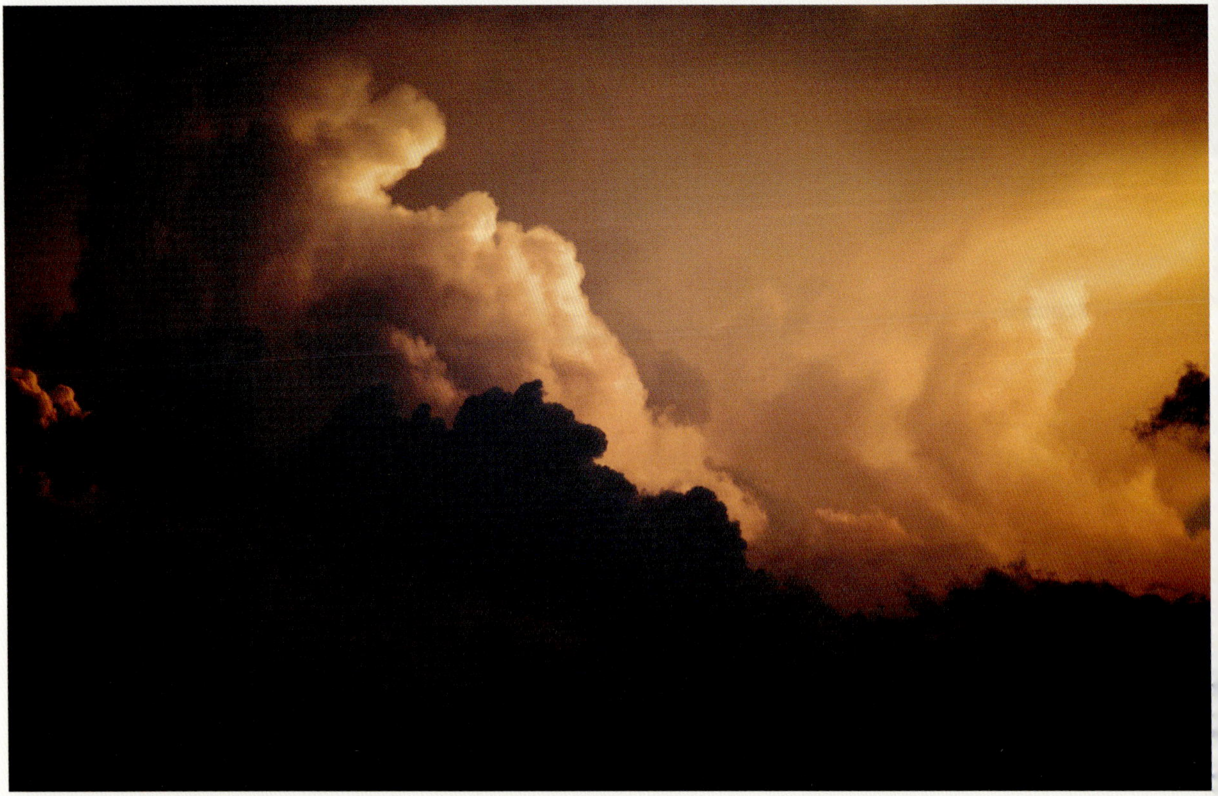

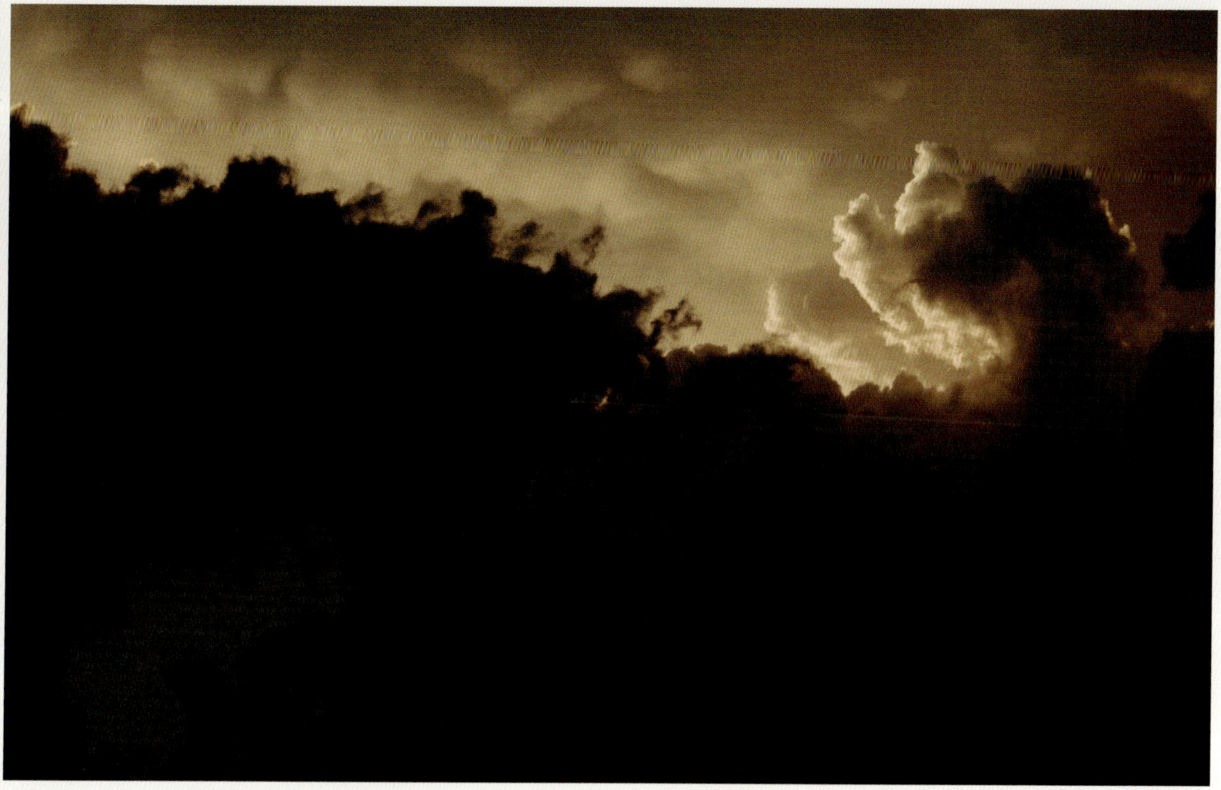

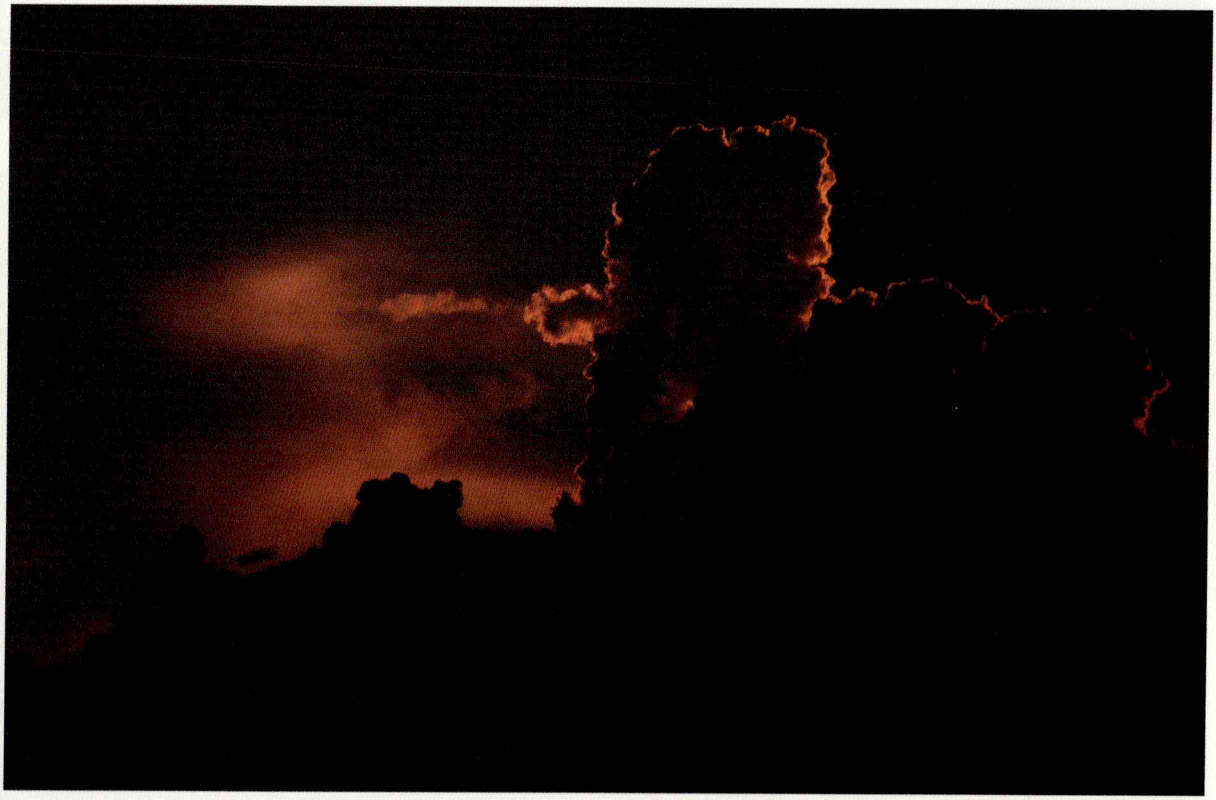

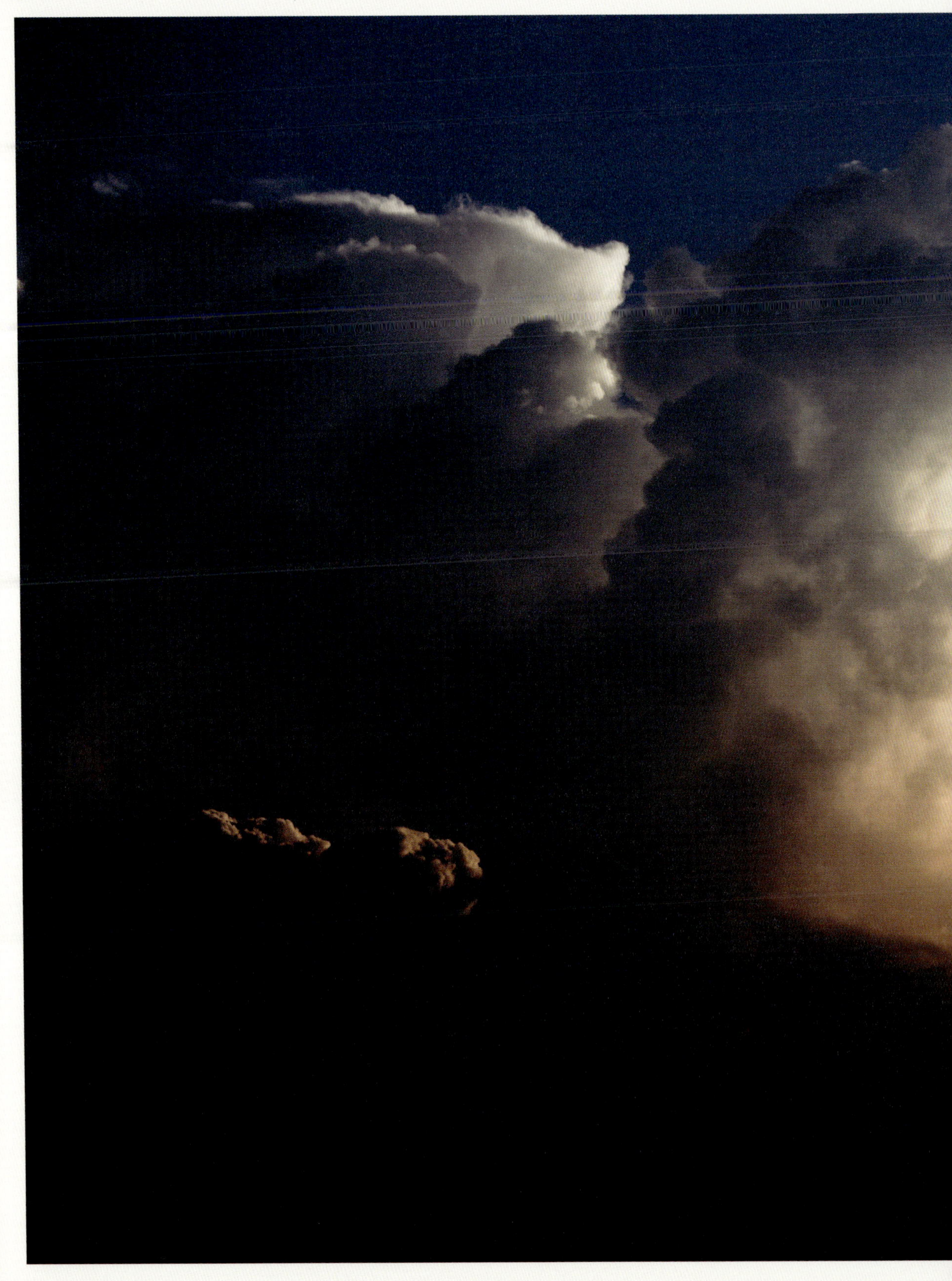

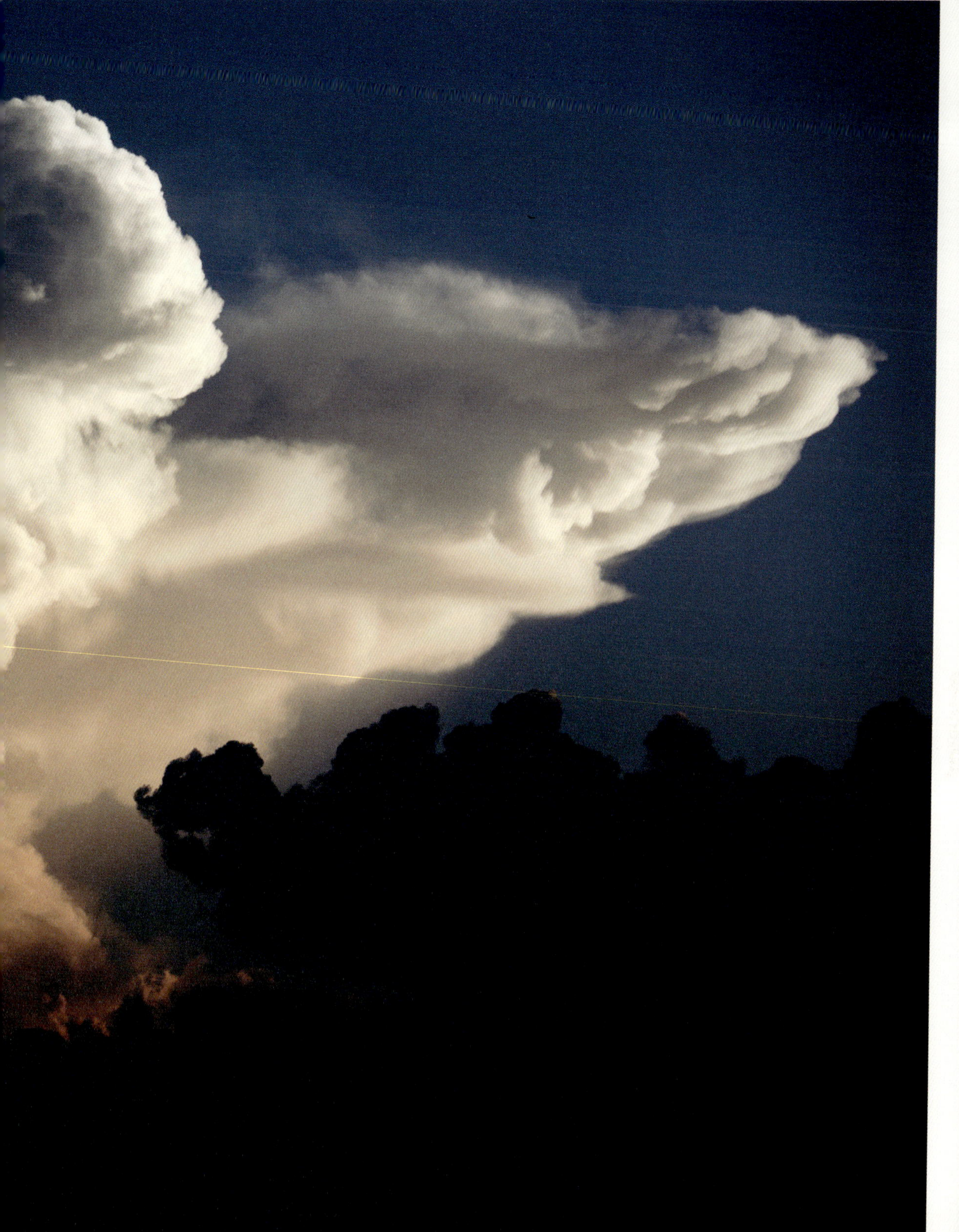

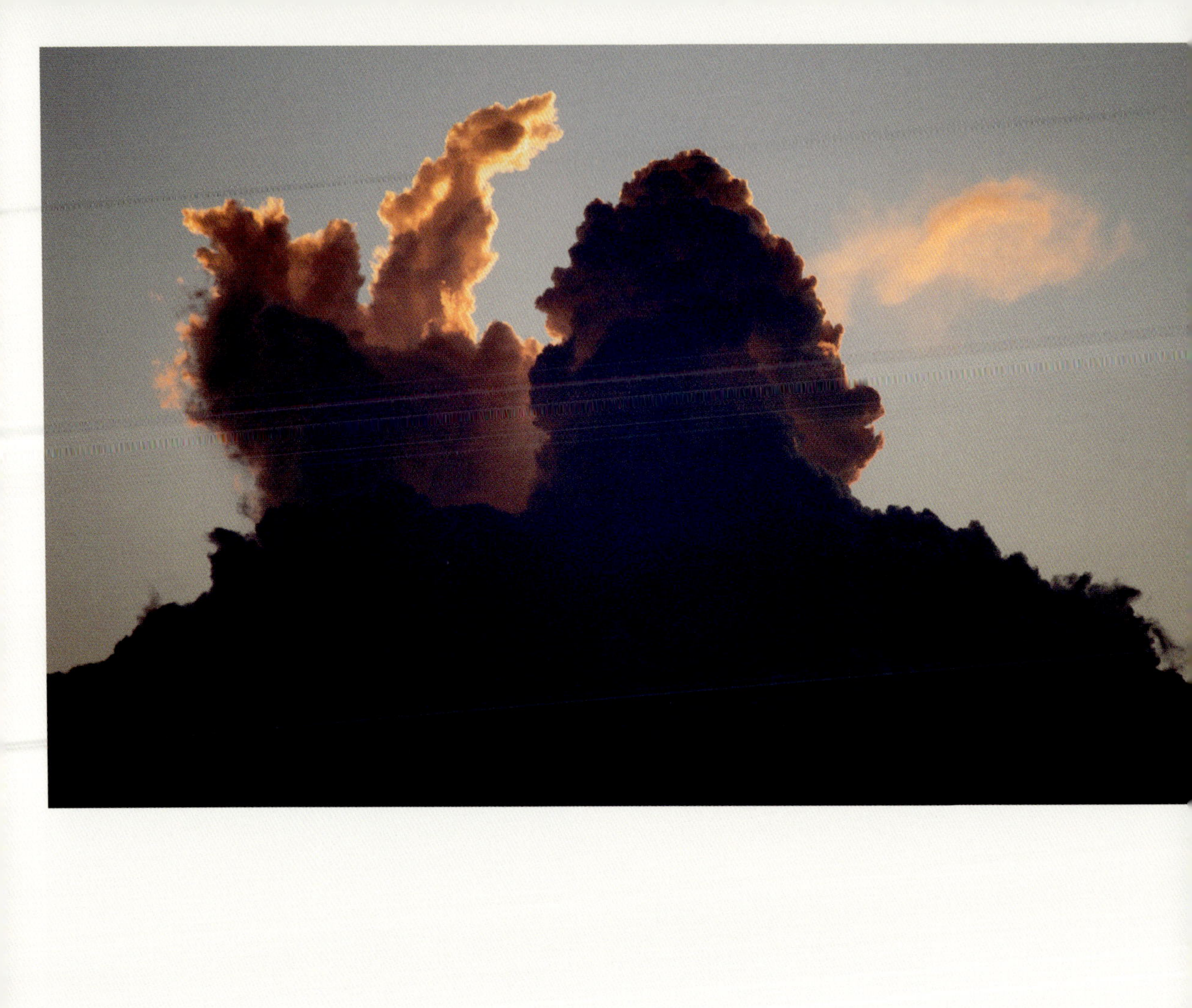

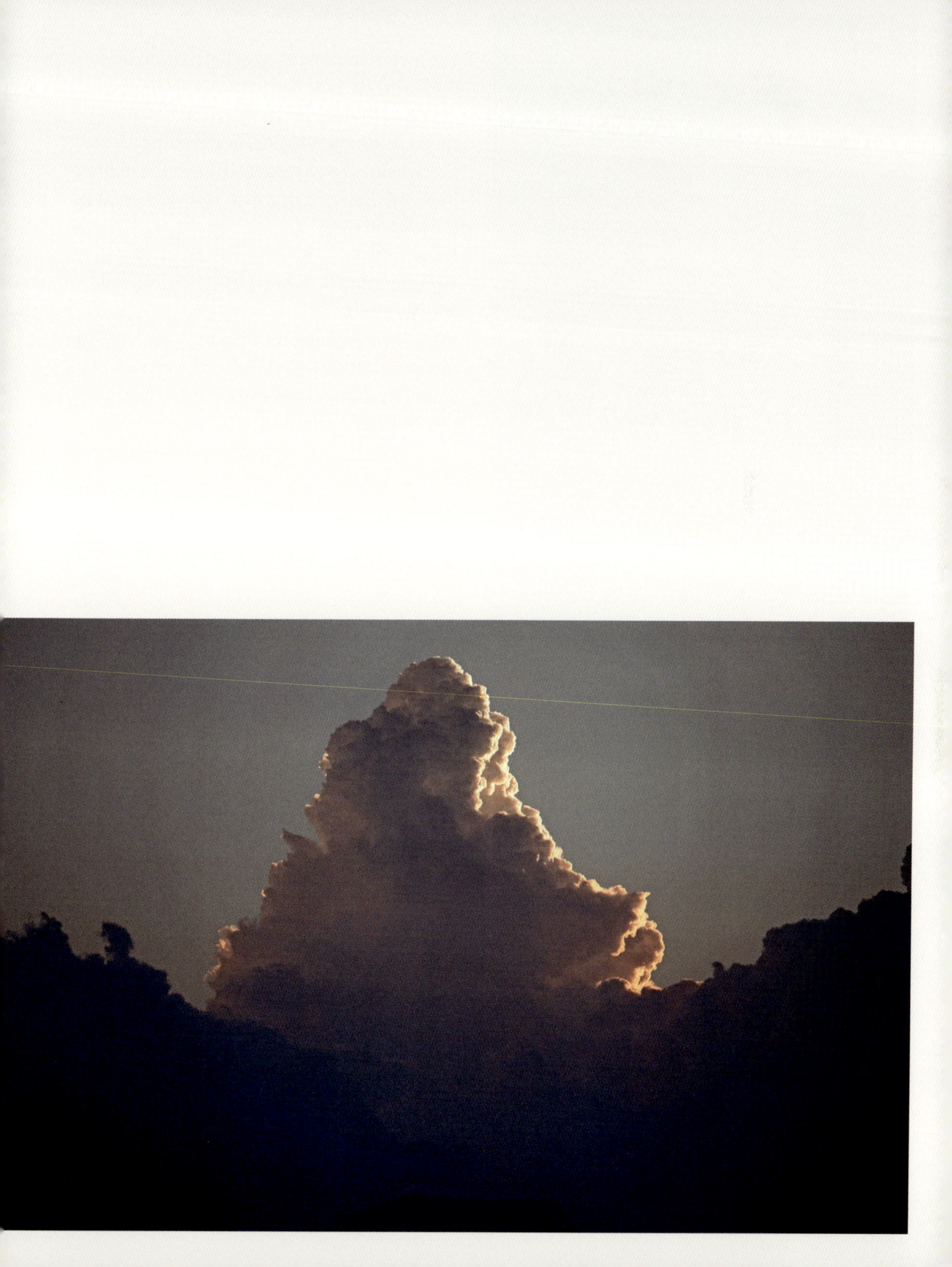

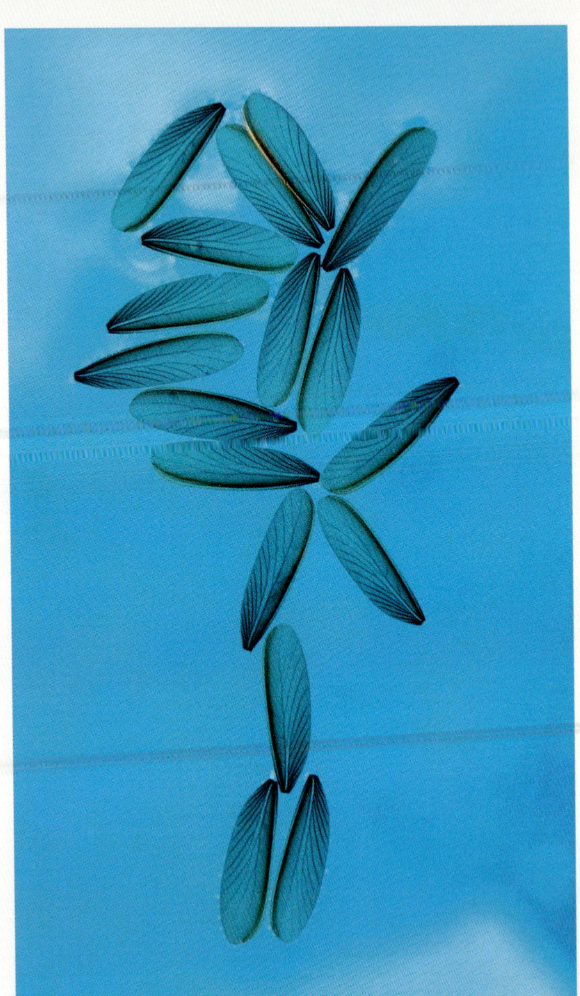

The arrival of rain changes the rhythm of the land. Life here has felt achingly slow; now everything starts to evolve at lightning speed. Without warning, one evening we are overwhelmed by a termite invasion as millions upon millions of flying insects swarm as far as the eye can see.

Termites release their wings when they land, and hundreds of these wings end up floating in the swimming pool of Casa Lyobaa, creating intricate, delicate patterns on the surface of the water. By the next morning, there is no trace of the termites—they have all dug themselves into the earth, and the wings in the swimming pool have all been sucked into the filter. Yesterday there were termites everywhere; today I do not see a single one. It is as if the whole spectacle was a dream.

SWARM

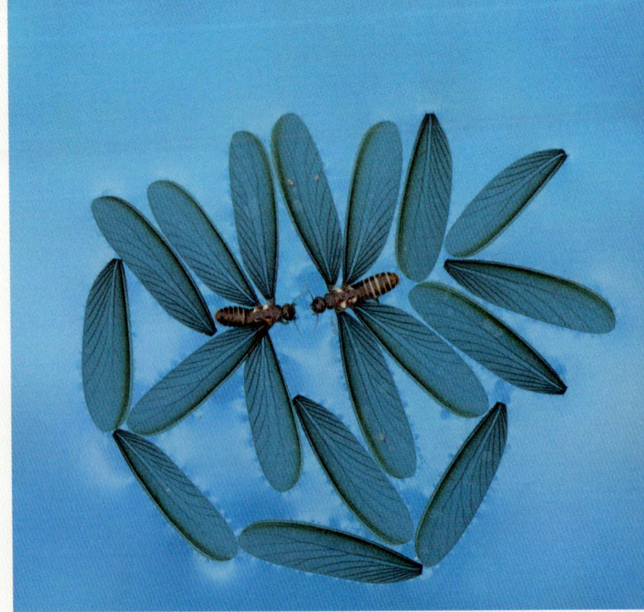

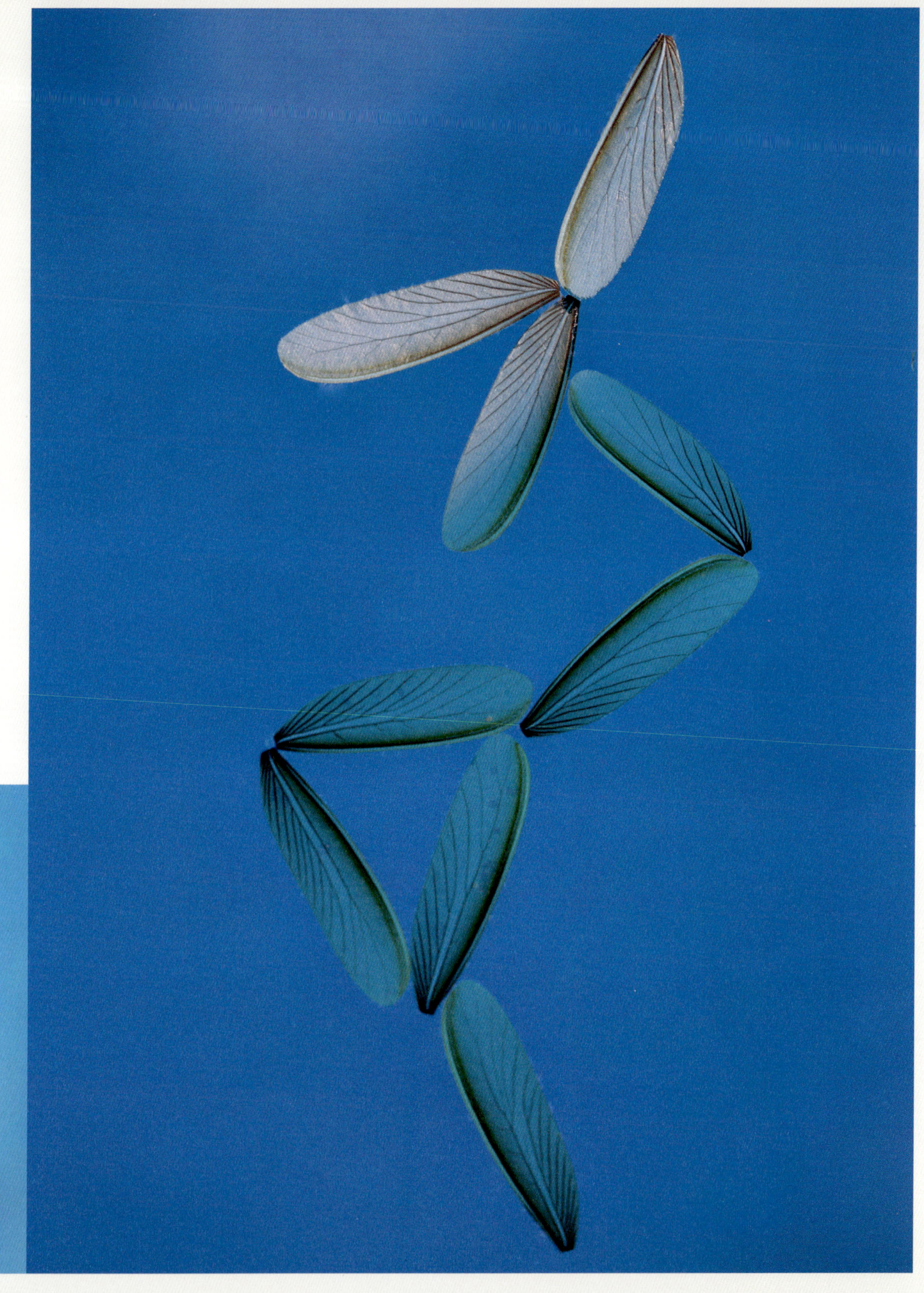

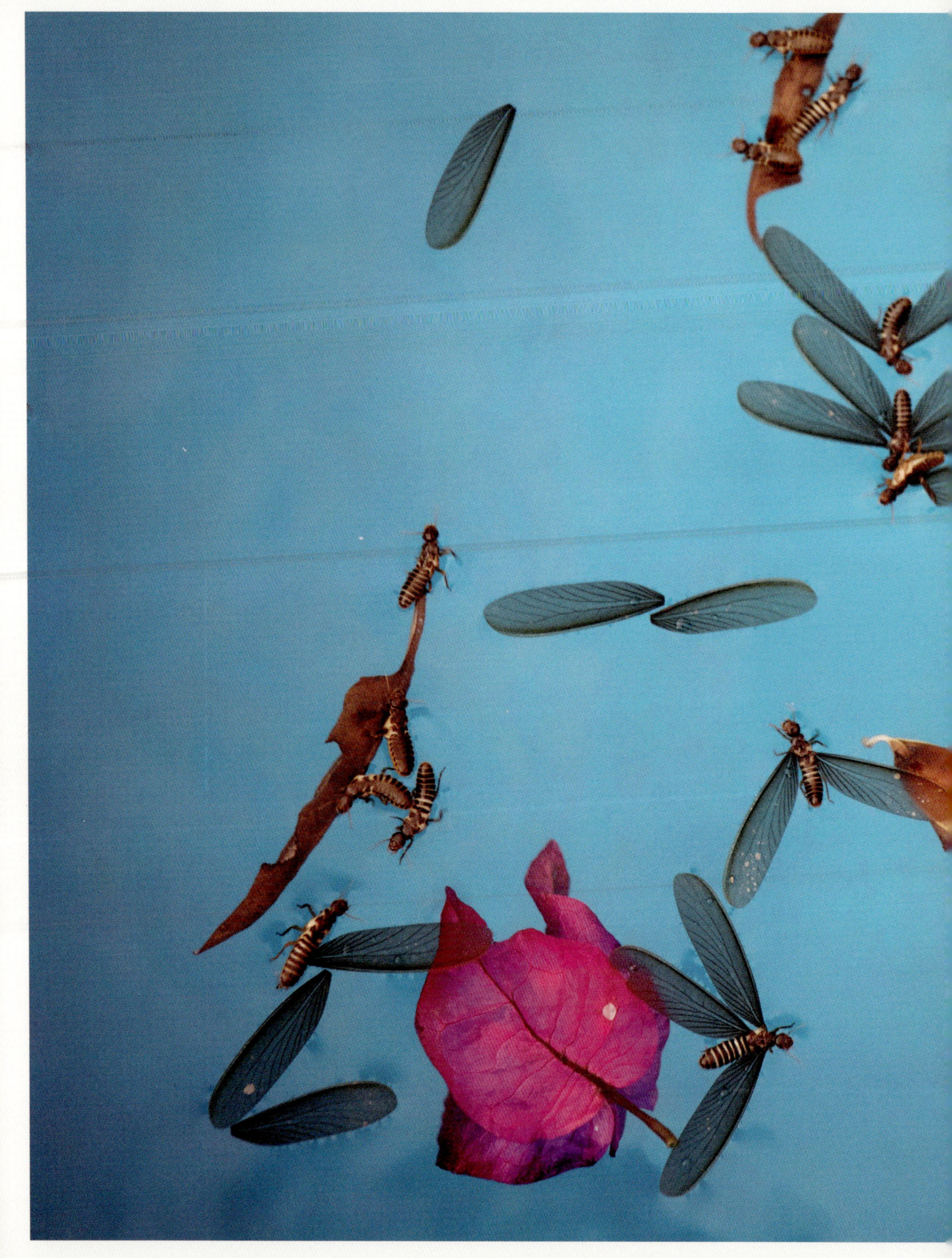

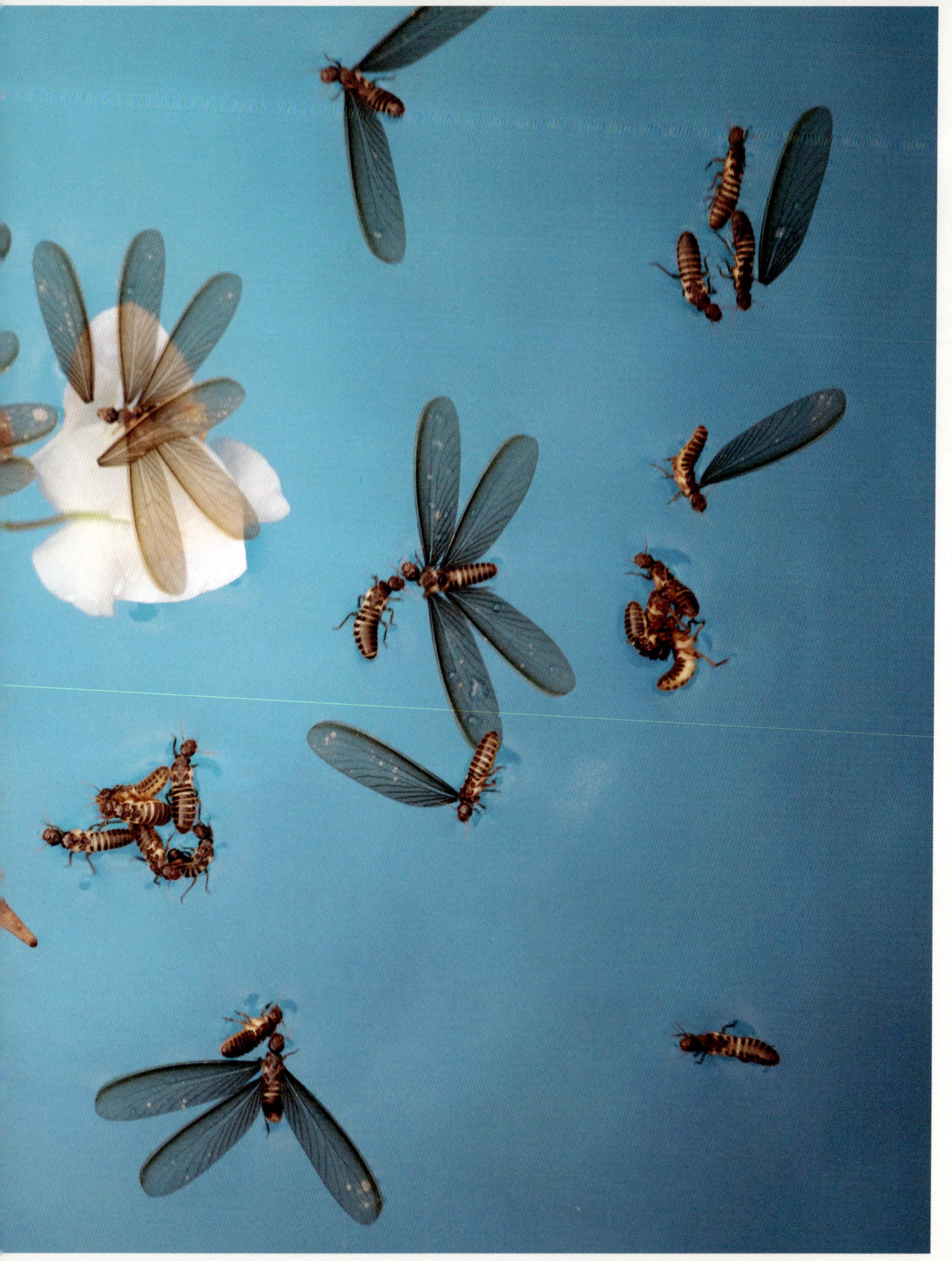

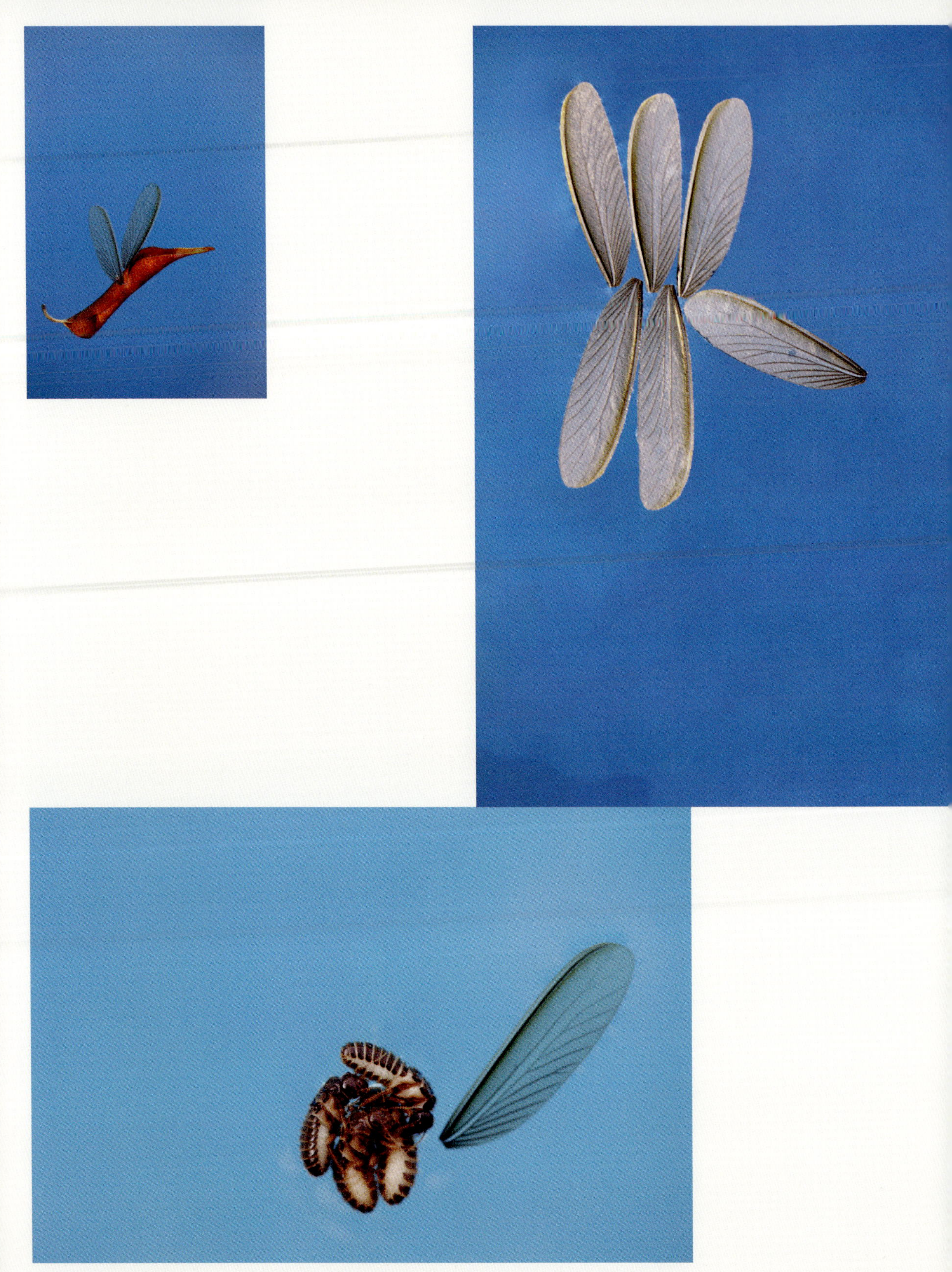

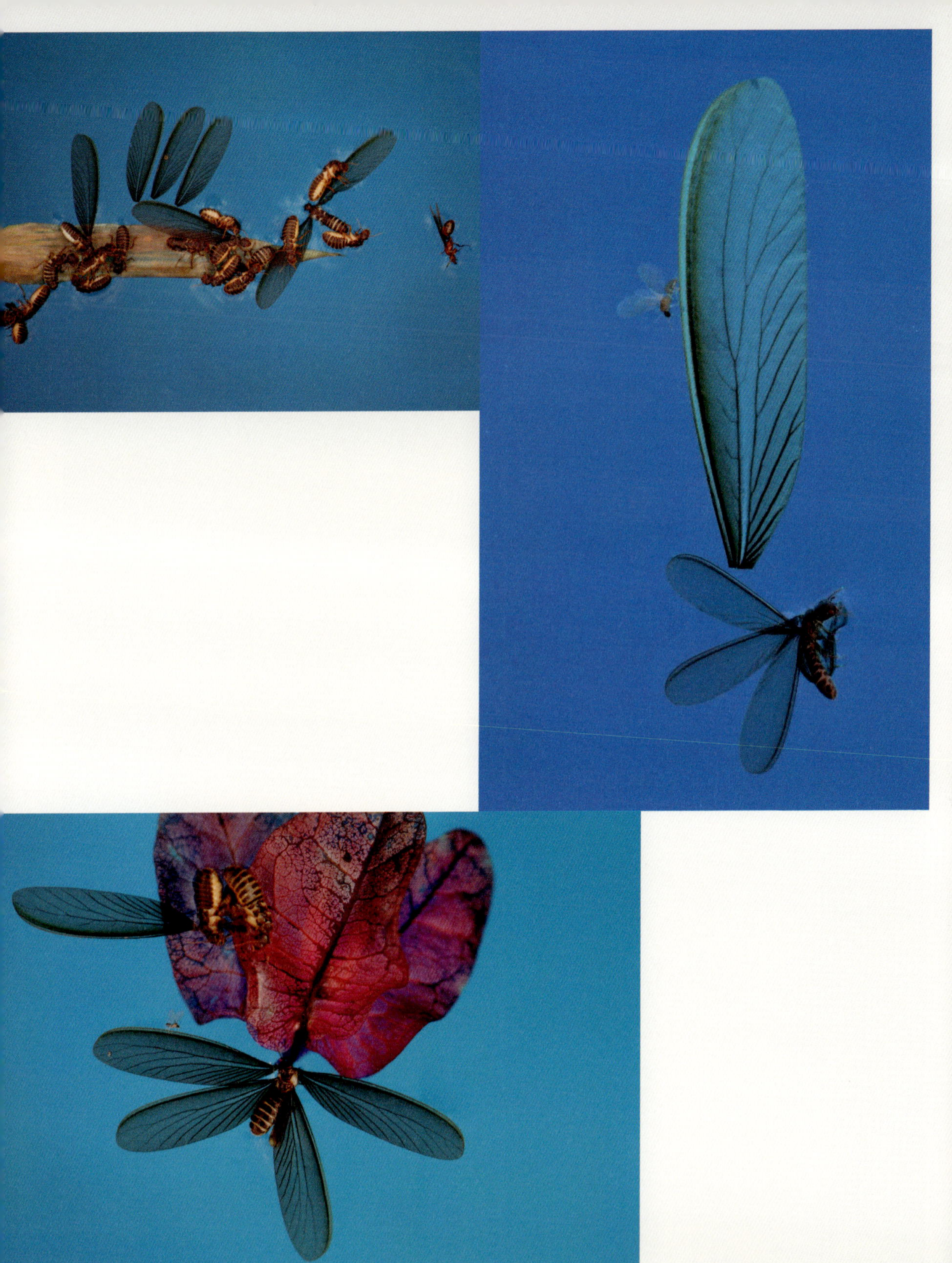

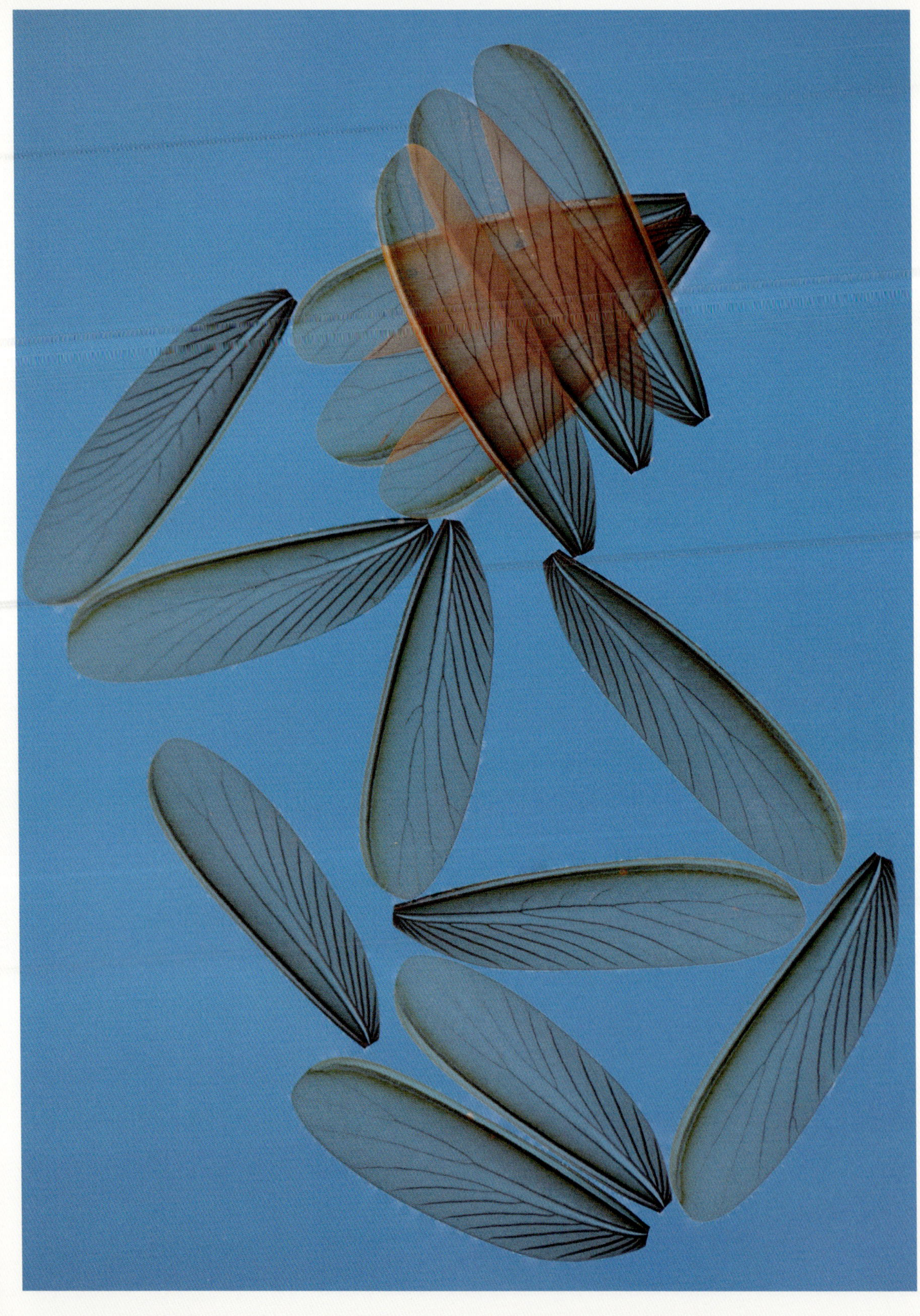

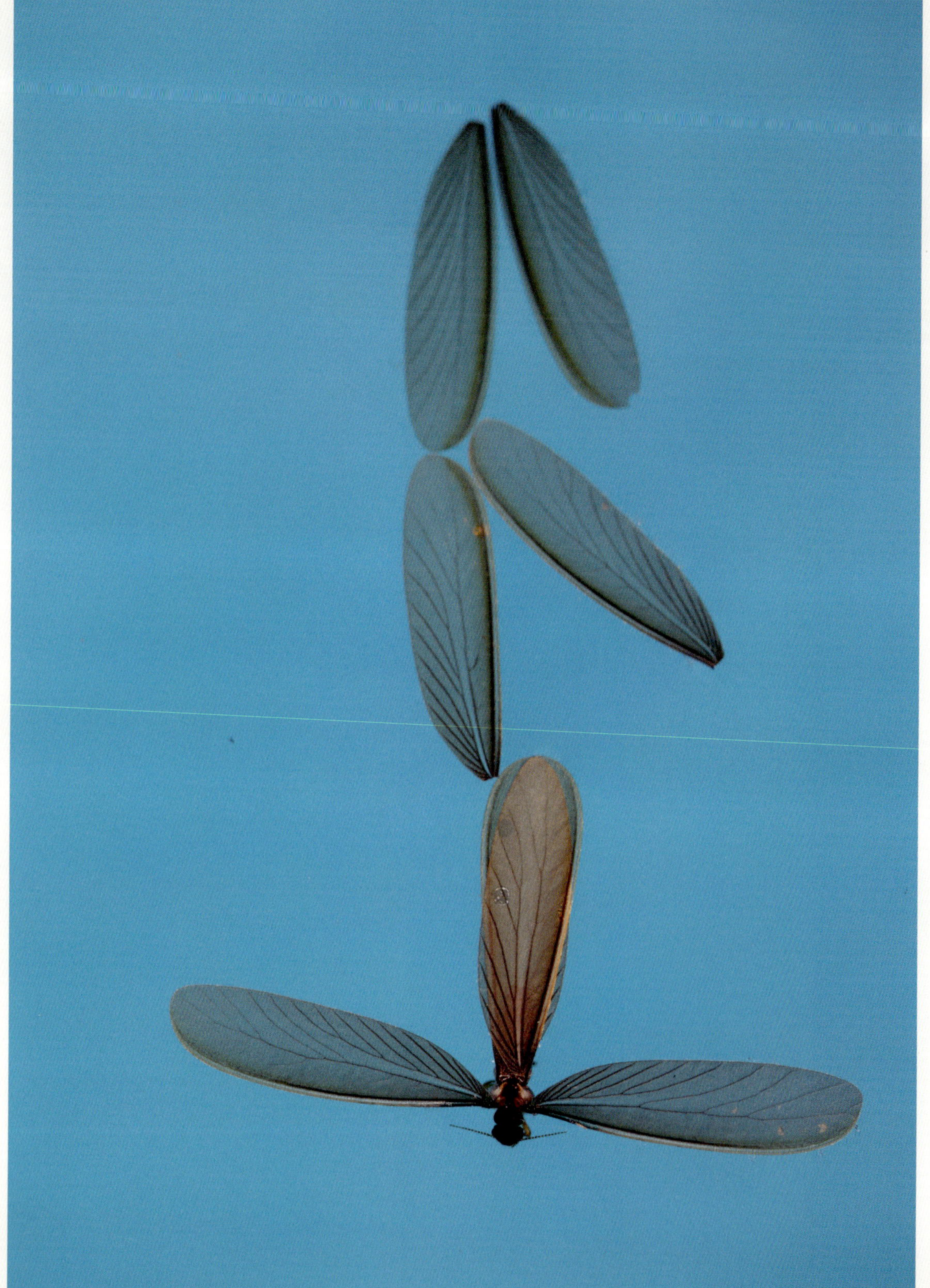

FLOWER
FRESH

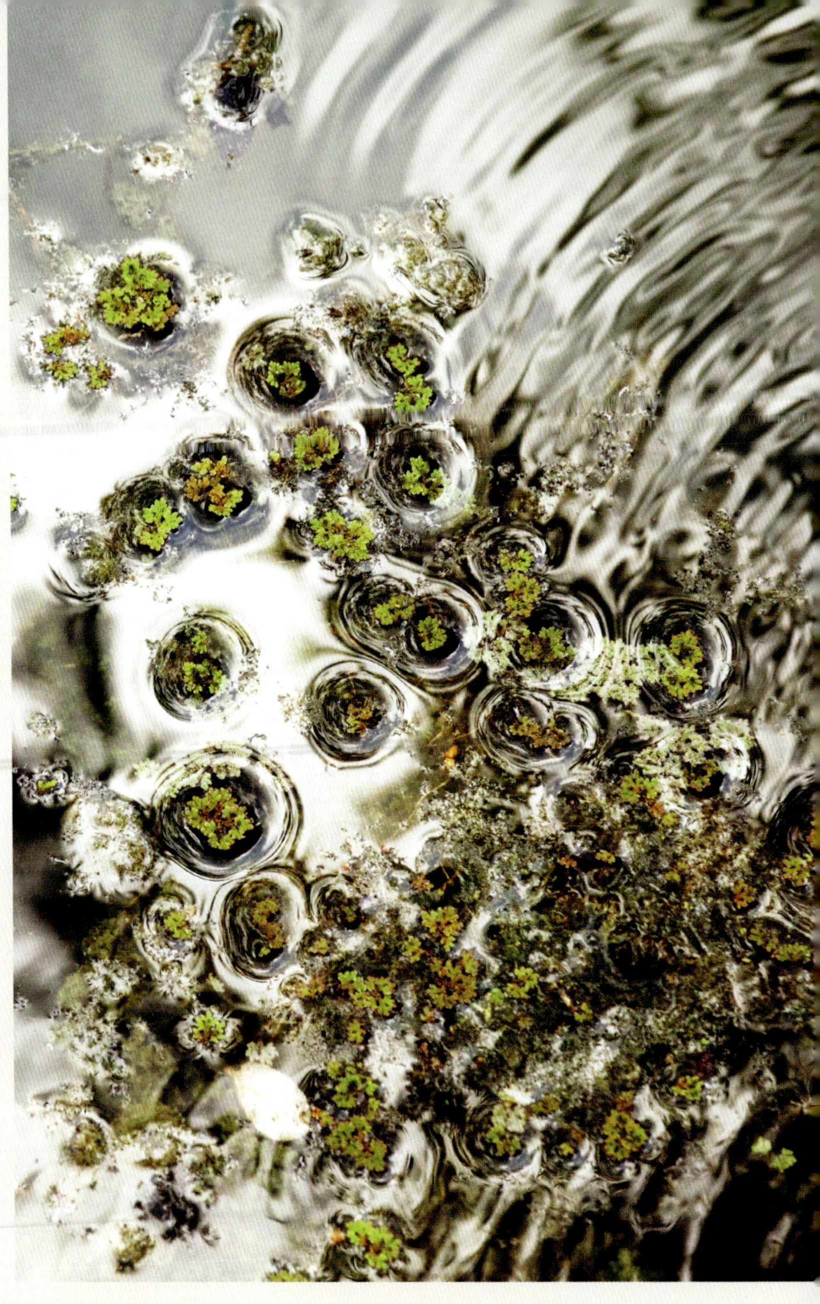

I have seen only a few seeds above the ground during my walks. It turns out I am completely unaware of the profusion of life below ground waiting for just the right moment to manifest. When the rains arrive, puddles form in dry river beds. After a few short days, a green carpet rolls out across the landscape.

Waterfalls and ribbons of water pepper the
mountains surrounding the Oaxaca valley.

Soon, wildflowers conjure themselves from
where a few days before had been only dust.
It feels like an artist has haphazardly splashed
paint on an empty canvas.

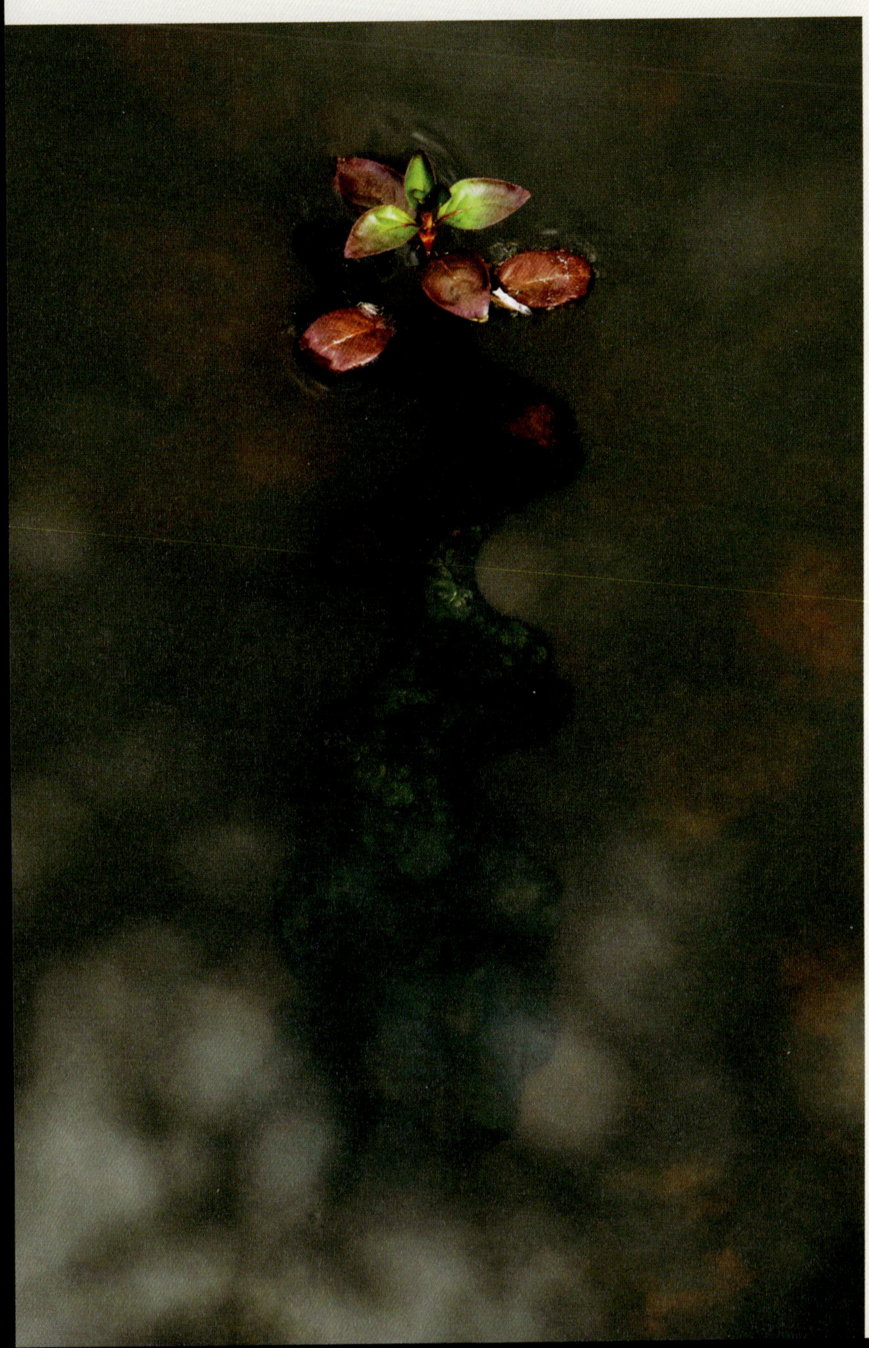

This sudden transformation mirrors the
workings of the mind as described in Buddhist
philosophy. The mind is seen as divided into two
zones: our store consciousness, which loosely
aligns with the Western understanding of the
unconscious, and our mind consciousness,
which contains what we are actively aware of.
In our store consciousness, numerous seeds
lie dormant. When watered by our thoughts,

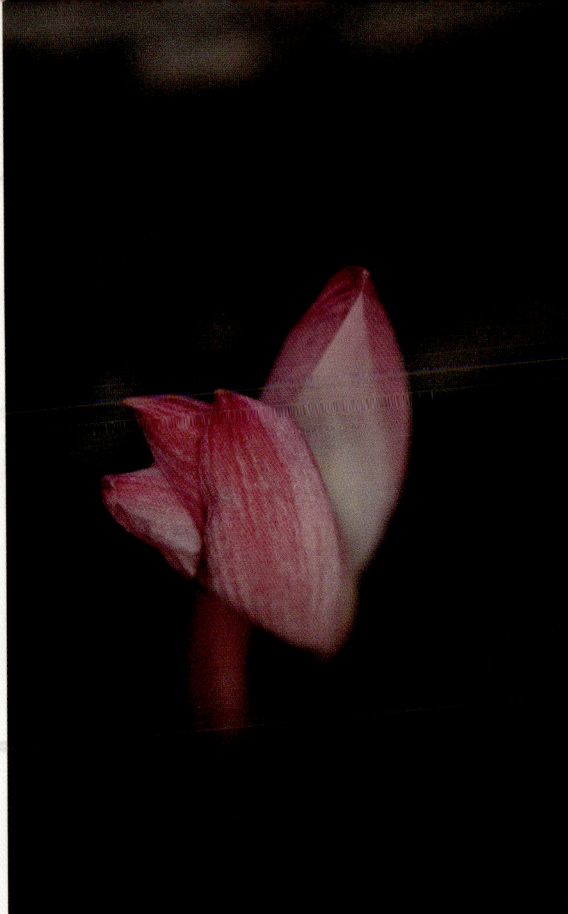

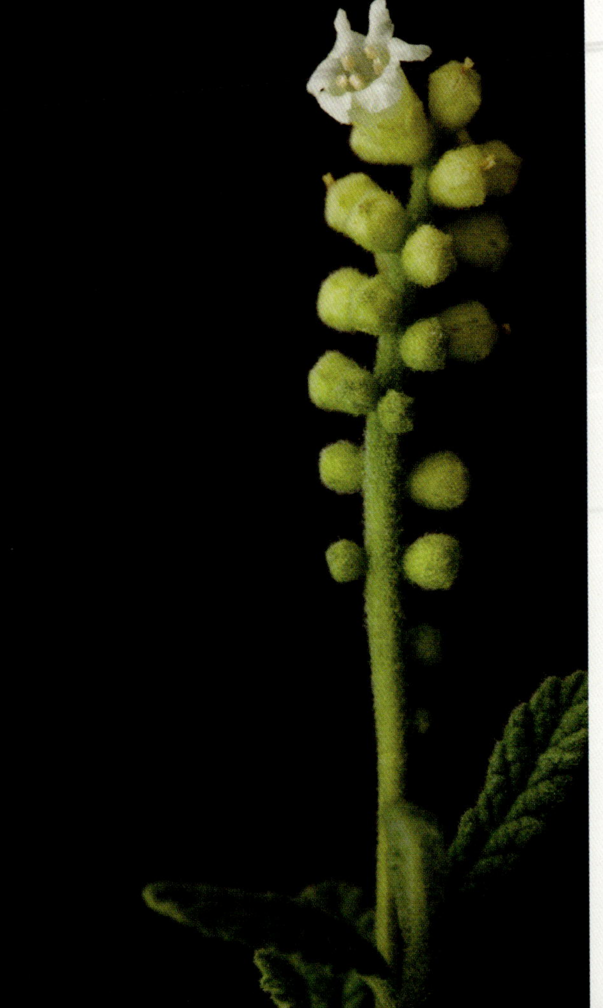

interactions, or the things we watch or listen
to, dormant seeds suddenly sprout roots and
shoot up into our awareness, after which we
often act on them. Some seeds are beneficial—
seeds of love, understanding, and generosity—
while others can be damaging—seeds of anger,
jealousy, and betrayal.

When a negative emotion gets watered and
rises into our mind consciousness, we can use
mindfulness to notice the feeling, name it,
understand its roots, and calm it, much like a
mother who cradles her baby when he or she
is suffering. For example, if I were to arrive
back at our room hot, sweaty, and exhausted,
it would be easy in that sensitive moment for
the seed of anger that lies dormant within me

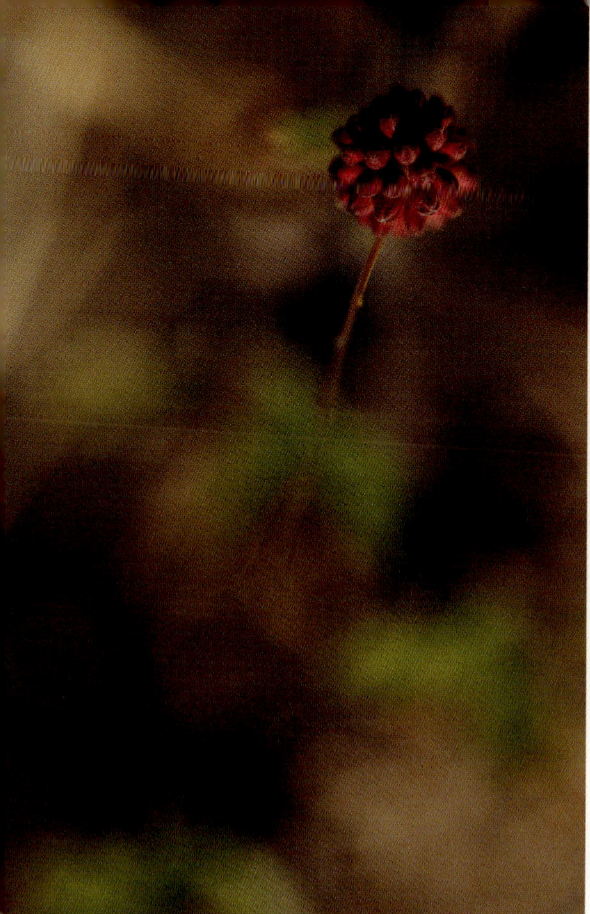

to rise up and express itself if my wife were to say something I consider insensitive. By recognizing the anger present inside of me, I can catch the sprouting seed before it takes over. I can pause and simply breathe with the sensation of it. Even if I am too slow to stop myself from reacting negatively, I can have the wherewithal to immediately apologize. As Thay would say, if you say something hurtful, you can send a positive thought or word after it to neutralize its impact.

This teaching has been instrumental in helping me work with the difficult emotions that have been arising in me so strongly since the start of the pandemic.

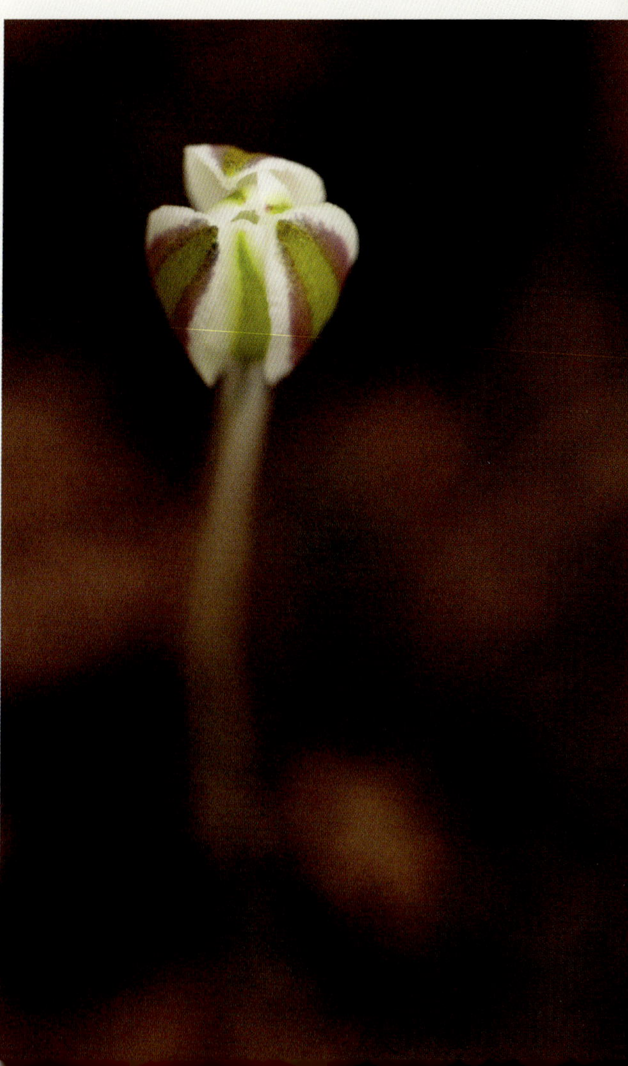

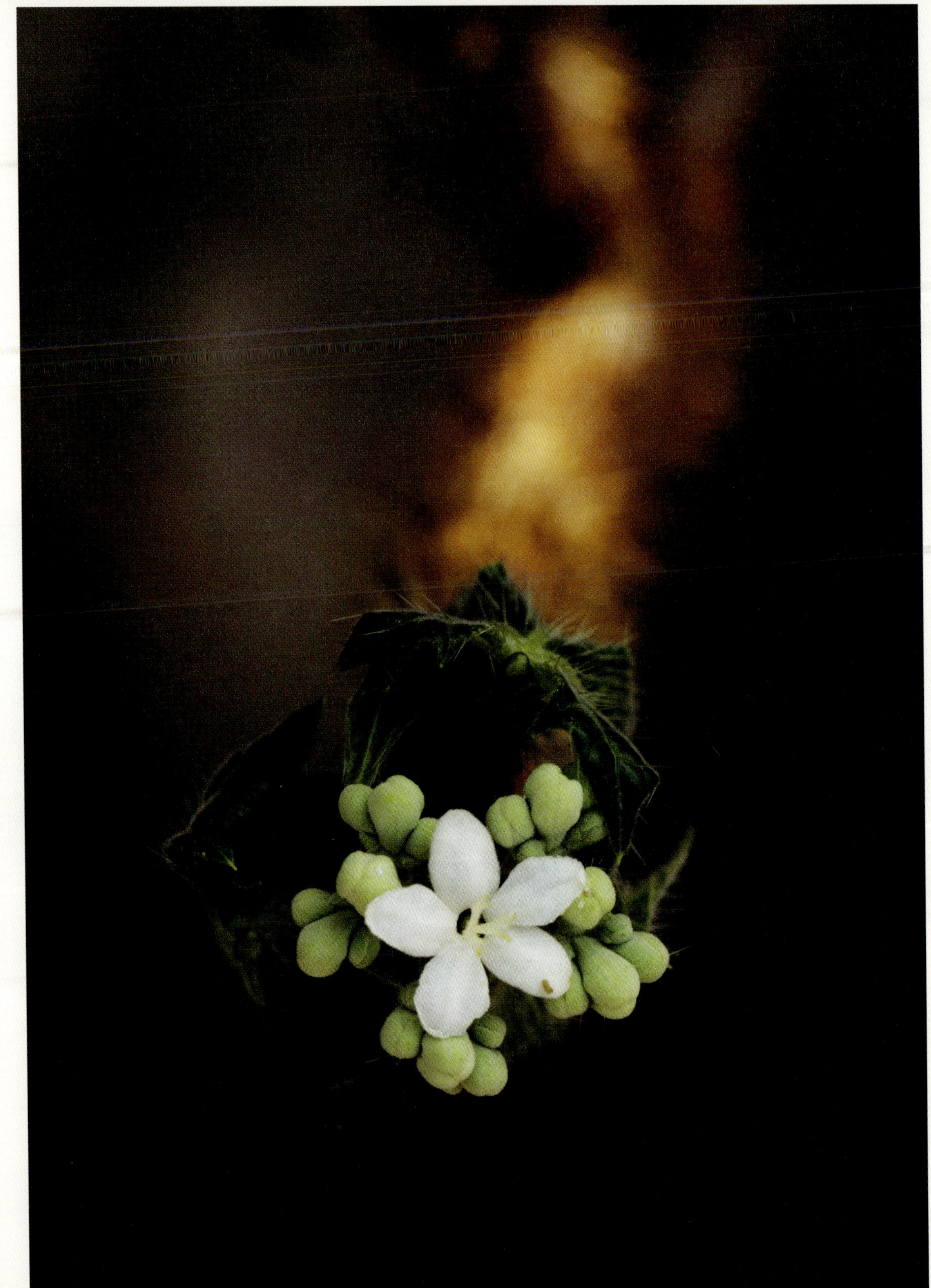

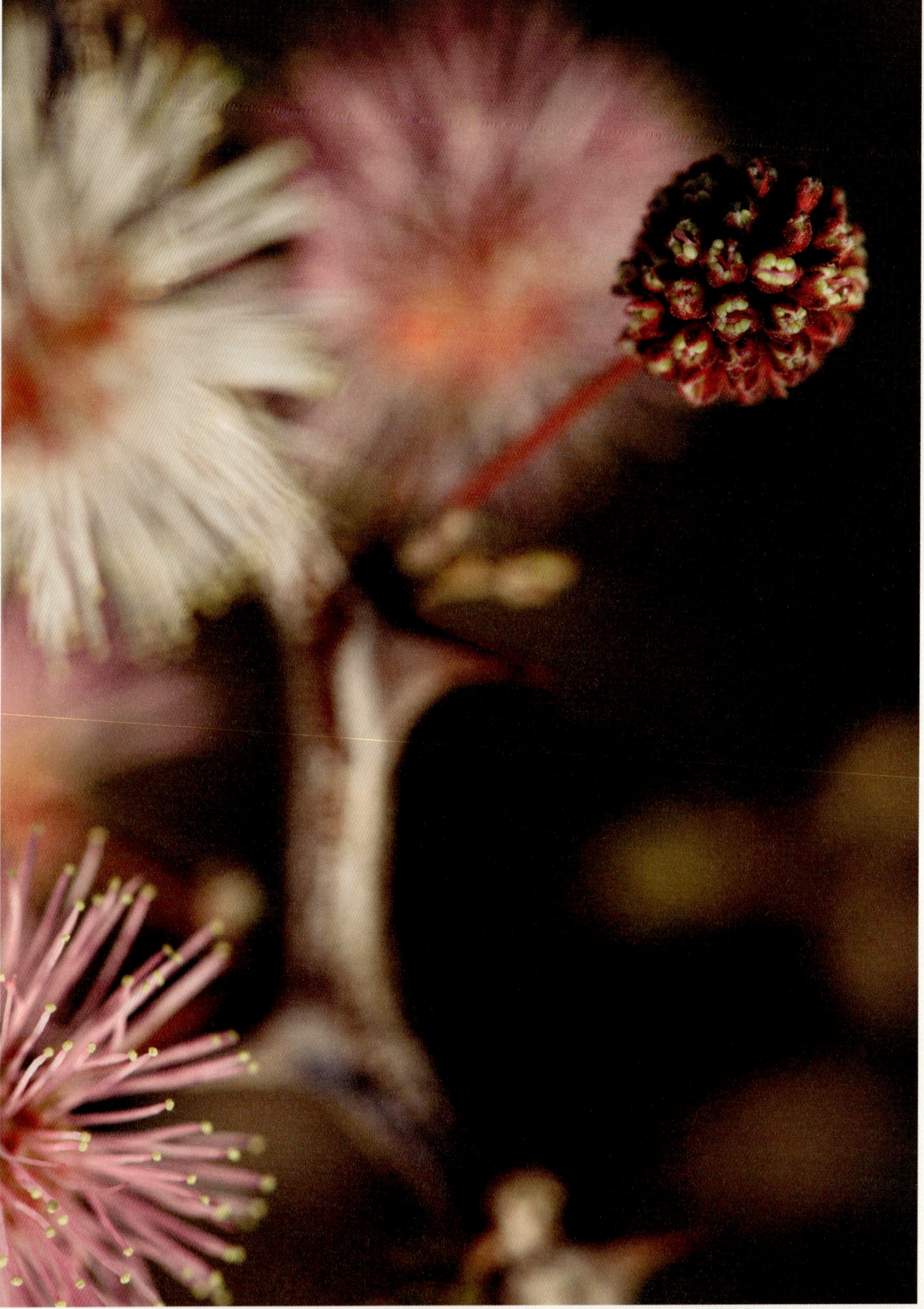

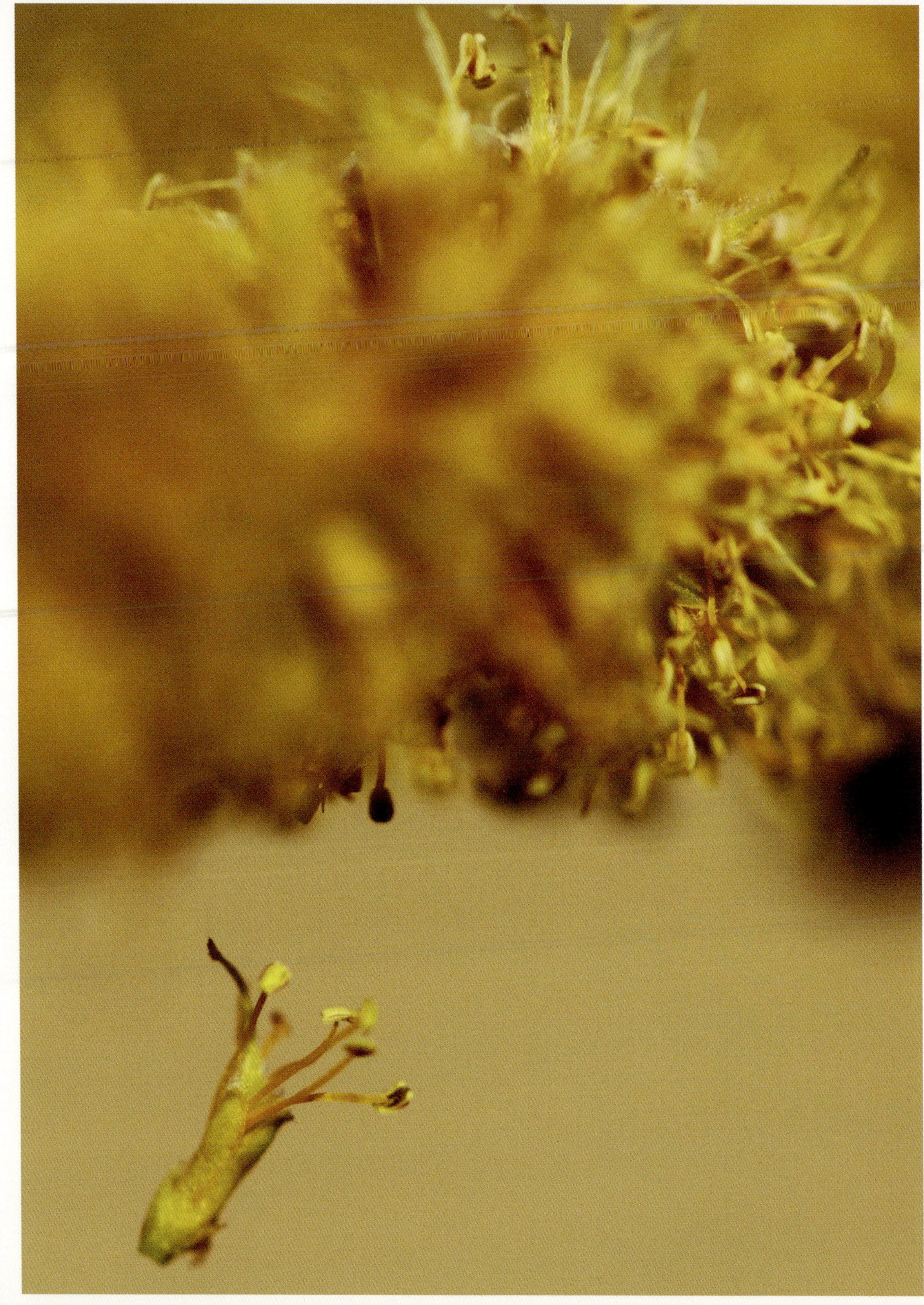

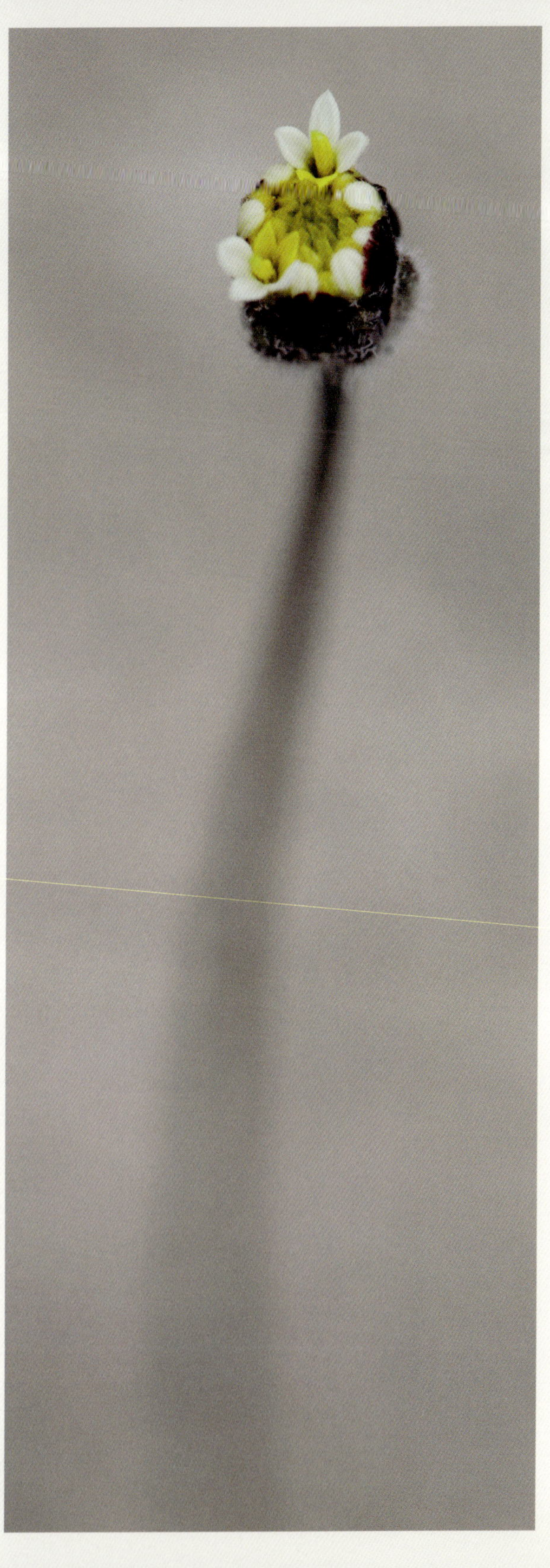

The transformation of the land around Mitla
acts as a bell of mindfulness for me in another
way. Much of my journalistic career focused
on raising the alarm about climate change
and biodiversity loss. In more recent years,
my worries multiplied as I saw these grief-
laden challenges interweave with deepening
crises of inequality, misinformation, mistrust,
and extremism to form what many now call
the *polycrisis*.

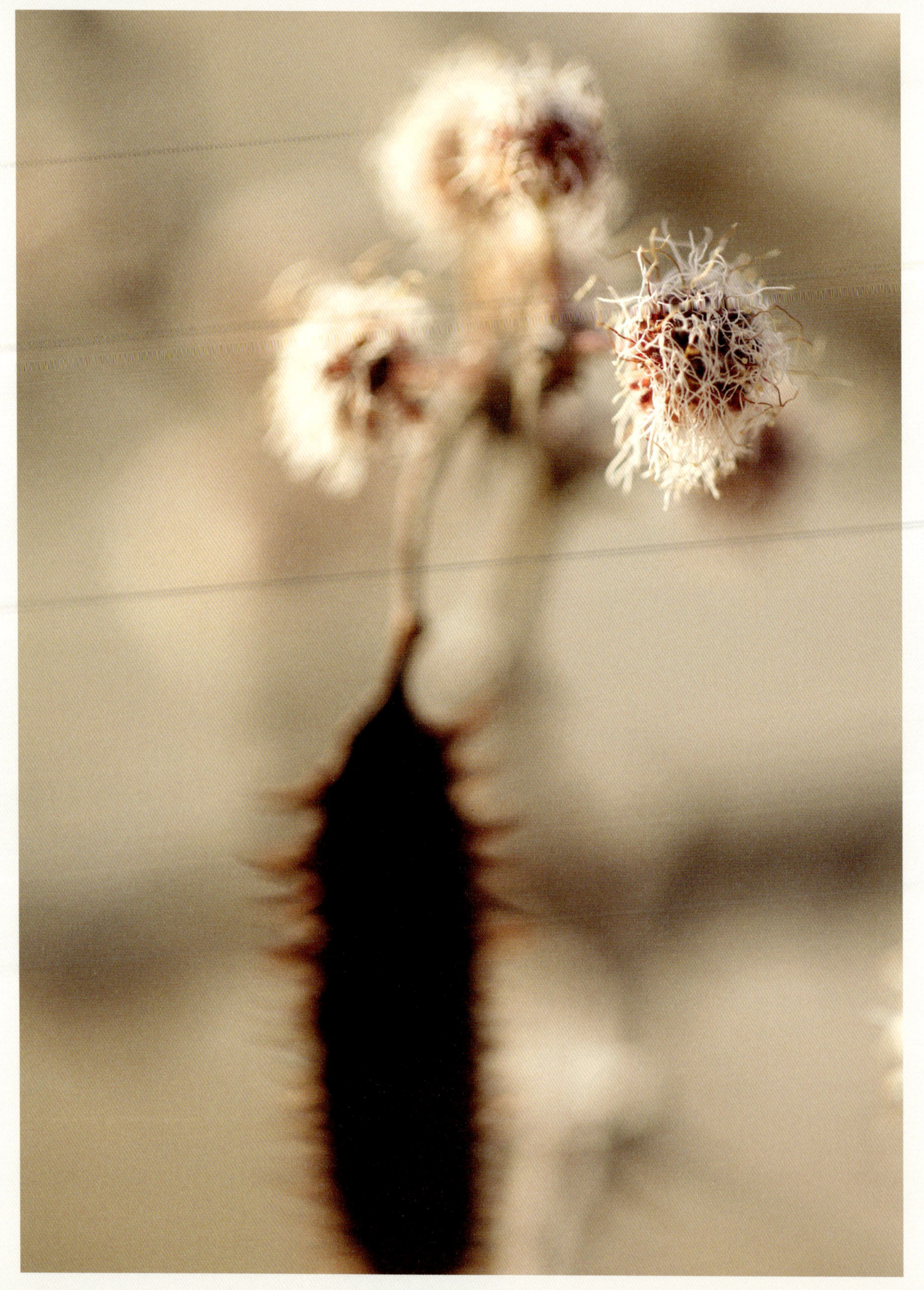

I do not think of myself as a doomsayer; at the same time, I see that the causes and conditions for a collapse of human society are present. This awareness sits heavily. In Mitla, the harshness of the dry season played into my fear that human-driven destruction of biodiversity combined with the climate emergency may turn many lush parts of the world into ecosystems like this scrubland, my fear that much of the natural world and diversity of life will recede into memory.

Seeing flowers emerge from dry dirt, I witness the extraordinary resilience of Mother Earth. I see her bring forth beauty in the most difficult of circumstances. It gives me hope that whatever damage we wreak on this jewel of a planet can somehow be rebalanced.

In one of my memorable conversations with Thay, I asked him how it is possible to hold the pain of the world without being crushed by it. This is what he told me: "For us, it is very alarming and urgent, but for Mother Earth, if she suffers, she knows she has the power to heal herself, even if it takes 100 million years. We have to accept that the worst can happen; most of us will die as a species, and many other species will die also. Mother Earth will be capable, after maybe a few million years, of bringing us out again—this time wiser."

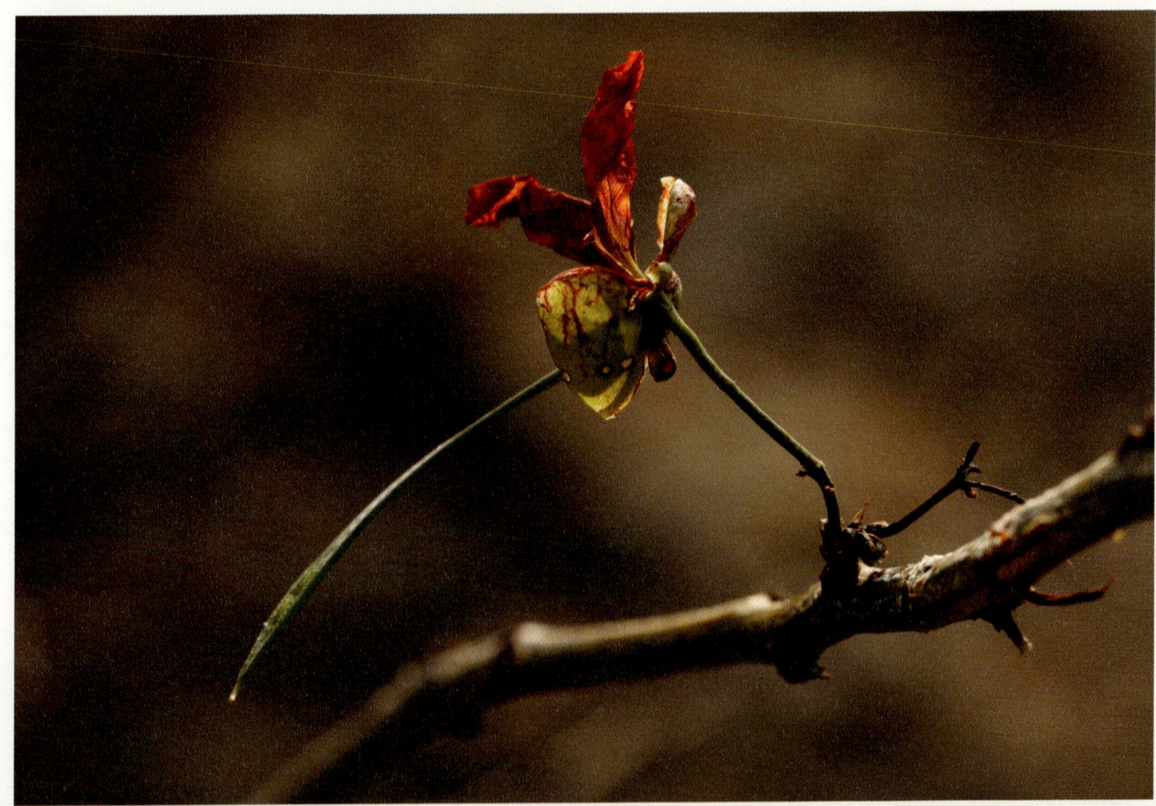

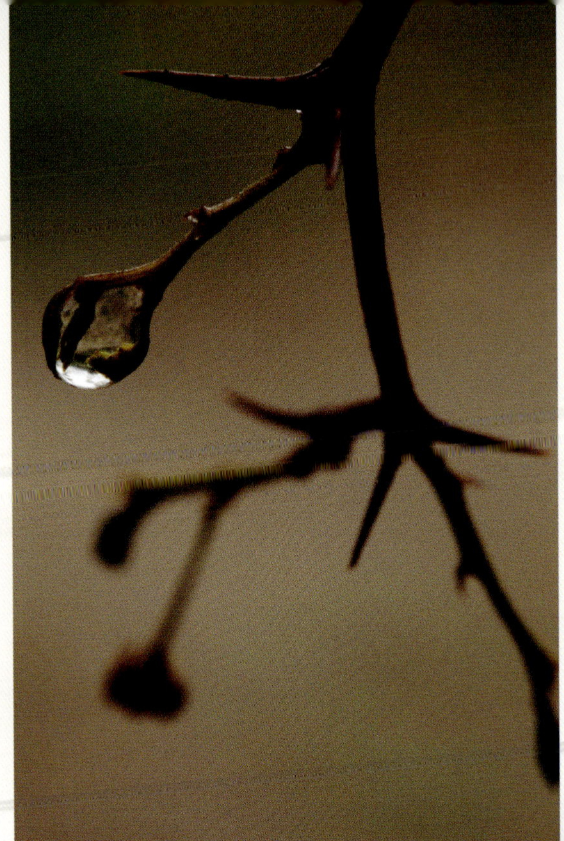

ALL THE WORLD
IN A DROP OF
WATER

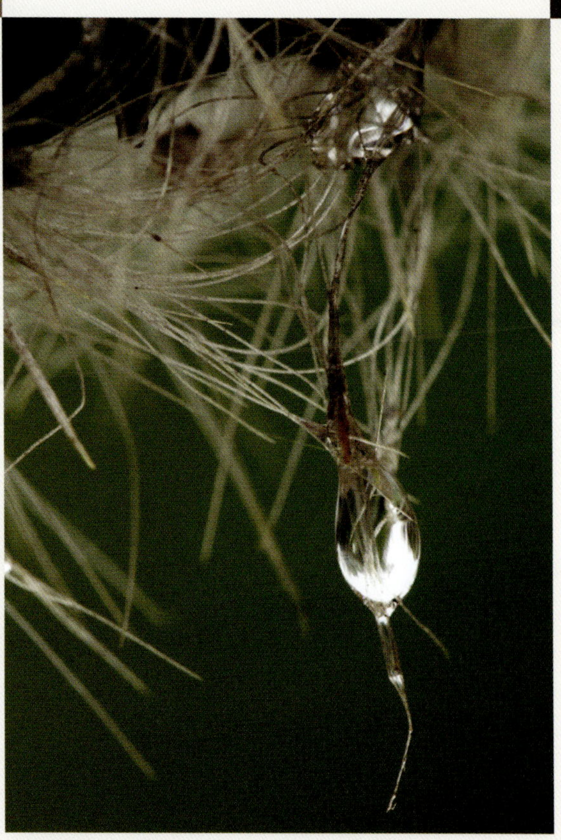

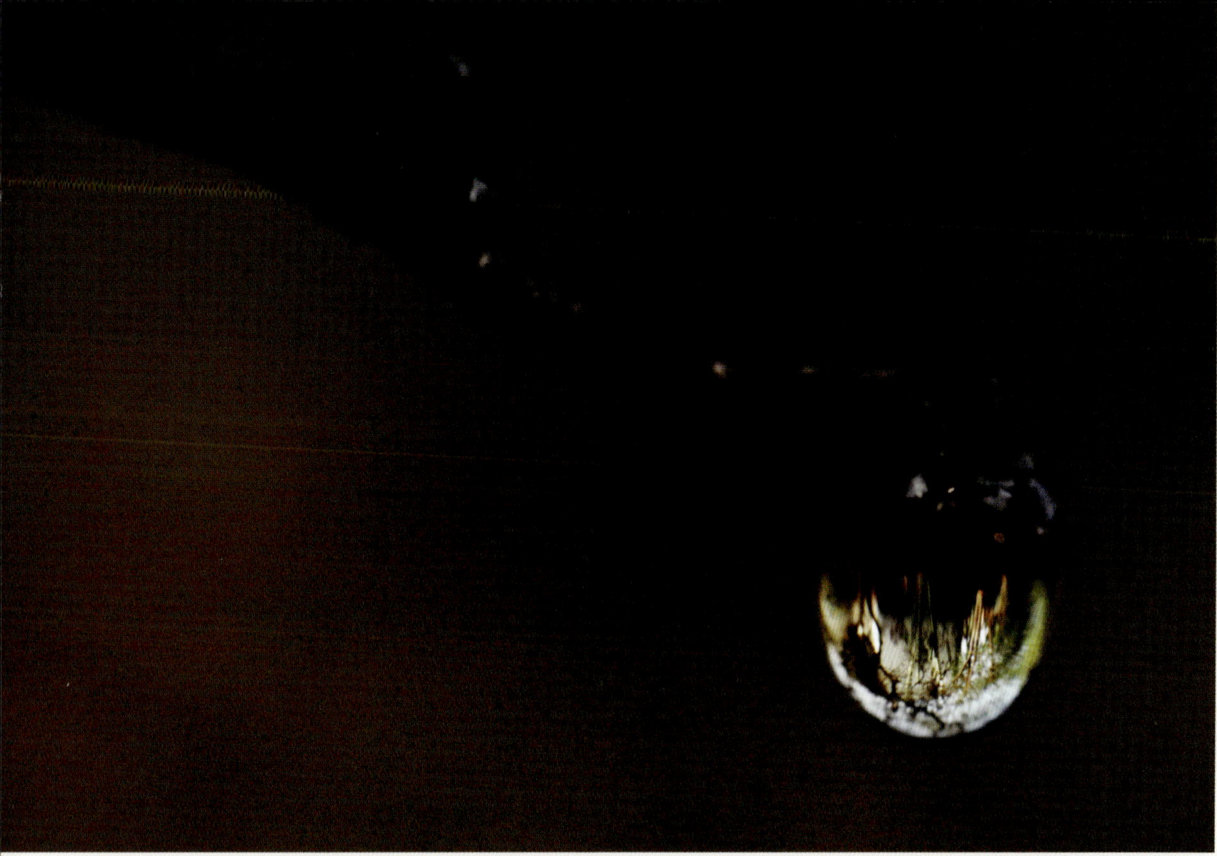

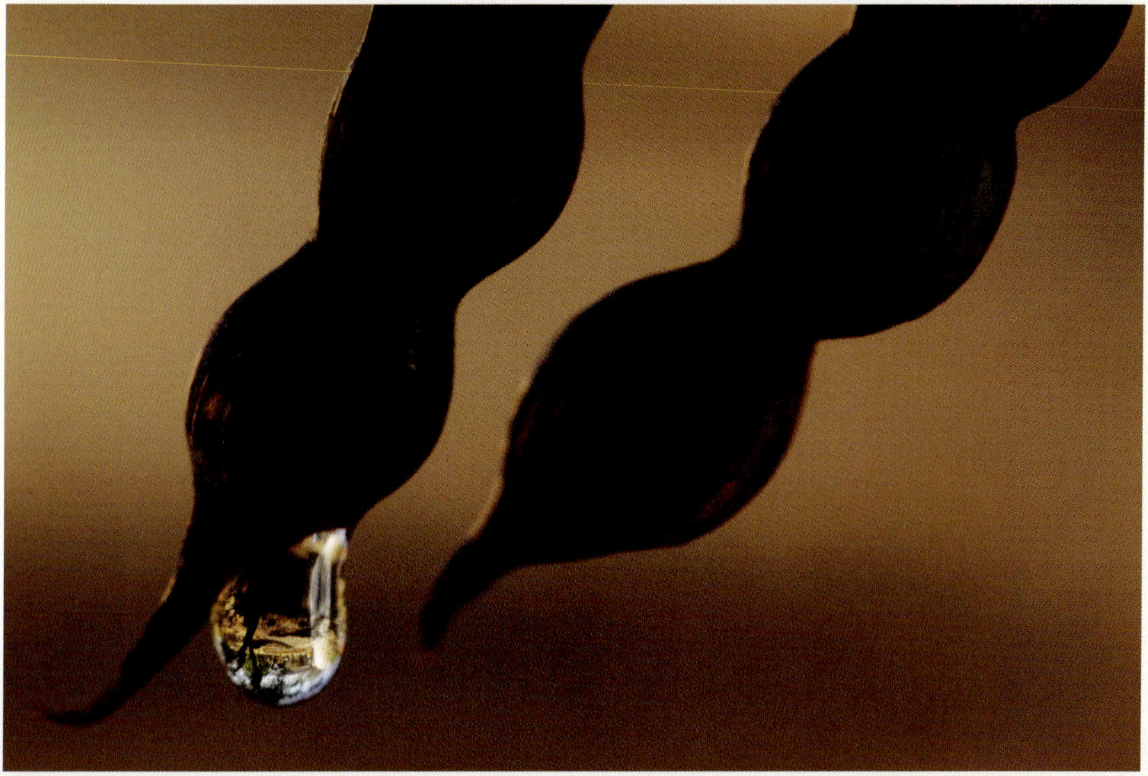

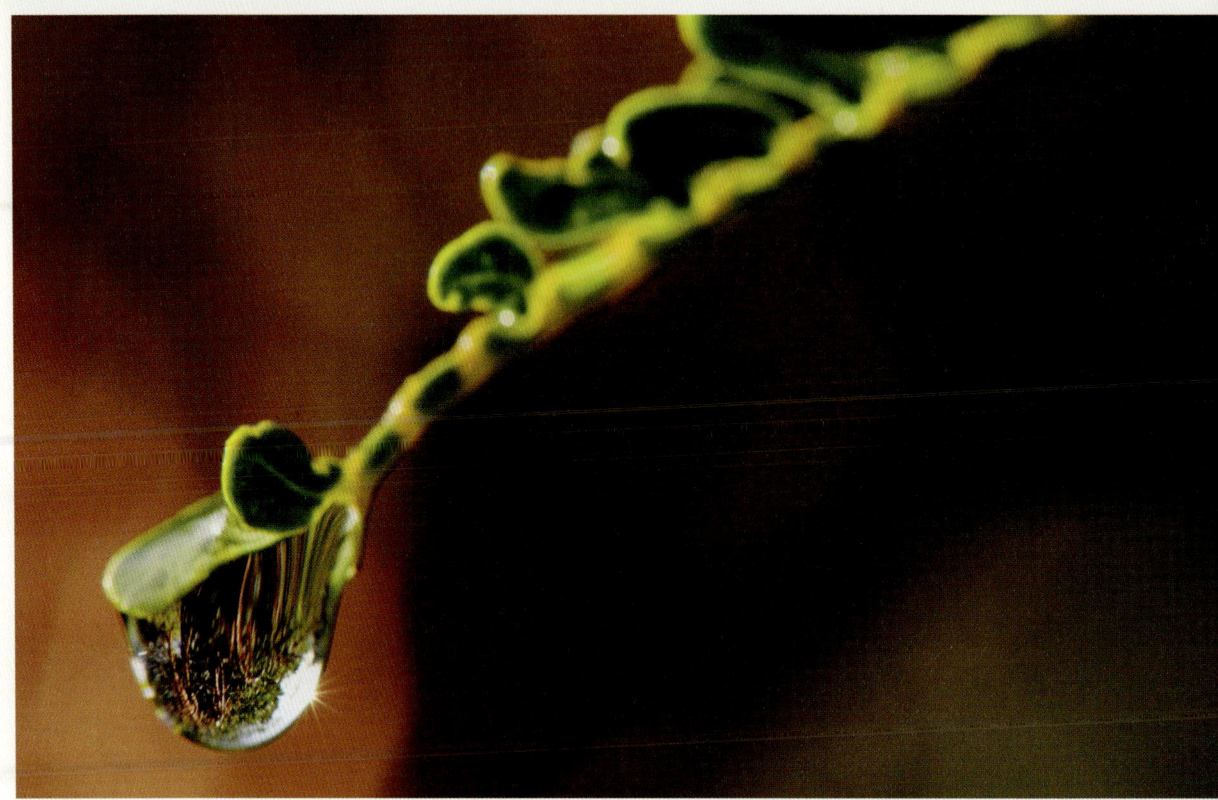

The rain comes down in sheets. I focus my
attention on individual raindrops, glittering
jewels that cling to twigs and leaves and then
let go and fall to the ground like autumn leaves
dropping from a tree.

I remember the quiet joy of taking my first
picture of a single rain drop, back in 2015
in Plum Village. It hung from a pine needle,
holding the vastness of the morning sunrise.

Now in Mitla, I am again drawn to how much
of the world each tiny bead of water is able
to contain and to reflect. There is something
magical about catching these moments in time,
knowing the surface tension will soon give
way and the water drop will slip away. These
fleeting gems remind me that beauty often
resides in the brief and the fragile.

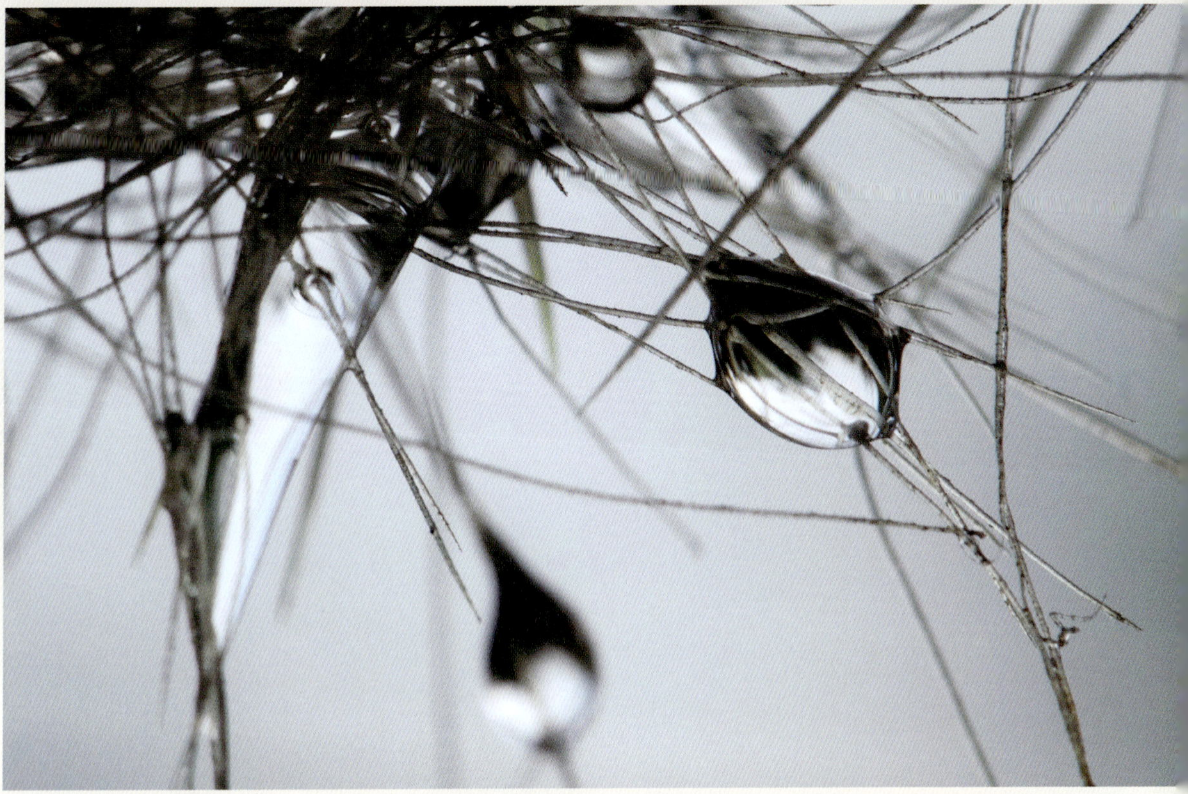

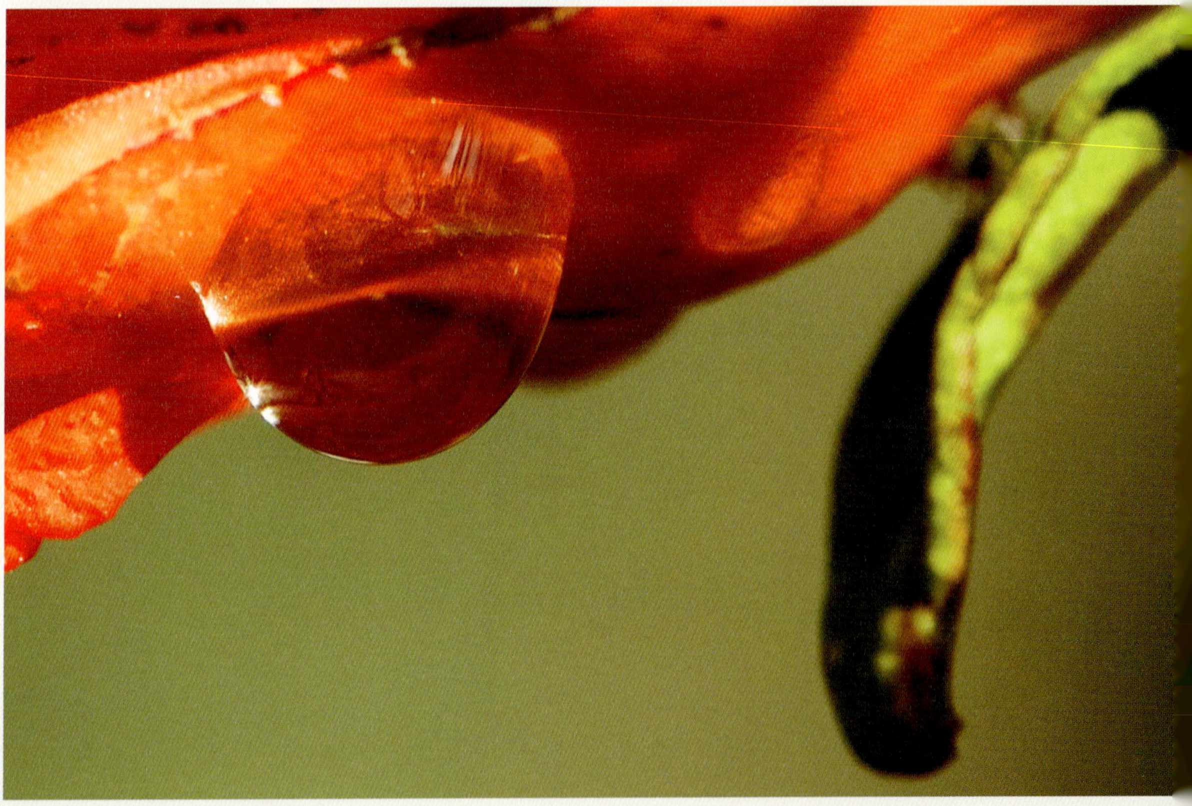

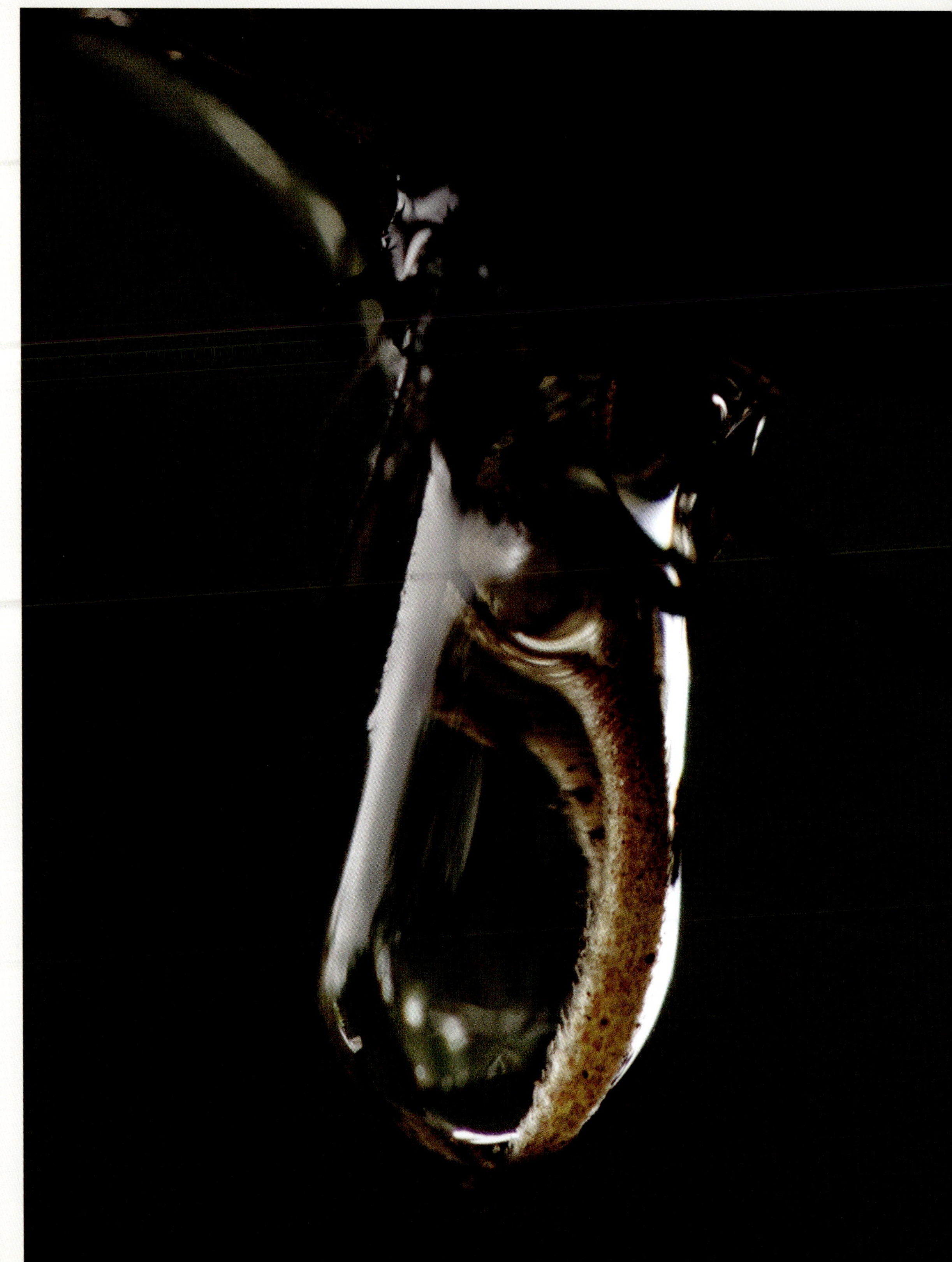

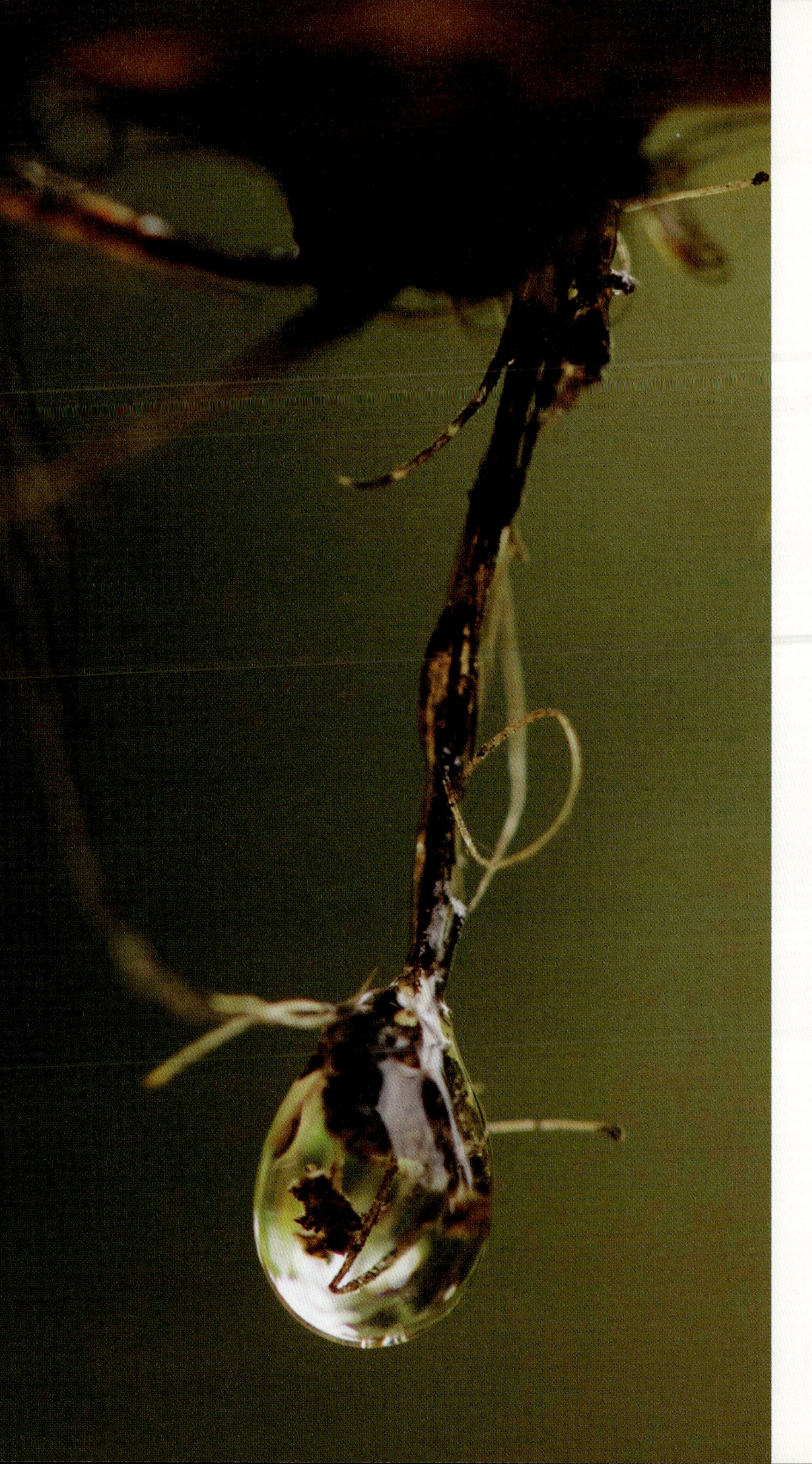

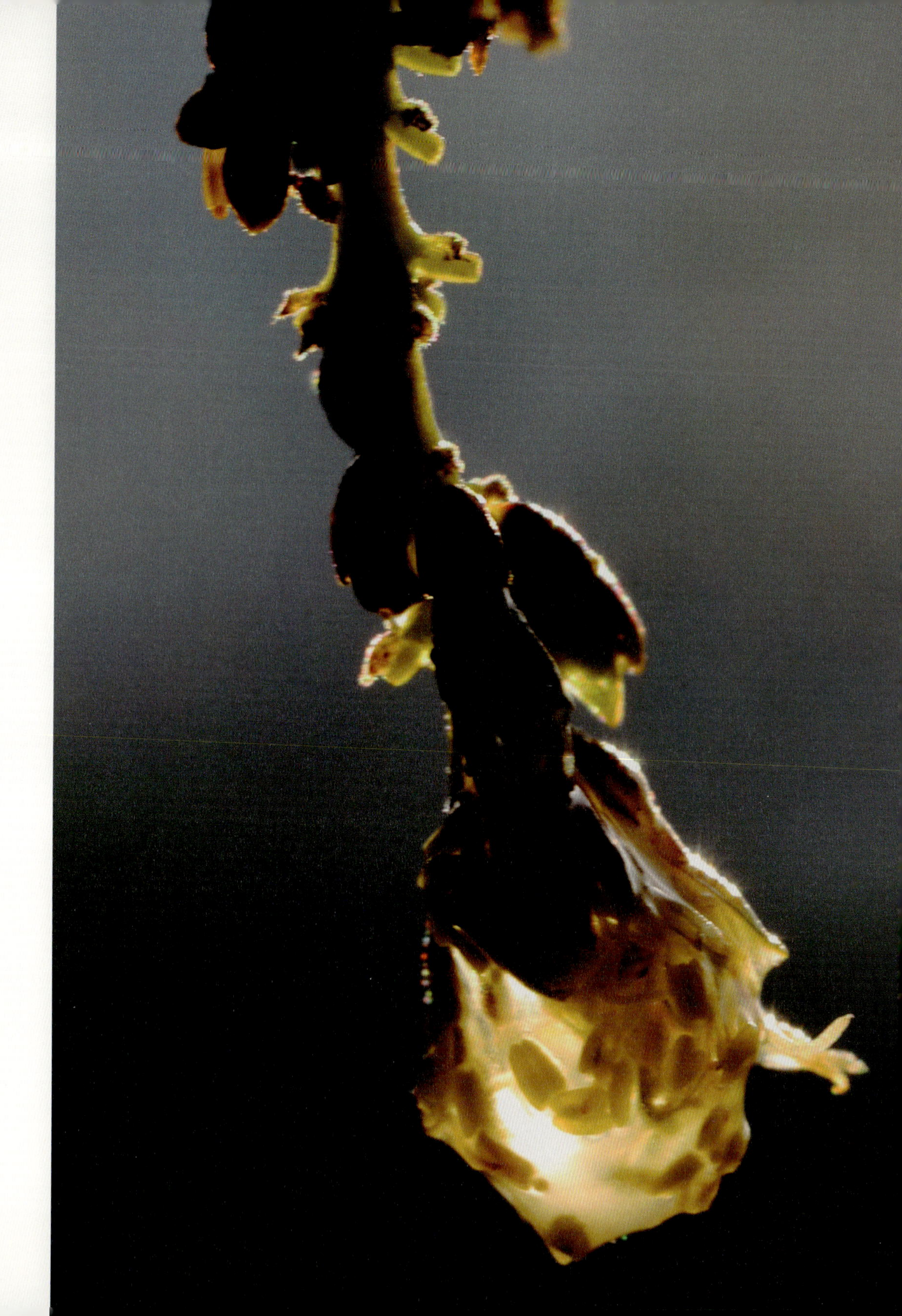

SOMEWHERE TO GO, SOMETHING TO DO

As the rains continue to transform the land and May rolls toward June, the town of Mitla itself also begins to come back to life, both grieving and hopeful. Shops open, many with black ribbons of mourning above their doors. The first visitors return. Some afternoons, the sound of music bursts through, a sign that life is starting to find its rhythm once more.

Part of me wants to stay and explore the archaeological sites and immerse myself in the local culture, things we were not able to do during lockdown. Yet a new adventure beckons.

On the day I lost my job in New York, I phoned my wife with the news, packed up my office, and went home carrying a box of belongings. I walked into our apartment and Paz and I looked each other in the eyes. Without saying a word, we both knew what our next move would be. That same morning, we reached out to a real estate broker in France whom we had met months earlier during a brief visit to Plum Village. She had shown us only one property, a seventeenth-century stone farmhouse. When we had viewed the house the previous fall, it had been out of simple curiosity—maybe one day, we thought, we'd want to be closer to the Plum Village community.

Standing in our apartment that winter morning in Manhattan, though, something deep within us told us that this farmhouse was our next home. Despite every piece of common-sense advice warning against making big decisions in the midst of upheaval, we called the broker and agreed to buy it on the spot. It was entirely unlike us, and yet felt completely aligned. The vague possibility we had considered months earlier had suddenly become our reality—but first, we would fly to Mexico.

Now, months instead of days later, it is time for what comes next. Casa Lyobaa had been an invaluable refuge, but we had known all along that one day we would move on. When news comes that France is reopening its borders, we decide it is time to leave—there may be only a small window of opportunity to move before another wave of infections shuts the world down again.

Plum Village is known for its songs. When I first encountered them, I was allergic to their simplicity—they seemed so childlike. But over the years, I have grown to appreciate these songs exactly for those qualities, for the lightness with which deep teachings are held. Once I let go of my self-consciousness, the songs touched a place of innocence inside of me that sophisticated lyrics tend not to. One song in particular comes to me in the final days before our flight, and I sing it quietly to myself to calm my nerves.

Happiness is here and now,
I have dropped my worries.
Nowhere to go, nothing to do,
No longer in a hurry.
Happiness is here and now,
I have dropped my worries.
Somewhere to go, something to do,
But I don't need to hurry.

From nowhere to go and nothing to do, we now have somewhere to go and something to do. Our belongings from New York sit in a warehouse, waiting for confirmation of our final address. In Mitla we've lived out of one suitcase each, and it has been more than enough—another reminder that we do not need much to be happy. Now it is time to pack these suitcases again, to tearfully say goodbye to the family who so warmly and generously welcomed us into their home despite existential danger, and to trade the seemingly endless space of Mitla for Mexico City's Benito Juarez International Airport.

Though the decision to leave is ours alone, it feels like being cast out of the Garden of Eden. From a place of quiet and solitude, we find ourselves in an airport filled with anxious people seeking to keep their distance. On the long overnight flight to France, everyone is squeezed tightly together, faces masked.

This chapter of our lives, the first lockdown, has come to an end. I check my calendar and realize that our departure comes exactly a hundred days after our arrival.

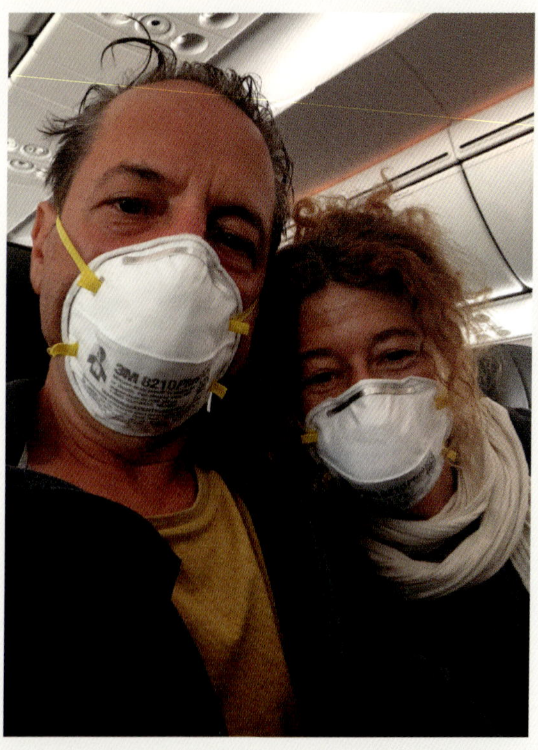

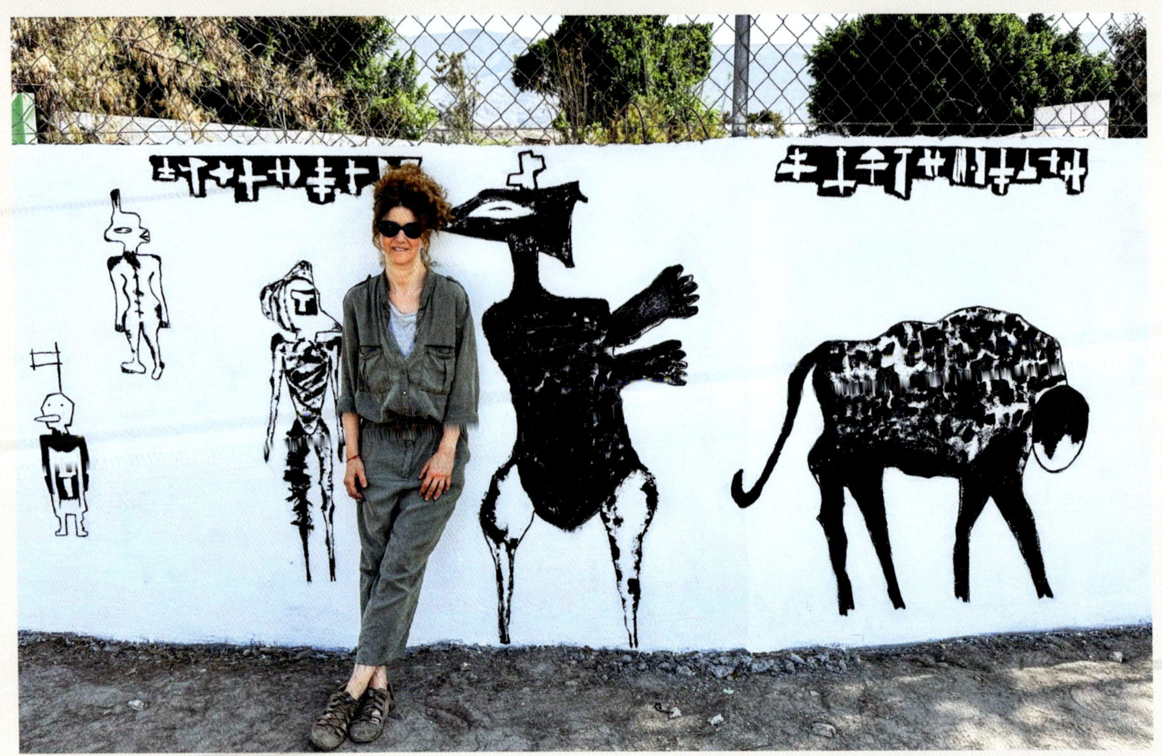

RETURNING

Four years after moving to be part of the Plum Village community, I return to Mitla. Paz has been commissioned to paint a twelve-meter mural of mythical "earth protectors" in the town, and I come along to support her. The return journey brings my original experience sharply into focus. It's wonderful to be back, but as I retrace my steps across the desert-like scrub, grief starts to grip me. It is the hottest week on record in Mexico, and I witness plants and animals experiencing deep stress. Cacti that taught me the power of resilience are shriveling, and there is a dearth of insect life.

I am taught one final lesson. I have brought my camera, intending to take new photographs, but I recognize the folly of trying to reenact the past. My first time here was a magical experience—I cannot, and should not, try to repeat it. I place my camera down and simply breathe.

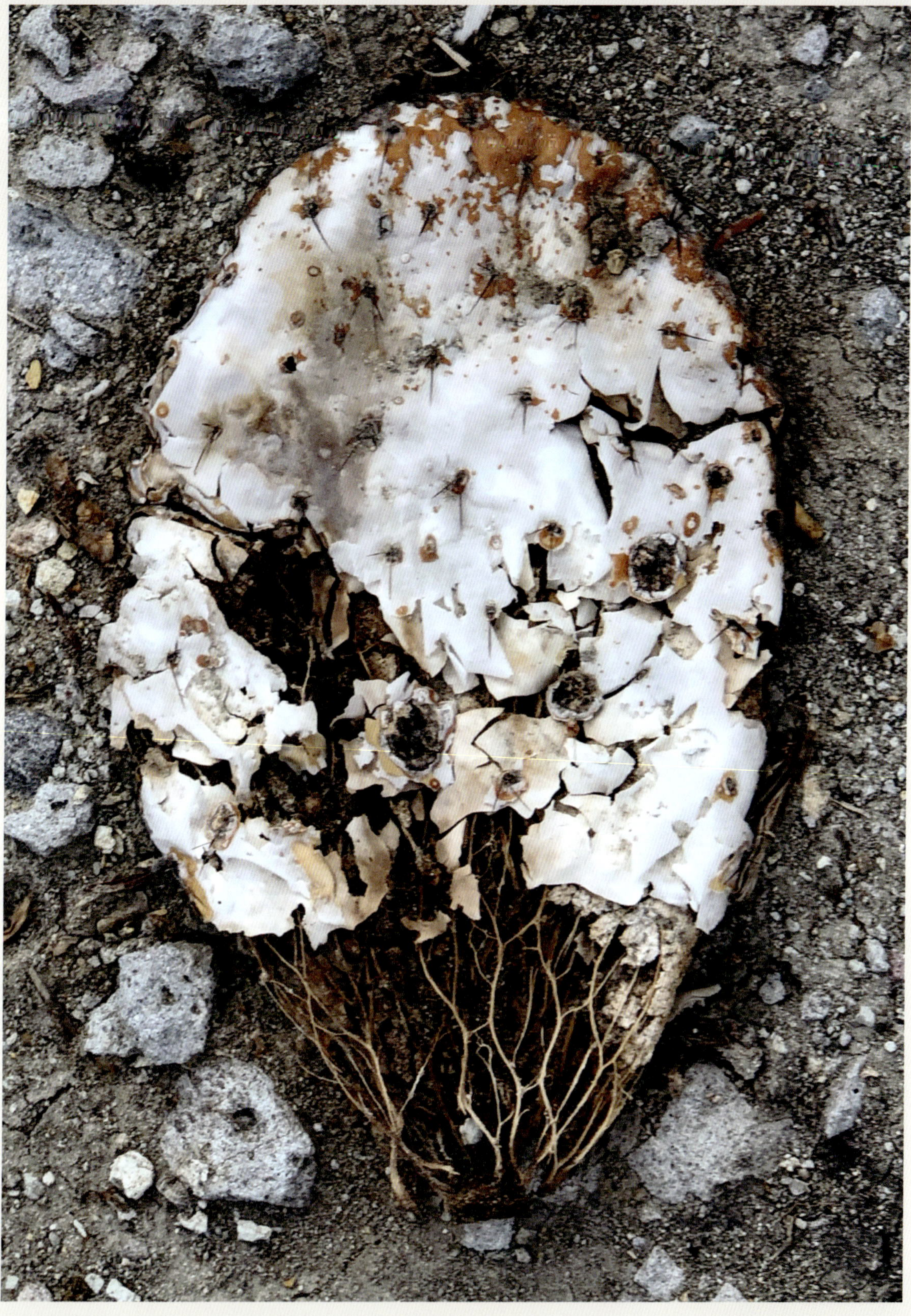

AFTERWORD:
THE QUIET BEAUTY
IN EVERYTHING

When we receive a gift, it is only natural
to express our appreciation and to offer
something in return. Indigenous cultures
around the world have long honored this
spirit of reciprocity. I consider this book my
offering, born of a desire to help others see the
extraordinary symphony of life right in front
of our noses—so often missed in our rush to go
from here to there.

During my time in Mitla, I took around 1,400
close-up photos of the sparse flora and fauna.
Before leaving New York, I had agreed to trade
in my macro lens—I rarely used it, and it was
gathering dust. I am so glad I changed my
mind at the last moment. That lens became my
close companion. It allowed me to discover
that intimacy is found in proximity. All the
photographs in this book were taken within
a three-mile radius of where we were based,
the distance I could walk each morning before
being forced to return by the intense heat of
the day. Despite my initial misgivings, it turned
out to be more than enough ground.

I come from a family of avid photographers. As
a child, mesmerized, I used to watch my father
and older brothers in our basement darkroom
as the black and white images appeared, as if
by magic, in the chemical trays.

I never learned to play an instrument, I could
not sing, and I was a failure at painting and
drawing. Photography gave me a language and

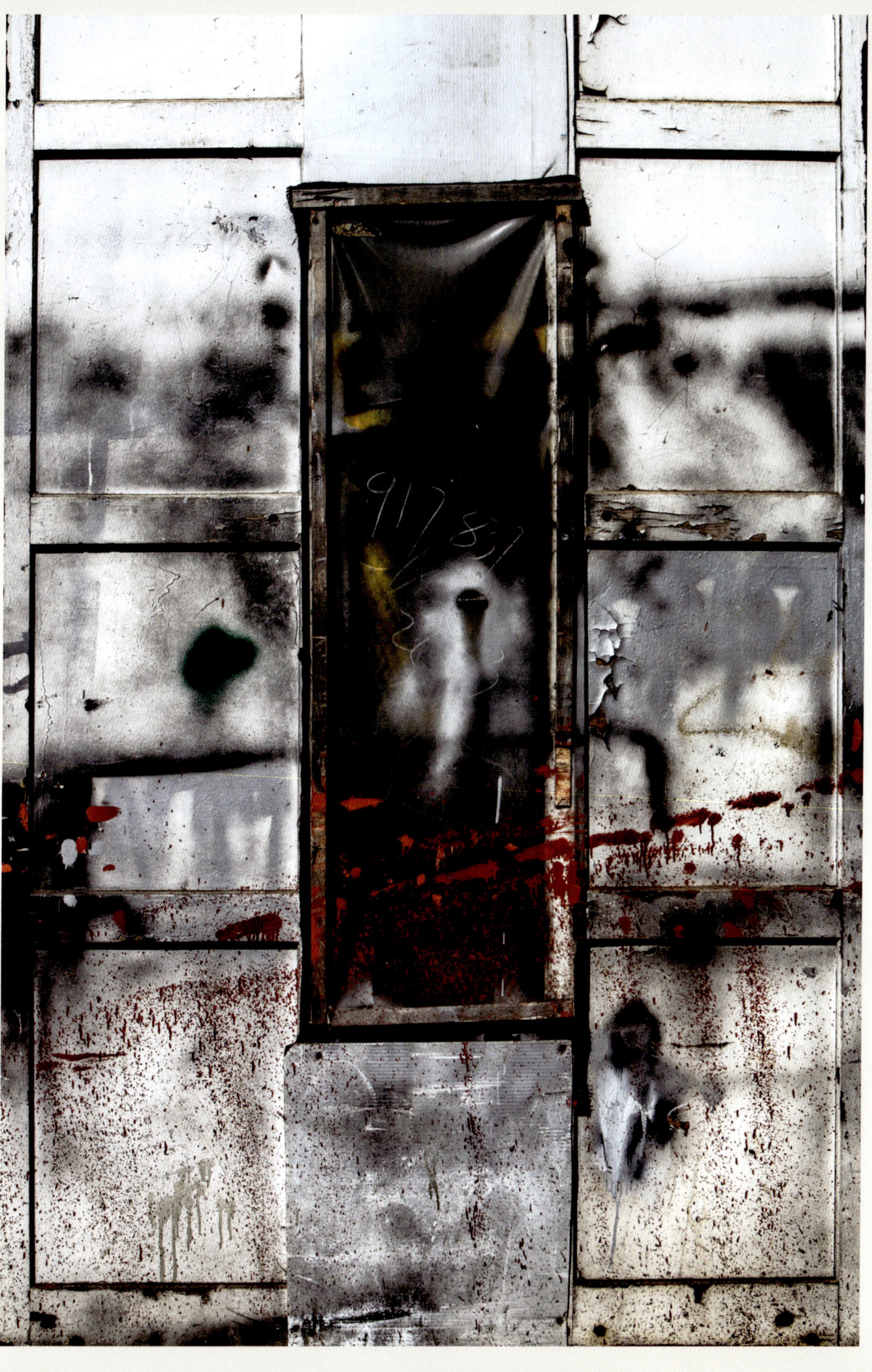

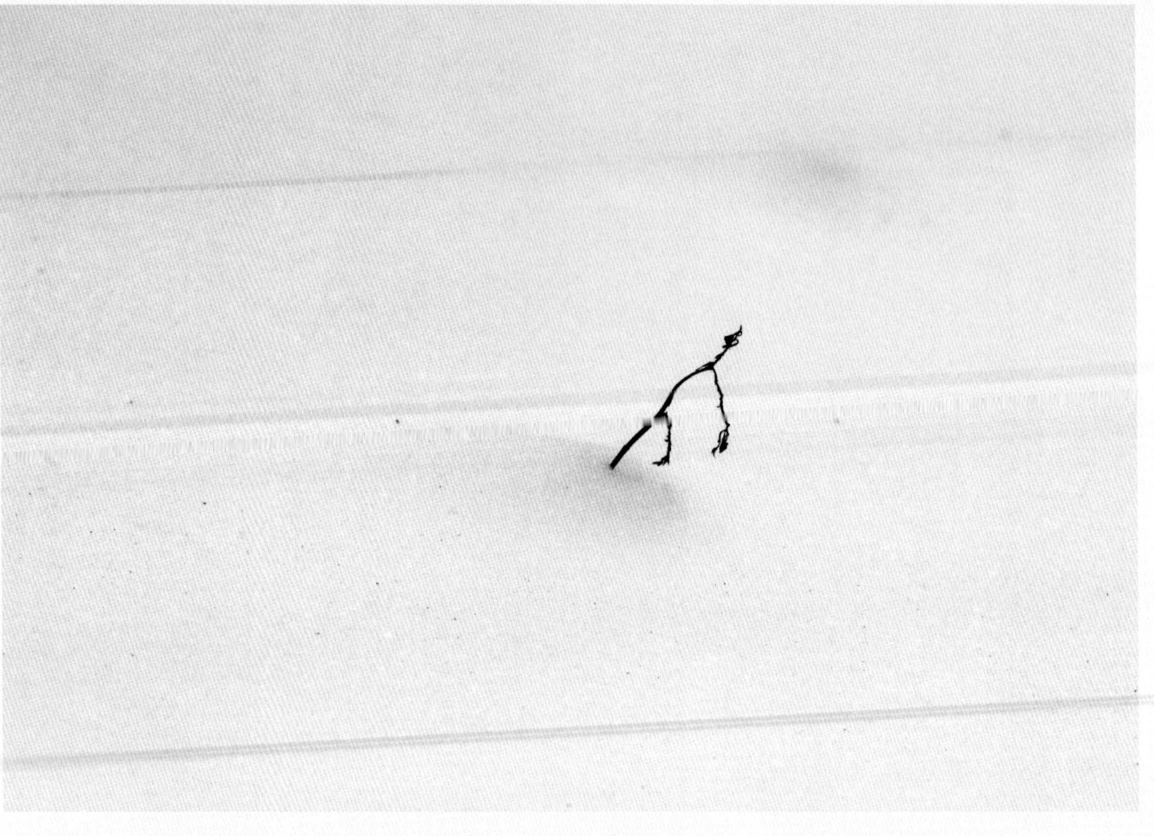

permission to express myself and play with light, color, and form. I fell in love with composition. I came to understand over the years that the pictures I take are a mirror of who I am. During my time in Mitla, I came to a deeper understanding: photography has been a quiet companion on my journey of personal healing.

One of my passions, which has developed over the years, is photographing objects that often go unnoticed and unacknowledged. Looking back, the genesis of this may have been an experimental acid trip at university, during which I spent many hours observing a single foxglove flower, allowing it to penetrate deep into my consciousness. I also vividly remember walking through an ancient forest on the West Coast of Scotland in my late twenties: while my friends were awed by the magnificent canopy above, I was drawn downward to the extraordinary beauty of the moss-covered forest floor. Getting down on my hands and knees, camera in hand, and becoming small myself, I discovered vastness. Within an area of just a few meters, I became immersed in a terrain of magical forests, ravines, and miniature mountain ranges.

It's easy for places like the Grand Canyon or the Himalayas to generate awe. But I discovered the same sense of wonder in the most ordinary things. During the five years I lived in New York, while most photographers were drawn to Manhattan's dramatic skyline, I focused on objects like the splattered doorway of a Brooklyn metal merchant, a dirty rag hanging from a pipe in a bus depot in Red Hook, and a

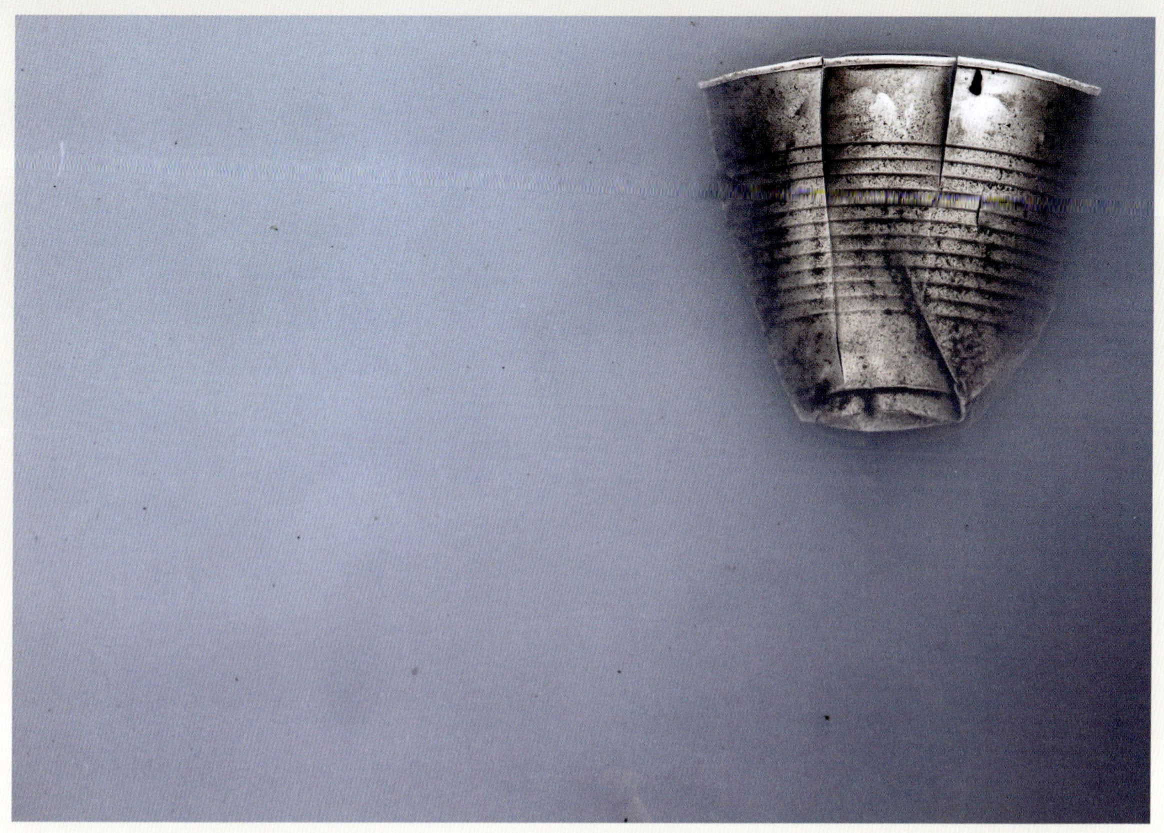

twig poking through the snow in Central Park that reminded me of the struggles of life.

I would cycle to industrial parks and photograph discarded objects, such as a crushed plastic cup floating in a puddle, giving them a sculptural dignity to help others see their quiet beauty. That same impulse to hold space for what often goes unseen or unacknowledged continues to animate my work.

This way of seeing the world is very much attuned to Thay's invitation to view our consciousness as an artist, painting our world into being. I spent my childhood believing I had nothing to offer—that I was small, insignificant, irrelevant, and ugly. I did not feel I had a place in the world; I did not feel at home. As I gradually healed my wounds, I learned first to like myself, and then to love myself.

My photography has evolved alongside my growing understanding of my place in the world. I want people to see the monumental in the mundane, to understand that what we often dismiss as ugly or worthless can embody profound beauty and deserves reverence. Sometimes all it takes is reframing the way we see ourselves—and the world around us.

Knowing so many people suffered greatly during the pandemic, I feel shy to say my time in Mitla, when I look back at the entire experience, was among the happiest periods of my life. I arrived full of fears and left full of hope. The deep lessons I learned while on my photographic walkabouts still resonate

years later and have proved instrumental in
reshaping my life. Sometimes they slip my
mind, but my foundational experience in
Mitla—there were moments when I looked
at the mountains and felt them looking back
at me—helps me to more easily reconnect to
peace and beauty in a landscape of confines
and impermanence when I veer off the path.
The scrubby, desert-like landscape still
speaks to me, as do the plants and the animals,
reminding me to take time and allow life to be
my teacher.

Those quiet months in Mitla taught me to listen
more deeply—not only to nature, but to my
own suffering and to the suffering of others.
That practice of presence became foundational
as I began accompanying others on their
journeys through my coaching and spiritual
mentoring as well as in the conversations
I have on *The Way Out Is In* podcast, and in
the books I've cowritten with Brother Phap
Huu, the abbot of Plum Village and a longtime
attendant of Thich Nhat Hanh.

I try to bring the spirit of spaciousness I learned
in Mitla to my work with clients and groups—
offering not answers, but the kind of grounded
attention that the cacti, the silence, and the sky
offered to me. As I often tell people I work with:
"If I'm full of busyness, that's all I can offer. But
if I've made space inside myself, I can offer that
space to you." For many, that's the very thing
they need most.

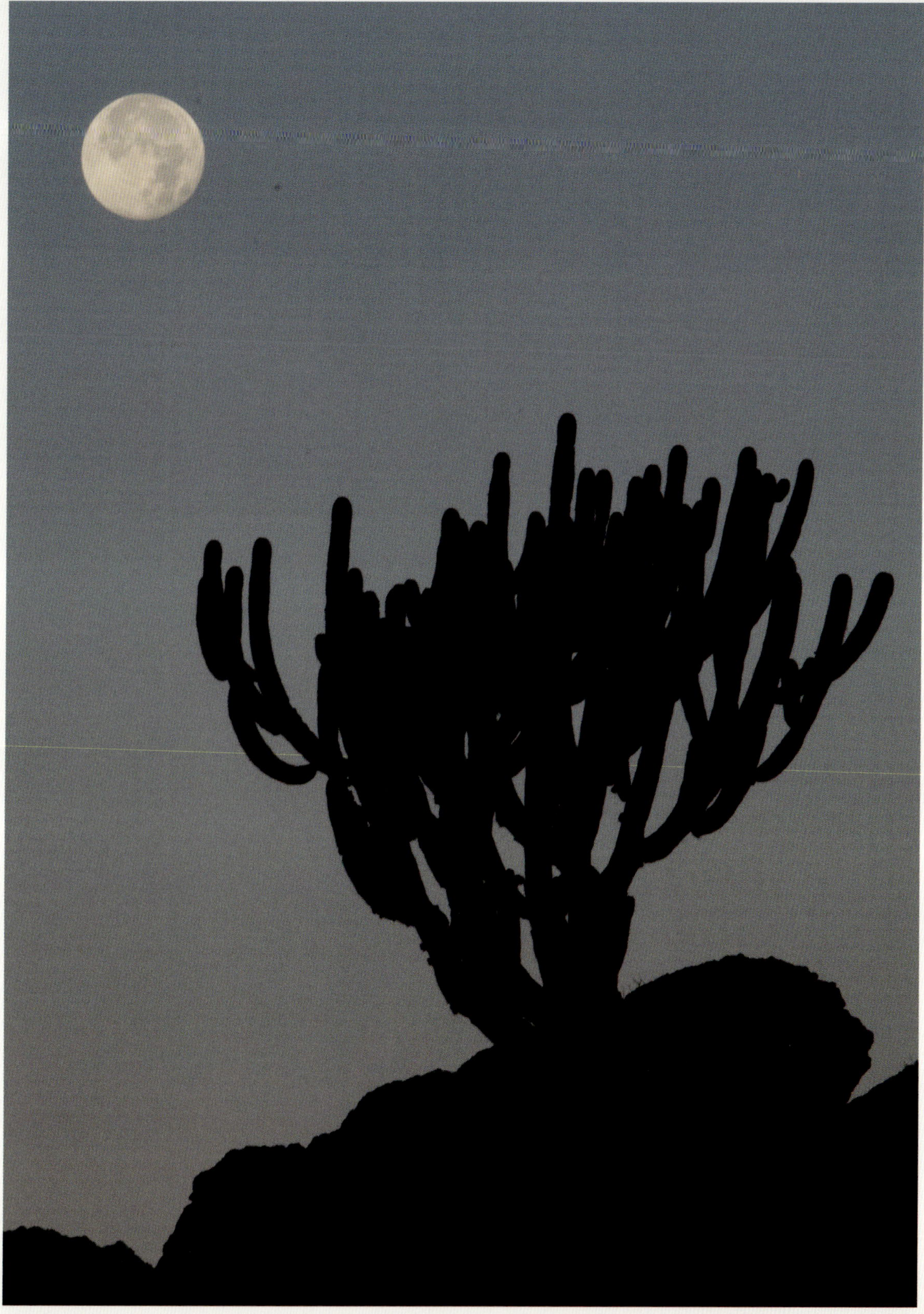

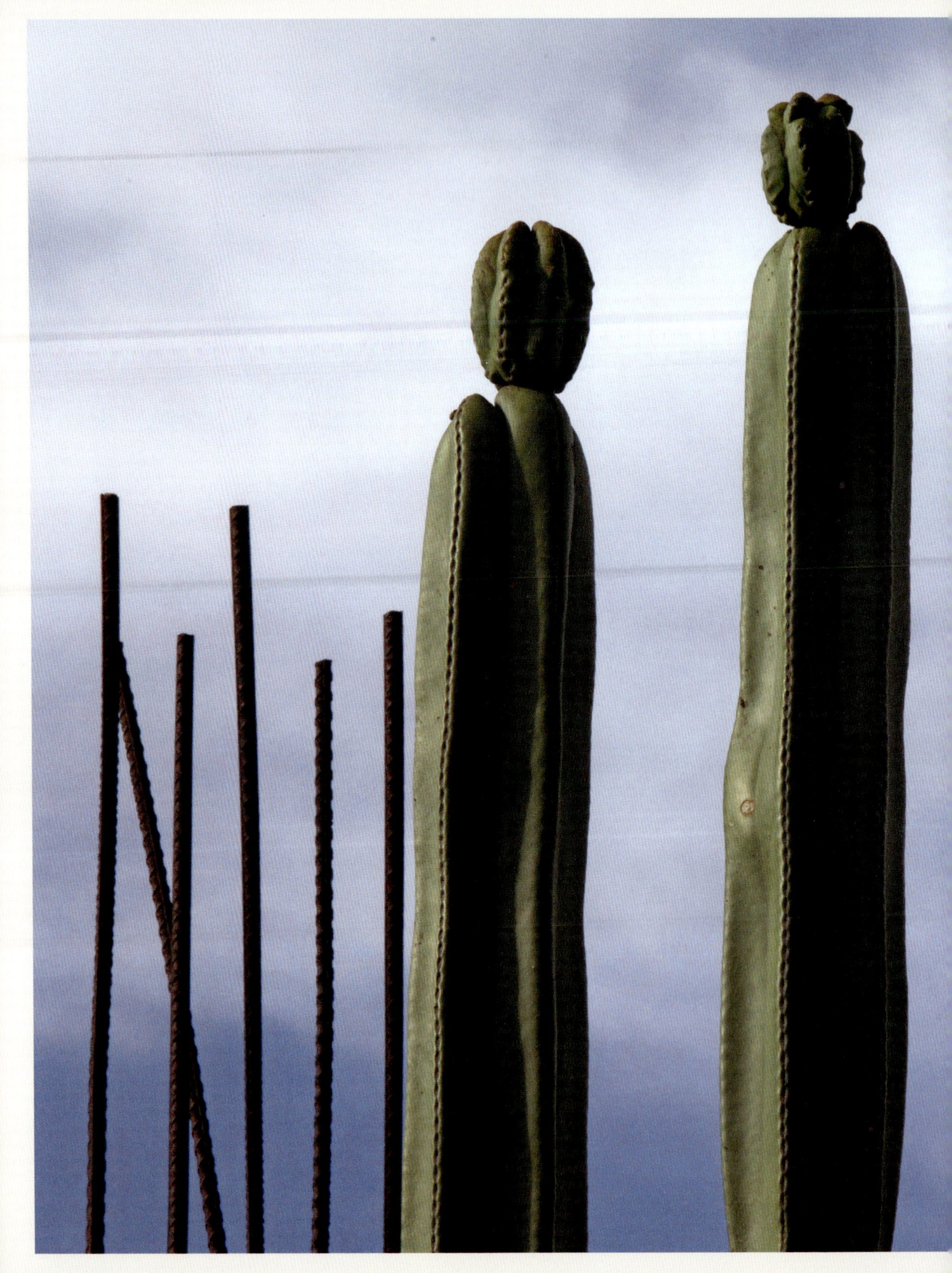

APPRECIATION

I am deeply grateful to my mother and father, both avid photographers, who inspired me to look beyond the obvious and to embrace photography as a practice of true self-expression. My brother Daniel and I have carried on the tradition of creatively making sense of ourselves and the world through a viewfinder, and it brings me great joy that my younger son, Isaac, is now creating his own path in still photography and documentary film.

This book would not have been possible without the kindness and generosity of the family who offered us refuge in Mitla. Paul, Sylvia, and their children, Hannah and Santiago, became our community during those months. We forged a close friendship that continues to this day. Paul's invaluable advice and thoughtful editing support have been essential to the creation of this book, and I am profoundly thankful.

My wife, Paz, was an enormous source of support during the fearful early days of the pandemic. Together we drew deeply from the teachings of Thich Nhat Hanh, which helped us to calm our suffering and find a place of peace.

I also wish to thank Katie Eberle, the designer of *Between Earth and Sky*, whose great love for books shines through her work—at once abundantly creative and spacious.

Finally, this is the second book I have had the joy of working on with Miranda Perrone, a poet whose deft touch and lyrical sensibility have made the editing process a true pleasure.

NOTES

Epigraph: Thich Nhat Hanh, interview by Jo Confino, "Zen Master Thich Nhat Hanh Explains Why Mindfulness Is Essential to Climate Action," the *Guardian*, February 20, 2012, https://www .theguardian.com/sustainable-business/blog/thich -nhat-hanh-mindfulness-environment-climate -change.

"A Bell of Mindfulness." The Five Remembrances can be read on the Plum Village website. Plum Village Community of Engaged Buddhism, "Daily Contemplations on Impermanence & Interbeing," Plum Village, accessed August 28, 2025, https://plumvillage.org/daily-contemplations-on -impermanence-interbeing.

"Patience and Perseverance." Quote from Thich Nhat Hanh's Dharma talk February 2013, https://www.parallax.org/mindfulnessbell/article /dharma-talk-no-birth-no-death-only -transformation-2/.

"Less Is More." Thich Nhat Hanh, *The Art of Living: Peace and Freedom in the Here and Now* (New York: HarperOne, 2017).

"Reverence." John Muir, *John of the Mountains: The Unpublished Journals of John Muir* (Madison: The University of Wisconsin Press, 1979), 331.
John Muir: Nature Writings (New York: Library of America, 1997), 245.

"The Miracle of Life." William Shakespeare, *Hamlet*, ed. Barbara A. Mowat and Paul Werstine (New York: Washington Square Press, 1992), 5.1.187–191.

"Somewhere to Go, Something to Do." Plum Village, "Happiness Is Here and Now" In *Chanting from the Heart: Buddhist Ceremonies and Daily Practices*, revised edition (Parallax Press, 2006).

ABOUT JO CONFINO

Jo Confino is a leadership coach, spiritual mentor, facilitator, journalist, author, and sustainability expert. He works at the intersection of personal transformation and systems change, and his coaching practice focuses on supporting leaders within the fields of climate, biodiversity, and social justice. As a journalist for more than forty years, he was executive editor as well as Impact, Innovation, and Editorial Director of "What's Working" at the *HuffPost* in New York. Before joining *HuffPost*, he was an executive editor of *The Guardian*, helping to create the environment, sustainable business, and global development websites as well as being responsible for ensuring the media organization lived its own values. A mindfulness advocate, Confino has worked closely with Zen Master Thich Nhat Hanh and his monastic community in southwestern France for nearly twenty years.

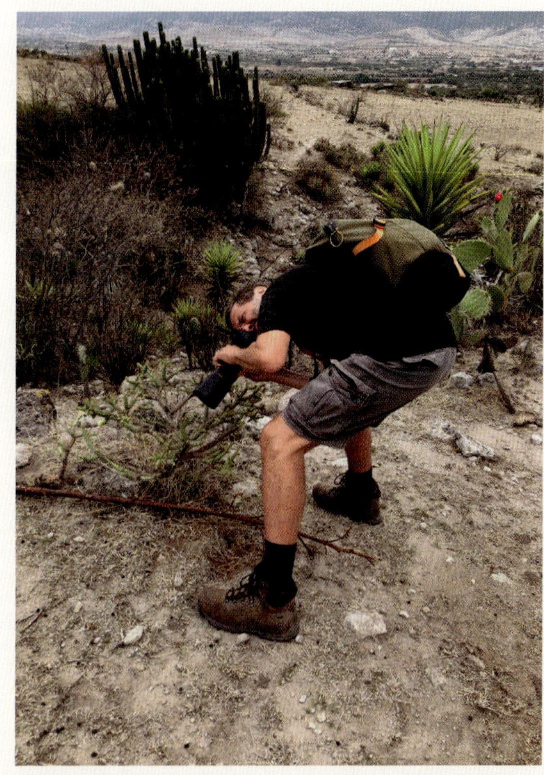

Parallax Press
PO Box 7355
Berkeley, CA 94707
parallax.org

Parallax Press is the publishing division of
Plum Village Community of Engaged Buddhism, Inc.
© 2026 by Jo Confino
All rights reserved

Cover and text design by Katie Eberle
Cover photos by Jo Confino
Author photograph by Paz Perlman

Printed in the United States by Versa Press on FSC-certified paper

Parallax Press's authorized representative in the EEA and EU is
SARL Boutique La Bambouseraie Point UH, Le Pey, 24240 Thénac, France
Email: europe@parallax.org

ISBN 978-1-967175-02-4
Ebook ISBN 978-1-967175-11-6

Library of Congress Cataloging-in-Publication Data

Names: Confino, Jo author
Title: Between earth and sky : 100 days of deep looking in the place of the dead / [Jo Confino].
Description: Berkeley, California : Parallax Press, [2026] |
Summary: "A transformative 100-day exploration through the seemingly desolate lands of Mexico's
"place of the dead" etches a path of collapse and renewal, documented in poignant, imaginative prose
and remarkable macro lens photography. A visually arresting and contemplative giftable object that
pairs luminous, full color macro photography from the stark, mythical deserts of Oaxaca, Mexico with
short, reflective prose rooted in mindfulness"—Provided by publisher.
Identifiers: LCCN 2025048820 (print) | LCCN 2025048821 (ebook) | ISBN 9781967175024 trade
paperback | ISBN 9781967175116 epub Subjects: LCSH: Confino, Jo—Psychology | Meditation—
Buddhism | Macrophotography—Mexico—San Pablo Villa de Mitla | Mindfulness (Psychology)
Classification: LCC BQ5620 .C66 2026 (print) | LCC BQ5620 (ebook)

LC record available at https://lccn.loc.gov/2025048820
LC ebook record available at https://lccn.loc.gov/2025048821

1 2 3 4 5 VERSA 30 29 28 27 26